3/07

Rumor
Psychology

Rumor

Psychology

Social and
Organizational
Approaches

Nicholas DiFonzo and Prashant Bordia

American Psychological Association • Washington, DC

Published by
American Psychological Association
750 First Street, NE
Washington, DC 20002
www.apa.org

To order
APA Order Department
P.O. Box 92984
Washington, DC 20090-2984
Tel: (800) 374-2721; Direct: (202) 336-5510
Fax: (202) 336-5502; TDD/TTY: (202) 336-6123
Online: www.apa.org/books/
E-mail: order@apa.org

In the U.K., Europe, Africa, and the Middle East, copies may be ordered from
American Psychological Association
3 Henrietta Street
Covent Garden, London
WC2E 8LU England

Typeset in Meridien by World Composition Services, Inc., Sterling, VA

Printer: Hamilton Printing, Castleton, NY
Cover Designer: Naylor Design, Washington, DC
Technical/Production Editor: Tiffany L. Klaff

The opinions and statements published are the responsibility of the authors, and such opinions and statements do not necessarily represent the policies of the American Psychological Association.

Library of Congress Cataloging-in-Publication Data

DiFonzo, Nicholas.
    Rumor psychology : social and organizational approaches / Nicholas DiFonzo and Prashant Bordia.—1st ed.
        p. cm.
    Includes bibliographical references and index.
    ISBN-13: 978-1-59147-426-5
    ISBN-10: 1-59147-426-4
    1. Rumor. 2. Social psychology. 3. Organizational behavior. I. Bordia, Prashant. II. Title.

HM1241.D54   2007
302.2′4—dc22   2006009552

British Library Cataloguing-in-Publication Data
A CIP record is available from the British Library.

Printed in the United States of America
First Edition

Dedicated to Mary Josephine DiFonzo and Manjula Bordia.

Contents

Acknowledgments

Several people have been especially helpful in the production of this volume. We are particularly indebted to Ralph L. Rosnow, our ever-helpful colleague and mentor at Temple University, a true pioneer in the study of rumor transmission. We also thank Charles Walker of St. Bonaventure University for his perspicacious advice on chapter 1. We thank the anonymous corporation, including workers, questionnaire administrators, and management, who participated in the longitudinal survey described in chapters 2 and 8. Credit with regard to this project is particularly due to Rob Winterkorn for his determined—and successful—efforts in data collection. We thank H. Taylor Buckner and Frederick Koenig for their comments on chapters 6 and 7. We appreciate comments on a draft of chapter 8 made by Kurt Dirks, Chip Heath, and Ralph L. Rosnow. We thank Eric K. Foster, Holly Hom, Frederick Koenig, Mark Pezzo, Charles Walker, Sarah Wert, and John Yost for consistently stimulating our thinking about rumor and gossip via the electronic discussion group, Rumor-GossipResearch@listserver.rit.edu. The first author (DiFonzo) acknowledges funding to assist in the preparation of this volume from two sources at Rochester Institute of Technology: the College of Liberal Arts Faculty Education and Development Fund and the Provost's Faculty Leave Fund. Research reported in chapter 9 was funded by the Australian Research Council and the University of Queensland Foundation. We are grateful to collaborators past and present. We thank Simon Lloyd Restubog and

Bernd Irmer for help at various stages in the preparation of this manuscript. We thank Emily Leonard, development editor, and Tiffany Klaff, production editor, in the Books department at the American Psychological Association, and two anonymous peer reviewers for their helpful comments on a draft of this volume.

Rumor
Psychology

Introduction

We are *swimming* in rumors.
> —*Manager at a small company facing severe downsizing*

Tropical Fantasy Fruit Punch contains a substance that causes black men to become sterile.
> —*False rumor circulating in New York City that caused sales to plummet 70% (Freedman, 1991)*

Israel warned 4000 Jews not to report for work at the World Trade Center on September 11th, 2001.
> —*False rumor circulating among anti-Zionist groups (Hari, 2002; U.S. Department of State, 2005)*

Rumors are an enduring feature of social and organizational landscapes. They attract attention, evoke emotion, incite involvement, affect attitudes and actions—and they are ubiquitous. A small example includes the groundless rumors that McDonald's uses worm meat in its hamburgers grounded sales in Atlanta (Goggins, 1979). Sober reports that Paul McCartney was dead were discussed with sadness and snowballed, even after a photo and interview with a very much alive McCartney was published in *LIFE* magazine (Rosnow, 1991). Office scuttlebutt often eats away at trust—and feeds on distrust—among organizational members (DiFonzo, Bordia, & Rosnow, 1994). False rumors that a Haitian coup leader was to be set free spurred angry riots that killed 10 people ("10 Die in Haiti," 1991). Seven million people heard the incorrect claim that Coca-Cola contains carcinogens (Kapferer, 1989). Two bizarre and fallacious rumors, widespread in Africa, were that the AIDS virus was developed in a western laboratory, and that a World Health Organization team inoculated 100,000 Africans with an untested vaccine that caused the continent's pandemic of AIDS (Lynch, 1989). Harmful or potentially harmful rumors reach the ears of top corporate public relations personnel nearly once per week on average (DiFonzo & Bordia, 2000). E-mailed computer-related hoaxes, such as the "Good Times" virus that will rewrite one's hard drive and the "teddy bear" icon that destroys your whole system, regularly alarm novice Internet users (Bordia & DiFonzo, 2004; "JDBGMGR.EXE," 2002). The catalog continues in abundance; rumors flourish, fascinate, and frustrate.

It is not surprising then that the record of scholarly interest in the psychology of rumor is long and illustrious; for over 7 decades social and organizational researchers in psychology and sociology have researched rumor. Some brief highlights we note include the early and substantial work of Jamuna Prasad (1935) who studied rumors circulating after a cataclysmic Indian earthquake. Interest in the subject of rumor psychology peaked during World War II and rumor researchers included such well-known social psychologists as Floyd H. Allport, Kurt Back, Dorwin Cartwright, Leon Festinger, Stanley Schachter, and John Thibaut (e.g., F. H. Allport & Lepkin, 1945; Back et al., 1950; Festinger et al., 1948; Schachter & Burdick, 1955). The standard work during this period was G. W. Allport and Leo J. Postman's *The Psychology of Rumor* published in 1947. The eminent Tamotsu Shibutani published the landmark sociological treatise *Improvised News: A Sociological Study of Rumor* in 1966. Ralph L. Rosnow and his associates refined the conceptual understanding of rumor and systematically investigated the dynamics of rumor transmission in the latter decades of the 20th century (e.g., Jaeger, Anthony, & Rosnow, 1980; Rosnow, 1974, 1980, 1988, 1991; Rosnow, Esposito, & Gibney, 1988; Rosnow & Fine, 1976; Rosnow & Georgoudi, 1985; Rosnow, Yost, & Esposito, 1986). Other social and organizational psychologists and sociologists contributed significantly to the body of knowledge regarding rumor as well during this period (e.g., K. Davis, 1972; Fine, 1992; Kapferer, 1987/1990; Knopf, 1975; Koenig, 1985; Morin, 1971; Pratkanis & Aronson, 1991; P. A. Turner, 1993; R. H. Turner & Killian, 1972). And within the past decade, social and organizational psychologists have paid increased attention to this topic (e.g., R. S. Baron, David, Brunsman, & Inman, 1997; Bordia & DiFonzo, 2002, 2004, 2005; Bordia, DiFonzo, & Schulz, 2000; Bordia & Rosnow, 1998; DiFonzo & Bordia, 1997, 2002b, 2006, in press; DiFonzo, Bordia, & Winterkorn, 2003; DiFonzo et al., 1994; Fine, Heath, & Campion-Vincent, 2005; Fiske, 2004; Heath, Bell, & Sternberg, 2001; Houmanfar & Johnson, 2003; Kimmel, 2004a, 2004b; Michelson & Mouly, 2004;

Pendleton, 1998; Pratkanis & Aronson, 2001; Rosnow, 2001; Rosnow & Foster, 2005). Indeed, an electronic discussion group of scholars interested in both rumor and gossip research was formed in 2003 (Rumor-GossipResearch@listserver.rit.edu).[1]

Therefore, some of what is known about rumor is quite old and some of it is quite new; and so rumor theory is due for synthesis into an updated whole. That is our first purpose in writing this book. We have made a concerted effort to integrate and update findings from all phases of rumor's long research history. Such a work is very much needed; during a recent electronic discussion among social psychologists, the topic of post-9/11 rumors surfaced. The conversation was perspicacious and insightful; however, it was informed mostly by G. W. Allport and Postman's seminal—but dated—*The Psychology of Rumor* (1947b). Another kind of integration is also needed; the existing body of scholarly and practitioner knowledge about rumor tends to be isolated from recent social–psychological theory. Rumor has become an eddy among mainstream currents. It is no longer included in popular social–psychological textbooks (although this is changing; e.g., Fiske, 2004, p. 517). This omission is unfortunate because rumor—an intrinsically fascinating topic in social psychology—is closely entwined with a host of social and organizational phenomena including social cognition, attitude formation and maintenance, prejudice and stereotyping, group dynamics, interpersonal and intergroup relations, social influence, and organizational trust and communication. These connections have not been clearly set forth; that is the second reason we have written this book.

In this volume, we address a series of questions—some old, some new—that surround rumor. We set these questions against a backdrop of current social and organizational psychological theory, and our approach has a strong empirical flavor. Following are the questions we tackle.

What Is Rumor?

Despite rumor's long history of inquiry, the rumor construct continues to elude clarification. In chapter 1, we attempt to bring conceptual clarity to rumor by presenting a new definition that takes into account

---

[1] Researchers wishing to subscribe to this list should send the following message in the first line of an e-mail to listserver@listserver.rit.edu: SUBscribe Rumor-Gossip Research *your name* (please insert your actual name [e.g., *Gordon Allport*] at *your name*).

the content, contexts, and functions of rumor, gossip, and urban legend. We develop these dimensions and present empirical evidence to buttress our contention that rumor, gossip, and urban legend tend to exhibit different information-dimension patterns.

What Are the Categories of Rumor, How Frequent Are They, and What Effects Do They Have?

Chapter 2 addresses these descriptive questions, overviews rumor categorization schemes, and presents evidence pertaining to how frequently various forms of rumor occur. In addition, this chapter addresses a basic question, rarely investigated in a systematic fashion: Do rumors cause or contribute to various outcomes of interest? This chapter reviews a series of published and unpublished studies exploring the correlates and consequences of rumor activity. We pay special attention in this chapter to rumor effects in an organizational context.

Why Do People Spread Rumors?

Rumor transmission has been perhaps the most studied aspect of rumor research, and several antecedents have been implicated (Rosnow, 1991). In chapter 3, we review these antecedents and conceptually integrate them within a more recent social–psychological motivational framework used by attitude formation and maintenance researchers. The result is a better understanding of both the causes (external antecedents) and reasons (internal motivations) for rumor transmission. We present research investigating how the pattern of motivation differs in different social contexts. This chapter integrates the work on rumor transmission by Rosnow (1991) and colleagues within a motivational reasoning framework familiar to social psychologists.

Why Do People Believe Rumors?

A puzzling question indeed, especially for fantastic tales! In chapter 4 we view the question using Egon Brunswik's lens model of judgment in which distal attributes are inferred from proximal cues. We review and meta-analytically combine studies bearing on this question to identify cues that people use to infer the truthfulness of a rumor. We present evidence from a field study of stockbrokers suggesting the existence of these—and other—belief cues. To our knowledge, this topic has heretofore not been systematically studied.

How Do Rumors Help People Make Sense of Uncertainty?

Rumors typically help people make sense of ambiguous situations. Chapter 5 explores the psychological mechanisms involved in this process at the individual and interpersonal levels. At the individual level, we explicate rumor sense making using frameworks within social cognition: explanation theory, illusory correlation, causal attribution, and antiregressive prediction. At the interpersonal level, we explore collective rumor sense making by examining the content, functions, and flow of rumor statements uttered in rumor discussions on the Internet. Rumor has often been referred to as a sense-making process; this chapter materially advances the field's understanding of that process. It represents a much-needed integration of rumor theory and social cognition and advances the seminal collective sense-making theories proposed by sociologists Shibutani (1966) and Ralph H. Turner (Turner & Killian, 1972).

How Accurate Are Rumors and How Do They Become More—or Less—Accurate?

Rumors have a bad reputation as being false. Is this reputation deserved? Chapters 6 and 7 address this question and several others related to rumor content change with respect to veracity. In chapter 6 we first present a review of decades of research on rumor content change and attempt to resolve two divergent findings: Some rumors seem to expand (become more detailed), whereas others seem to level (become less detailed) over their lifetimes. We then present a sorely needed conceptualization of the term *accuracy* and discuss how accuracy is measured. Next, we pose a seldom-asked, but epistemologically important, question: Overall, how accurate are rumors? We review rumor accuracy studies and report three investigations into organizational rumor accuracy. In chapter 7 we review literature concerning the processes by which rumors become more accurate and less accurate: Cognitive, motivational, situational, group, and network mechanisms are proposed. We present data from our accuracy investigations to explore these processes. This chapter materially advances theory about accuracy and revives the lesser known work of the sociologist H. Taylor Buckner (1965) on this topic.

How Does Trust Affect Rumor Transmission?

In our investigations of rumor, we have frequently observed that where distrust grows, rumor flows—yet rumor research has not systematically investigated this connection. In chapter 8 we present a longitudinal study of the relationship between rumor and trust in an organization undergoing radical downsizing. We use a framework proposed by organizational trust researchers Kurt Dirks and Donald Ferrin (2001) in which trust is proposed to have both direct and moderating effects. This chapter is a new avenue for understanding the dynamics of rumor transmission from the vantage point of interpersonal trust.

How Can Harmful Rumors Be Managed?

Popular literature about how to handle rumor is fairly common—but almost all of it is nonempirical; it relies on intuition and individual experience. In chapter 9, we summarize and synthesize empirical research on rumor management strategies. Factors that moderate the effectiveness of rumor denials are examined. Along the way, recurring questions are addressed: Should a no-comments strategy be used? Should one repeat a rumor when rebutting it? We apply research on persuasion and causal attribution in addressing these questions.

What's Next in Rumor Research?

Finally, in chapter 10 we summarize the main elements of previous chapters, propose an integrative model of rumor processes, and set forth a comprehensive agenda for future research. We hope that our efforts in this volume will encourage and enable a renewed interest in the social and organizational psychology of rumor.

Defining Rumor

1

Anyone living in the United States during the weeks following the terror attacks of September 11, 2001, remembers two things: trying to make sense of these senseless acts, and feeling threatened. As people huddled in engaged conversations, rumors circulated widely:

Avoid Boston on September 22nd because drunken Arabs at a bar let it slip that there would be a second wave of attacks that day.

—Marks, 2001

A hijacked plane is headed for the Sears Tower in Chicago!

—Deener, 2001

Osama bin Laden owns Snapple (Emory, n.d.) and Citibank (Cantera, 2002) and was sighted in Utah.

—Mikkelson, 2001a

Federal Emergency Management Agency personnel were dispatched to New York City the day *before* the September 11 attacks, proving that the government knew of them in advance.

—"Monday, Monday," 2002

All of these rumors were false.

irthful friends posed the following question to one of us (DiFonzo) after revealing my research interest in rumor: "So, what's the latest on Ben and JLo?" They were referring to what, at the time, was the much publicized breakup of film stars Ben Affleck and Jennifer Lopez. My reply,

"Actually that's gossip—not rumor," was greeted with further merriment. I understood how I had tickled their funny bone: They were amused that such a shadowy and often humorous topic—rumor—was studied in a serious academic fashion. The conversation took an educational turn while maintaining its jovial spirit: Using Socrates's methods, I helped them "recall" that rumor had more to do with making sense whereas gossip had more to do with evaluative social talk. We attempt to do this and more in this chapter (and likewise retain our sense of humor!).

My friends' reactions were understandable: Rumor is often lumped with other genres of informal communication such as gossip, innuendo, urban legend, and idle chitchat. Among the general public, "Have you heard any rumors lately?" might elicit a juicy bit of office tattle, any statement thought to be false, a pejorative stereotype, a morality tale, or an anxious prognostication of office downsizing. Failing to distinguish rumor from gossip is also the case among the broader psychological public; indeed, *rumor* in the American Psychological Association's Psyc-INFO *Thesaurus* is currently subsumed under the term *gossip*. And among academics studying these forms of communication there is some disagreement about what constitutes rumor. This conceptual murkiness is not new; the Indian psychologist A. B. Ojha once observed that academic definitions of the term *rumor* varied greatly, thereby leaving the reader "in a fix" (1973, p. 61). Progress has been made (e.g., Rosnow & Georgoudi, 1985), but in some ways ambiguity persists: While dining together at a recent conference of social psychologists, rumor and gossip researchers disputed for an entire evening over whether rumor and gossip really are two different forms. And at a recent interdisciplinary conference on rumors and legends, rumor and legend researchers contended—again during meals—over whether rumor and urban legends differed in their essential features. Digestion notwithstanding, is this ambiguity a problem?

Yes, it is. Conceptual ambiguity has contributed to problems in rumor theory, research methodology, and management. For example, requesting participants to think of a rumor may actually produce a set of gossip statements; study results would then not be generalizable to rumor. A second example is telling an urban legend about tourists in Australia dressing up a stunned kangaroo who then awakens and hops away with one of their wallets is likely to serve different social functions than would telling a rumor about impending layoffs. In a similar way, remedies for common gossip about a friend's extramarital affair may not be a proper prescription for a rampant rumor about contaminated soda pop. Glossing over the differences between these genres of informal communication leads to inadequate conceptualizations of how they operate, how they are validly studied, and how they are effectively prevented and managed.

Meaningful distinctions between rumor and other forms of informal communication do exist (Rosnow & Georgoudi, 1985; Rosnow & Kimmel, 2000), although remarkably these have rarely been empirically investigated. In this chapter, we further sharpen the concept of rumor by defining it, comparing and contrasting it with gossip and urban legend, and presenting empirical evidence investigating the dimensions of these types of informal communication. In particular, we focus on the contextual, content, and functional elements of each form of communication. We begin with a definition of rumor.

Rumor

We define *rumors* as unverified and instrumentally relevant information statements in circulation that arise in contexts of ambiguity, danger, or potential threat and that function to help people make sense and manage risk. In this definition, we focus on the contexts in which rumors crop up, contents of rumor statements, and group functions that rumor serves, all of which are summarized in Table 1.1 along with the contexts, contents, and functions of gossip and urban legend.

RUMOR CONTEXTS AND FUNCTIONS

Rumors arise in situations that are ambiguous or threatening in some way (G. W. Allport & Postman, 1947b; Rosnow, 1991; Shibutani, 1966). Ambiguous situations are those in which the meaning or significance of events is unclear, or in which the effects of events are not certain. Ambiguity is problematic for people. Why? In any context, humans have a core social motive to understand and to act effectively (Fiske, 2004). Culturally defined categories ordinarily help individuals do this (R. H. Turner, 1964). Yet sometimes events do not fit well together or fail to convey meaning. In these cases, individuals refer back to the group to understand the situation and to act (Asch, 1955; Sherif, 1936). This referring back to the group—or *group thinking*—is rumor discussion. Thus, rumors occur when a group is attempting to make sense of ambiguous, uncertain, or confusing situations. Sociologist Tamotsu Shibutani (1966) proposed that when formal information is absent, people compensate by informally interpreting the situation (cf., Bauer & Gleicher, 1953; R. H. Turner & Killian, 1972). Rumor discussion is a process of group interpretation; rumor is a product of that process (Rosnow, 1974).

Rumor activity in ambiguous contexts therefore functions to make sense; it is a response to the core human motivation to understand (Fiske, 2004). The resolving of ambiguity is always a sense-making explanation of events that are unclear for some part of a group or community. As G. W. Allport and Postman put it in their seminal text, *The Psychology of Rumor*, "in ordinary rumor we find a marked tendency for the agent to attribute *causes* to events, *motives* to characters, a *raison d'etre* to the episode in question" [italics in original] (1947b, p. 121). Explanations primarily attempt to make reality perceptible and meaningful (Antaki, 1988); rumors are a collective effort at such explanations when a group—or subset of a group—is faced with uncertainty (Di-Fonzo & Bordia, 1998). To some extent, these explanations must pass some group norm of plausibility. When group standards of plausibility are high, rumor discussions look very much like fact finding. When the group standards are low, rumor discussions look very much like contagion or panic. Rumor is thus part of *"normal collective information seeking"* [italics in original] (R. H. Turner, 1994, p. 247) wherein the group is trying to define an ambiguous situation with a *"lower degree*

TABLE 1.1

Contexts, Content, and Functions of Rumor, Gossip, and Urban Legend

	Context	Content	Group function
Rumor	Ambiguous or threatening events or situations	Instrumentally relevant information statements that are unverified	To make sense of ambiguity To manage threat or potential threat
Gossip	Social network building, structuring, or maintaining	Evaluative statements about individuals' private lives	To entertain To supply social information To establish, change, or maintain group membership, group power structure, or group norms
Urban legend	Storytelling	Entertaining narratives	To entertain To establish, maintain, or impart cultural mores or values

Note. Each genre of communication may exhibit all contexts, contents, and functions in this table (e.g., rumor also functions to impart cultural mores and gossip also functions to help the group make sense of ambiguity), though each genre's quintessential contexts, contents, and functions are listed here.

of formalization of many of its component acts" [italics in original] (Shibutani, 1966, p. 23). Norms for verification, sources, and other aspects of fact finding are typically relaxed, but it remains a group sense-making activity.

Rumor also functions to manage threat; it is a response to the core human motivations to control one's environment or to protect one's self-image (Fiske, 2004). Threatening situations are those in which people feel that their welfare or sense of self is endangered. Threatening situations may indeed imperil one's welfare, as when a company faces possible layoffs. They may also involve threats to one's health or life, as with catastrophic situations such as earthquakes, floods, and nuclear accidents. Prasad (1935) documented one such outbreak of catastrophic rumors after the great Indian earthquake of 1934. Rumors also abounded after the Chernobyl nuclear accident in 1986 (Peters, Albrecht, Hennen, & Stegelmann, 1990). In the face of such threats to welfare, rumors help groups to make sense of the situation and thereby prepare for or act effectively against the threat. The preparation for threat may take the form of "secondary control" whereby simply interpreting events within a framework that makes sense to people helps them gain a sense of control (Walker, 1996). Threatening situations may also be those in which one feels emotionally endangered, in which one's sense of self—or indeed anything that one cherishes—seems threatened. "Eleanor Club" rumors (among Whites) that Black servants were found using the "lady of the house's" combs occurred during times of racial turbulence in American history (these rumors were so named after Eleanor Roosevelt; G. W. Allport & Postman, 1947b). The context of these rumors was a sense that one's identity as a White person was under attack. In a similar way, at the heart of *wedge-driving* rumors—rumors that derogate other groups or classes of people—is a defensive sentiment: one feels threatened. To cope with such feelings, the wedge-driving rumor monger enhances his or her sense of self by putting others down. Thus, in the face of threats to one's sense of self, rumors that portray other groups in a negative light help people think of themselves in a more pleasing way.

Rumor may also fulfill other functions such as entertainment, wish fulfillment, alliance making and maintenance, and enforcement of communal norms, but these are secondary. For example, rumors speculating about the identity of the person who murdered a babysitter (Peterson & Gist, 1951) may be entertaining for some, but this rumor function takes second place behind attempts to ascertain "whodunit," how it could have happened in one's community, what the implications are for future community safety, and so on. In short, the essence of rumor has to do with sense making and threat management amid uncertainty.

RUMOR CONTENT

Rumor content refers to the substance of rumor—what type of statement constitutes a rumor? Rumors are information statements that circulate among people, are instrumentally relevant, and are unverified.

Instrumentally Relevant and Communicated Information Statements

Rumors are first of all information statements. They tell rather than interrogate or command (although a rumor statement may indeed raise questions or direct behavior). The kernel of a rumor is an idea conveyed by a meaningful statement or set of statements. "Carter Hawley is bankrupt" (Lev, 1991), "The Haitian coup leader will be released from prison" ("10 Die in Haiti," 1991), and "Paul McCartney is dead" (Rosnow, 1991) are fundamentally subjects and verbs. Second, rumors are communicated information. A rumor is not seated at rest inside an individual; it moves among and through a set of persons. A rumor is never merely a private thought. Rumors are threads in a complex fabric of social exchange, informational commodities exchanged between traders (Rosnow, 2001). In this sense, rumors are a subclass of *memes*, ideas that survive through processes similar to those of natural selection; "unfit" rumors die—they stop circulating—whereas "fit" ones persist (Heath, Bell, & Sternberg, 2001).

Third, rumor is information that is circulated because it is instrumentally relevant to rumor participants; the information relates to, affects, interests, or threatens them in some way. We mean *instrumental* in the sense that Dewey (1925) intended: having some weighty purpose, rather than being entertaining, sociable, or aimless. That is, rumors tend to be about topics of significance to participants (Rosnow & Kimmel, 2000). This instrumental relevance may be of a recent nature, that is, it may pertain to current events. Rumor is similar to news in this way; it tends to be information that is new. Relevance of this sort often stems from potential consequences to persons (Rosnow & Fine, 1976); Rosnow (1991) dubbed it *outcome relevance*. For example, organizational rumors in a study by DiFonzo et al. (1994) arose from collective concerns such as job duties and advancement opportunities (turnover rumors), job security and compensation (layoff rumors), and deleterious health effects (contamination rumors). However, the relevance may be of an established nature. Rumors may pertain to topics of long-standing interest such as ritual murder and flying saucers (Rosnow & Kimmel, 2000). To the extent that participants considered such topics to relate to, affect, or threaten them in some way, such statements would be considered rumors. Put another way, although they sometimes make people laugh, rumors are not primarily jokes; although they may make people more sociable, they are not primarily meant to pass the time. Rumors are about topics that people consider relatively more urgent, significant, purposeful, or important.

Unverified Statements

Fourth—and most central—rumor is important communicated information that is unverified. To verify is "to prove to be true by demonstration, evidence, etc.; to confirm" (Agnes, 1996, p. 683); unverified statements, therefore, are unproven, not demonstrated to be true, and unaccompanied by "secure standards of evidence" (G. W. Allport & Postman, 1947b, p. ix). As Rosnow put it, rumor is "constructed around unauthenticated information" (1974, p. 27). Note that this is not to say that rumors never have a basis; they often do. Rather, the basis is simply weak or absent—it is not secure evidence. Secure or stable evidence is usually empirical in nature or consists of testimony from a credible source. This type of evidence coheres even under scrutiny, testing, and questioning. The difference between news and rumor is helpful here; news is always confirmed, but rumor is always unconfirmed (Shibutani, 1966).

To some people, statements appear to possess secure evidential moorings but on further scrutiny do not. Case in point: In 1981, a false rumor spread that the president of the Procter & Gamble Corporation (P&G) appeared on a nationwide talk show and proclaimed that P&G donated to the Church of Satan; the rumor was spread by means of a paper flyer (Koenig, 1985). The flyer proclaimed there was evidence: It directed people to call the talk show and obtain for $3.00 a transcript of the alleged broadcast. Anyone who took the time to call, of course, discovered that the event never happened; indeed, P&G's president has never appeared on any talk show. Thus, rumor includes what is sometimes called *misinformation,* or false statements thought to be true by some people. The implications of this reflection are sobering and (rightly) lead to a general sense of caution about what is heard: Evidence that initially seems firm may in fact easily crumble.

This characteristic of being unverified highlights the fact that some rumors are more vulnerable to reality testing than are others.[1] The eminent philosopher of science, Karl R. Popper (1962), proposed that a scientific theory is vulnerable to falsification; nonscientific theories are not. This is the principle of falsifiability. Like scientific theories,

---

[1] We are indebted to Charles Walker for the ideas and first example contained in this paragraph.

some rumors are observable or specific in character. For example, "Sam Dickson at corporate headquarters in Atlanta has asked all the branch offices in New York to cut clerical staff by 20%" can be refuted; it is a risky rumor. Mr. Dickson can rebut the rumor, clerical staff records can be combed, and human resource personnel can deny receiving cutback directives. In contrast, "Management are aliens!" is the kind of claim that is difficult to disprove. Less risky rumors—like some nonscientific theories—might be more immune to falsification because they assert nonobservable phenomena. This Popperian aspect of rumor may help to explain why some rumors are quite long-lived.

Mode of Transmission and Structure

Attempts have been made to define rumor on the basis of transmission mechanisms. G. W. Allport and Postman (1947b) stated that rumors were "passed along from person to person, usually by word of mouth" (p. ix). Rosnow (1980, 2001) pointed out that this definition was outdated. Today, print, electronic media, and the Internet may be added to word-of-mouth channels of communication through which rumors flow.

Attempts have also been made to define rumor by its structure. For example, rumors are often prefaced with a cautionary statement indicating lack of verification such as "I don't know if this is true . . ." or "I heard that. . . ." Because these prefaces indicate a lack of verification, however, they are attached only to those rumors for which the transmitter perceives the statement to be a rumor. They are thus only a subset of statements constituting rumor because they signal only those statements about which people are unsure. In addition, some researchers propose that rumors are simply short expressions. Rumors are nonnarrative in structure, that is, they tend not to have a plot sequence. They are one-liners. In contrast, longer tales are classified as legends, tall tales, fables, or myths. There is some merit in this distinction, although the storylike quality of rumors varies considerably. For example, we have collected many rumors that can be encapsulated in a single sentence (e.g., see Tables 4.3, 4.4, 6.3, 6.4), but Caplow (1947) observed that military rumors were typically composed of three statements rather than one. Also, Peterson and Gist (1951) reported rumors surrounding the murder of a babysitter; these rumors had snowballed—become very elaborate—and were quite storylike in nature. The distinction in structure stems from the differential functions of these statements. Rumors tend to relate information that pertains to an ambiguous situation or event of which people are already apprised and in which they are involved in ferreting out the facts; legends and myths tend to provide a setting, plot line, and interpretation all-in-one. Viewed in this way, rumors are like plot twists revealed serially over time rather than prepackaged as a coherent story. We return to this distinction in our comparison of rumors and legends later. We turn now to rumor's cousin, gossip.

Gossip

Gossip is evaluative social talk about individuals, usually not present, that arises in the context of social network formation, change, and maintenance—that is, in the context of building group solidarity. Gossip fulfills a variety of essential social network functions including entertainment, maintaining group cohesiveness, and establishing, changing, and maintaining group norms, group power structure, and group membership.

CONTEXTS AND FUNCTIONS

Gossip arises in the context of social network formation, change, and maintenance (L. C. Smith, Lucas, & Latkin, 1999), that is, in situations concerned with building group solidarity (Foster, 2004). One core human motivation is to belong, to fit in and be part of a group (Fiske, 2004). Gossip is talk that helps people do that by informing persons about the group and individuals within it, helping one to keep track of people in one's social network, advertising oneself as a potential friend or mate, influencing people to conform to group norms, and providing mutual enjoyment of an entertaining tidbit together (Dunbar, 2004; Foster & Rosnow, 2006; Rosnow & Georgoudi, 1985). Like primate grooming, activity that promotes interpersonal bonding is essential to group cohesion; gossip is thus a very important activity—without it, societies would not be sustainable (Dunbar, 1996, 2004).

Gossip performs several functions key to social network formation and maintenance (Foster, 2004). Gossip first of all provides information about complex social environments; it informs people about aspects of the group (Levin & Arluke, 1987). An organizational rookie benefits from gossip such as "By the way, the boss is a real fascist."[2] Wert and Salovey (2004) claimed that all gossip is information gained by social comparison with other people. For example, gossip informs people

---

[2] We thank Eric Foster for providing this illustrative example of the informative function of gossip.

about what to do and what not to do in a given social setting (Don't get drunk at the Christmas party!) and who is to be included or excluded in one's social group (Johnny is "cool"; Jason is a nerd). In most general terms, gossip has been proposed as information gained through observing the "adventures and misadventures of others"; gossip thus provides cultural information in a second- (and third- and fourth- and fifth-) hand fashion (Baumeister, Zhang, & Vohs, 2004, p. 112). Some examples of such cultural information include "'Just don't drink'; 'Don't forget your true friends'; 'Infidelity will eventually catch up with you'" (Baumeister et al., 2004, p. 119).

A second way that gossip builds group solidarity is by providing social entertainment (Litman & Pezzo, 2005; Rosnow & Fine, 1976). Gossip is a mutual mood enhancer—together people laugh at other people's peccadilloes. They enjoy a bit of private information about someone else (Rosnow & Georgoudi, 1985); sharing such information helps to pass the time. Tales of the office Don Juan's weekend escapades are amusing; gossip therefore fulfills an entertainment function (Gluckman, 1963).

Another primary function of gossip is to define intimacy boundaries and group membership; gossiping with another makes members feel closer (L. C. Smith et al., 1999) or bonded (Hom & Haidt, 2002). It has been argued that gossip is an efficient means of social bonding, enabling friendship groups to include many members (Dunbar, 2004). Gossip helps people affiliate with others by helping them keep track of people in the social network and by helping them to advertise their own desirability as a friend or mate (Dunbar, 2004). One knows that he or she is part of the social group when someone whispers some delightful inside information; one at last becomes an insider. One does not gossip with one's enemies, but with friends or people with whom one wishes to be more strongly affiliated. Thus, through gossip people gain friendships and alliances. Of course, the darker side of delineating intimacy boundaries is exclusion: Through gossip, people ostracize (L. C. Smith et al., 1999). Thus, gossip is evaluative talk behind someone's back (Foster, 2004; Sabini & Silver, 1982). It often evaluates the behavior of a person or persons known to the participants—that is, in their social network—in a conversational context in which the "evaluative talk [is] about a person who is not present" (Eder & Enke, 1991, p. 494). Gossip is a key weapon in "relational aggression" (Crick et al., 2001). These painful experiences of exclusion are often the most memorable aspects of childhood gossip experiences. Consistent with gossip's usefulness in excluding others is the finding that people sometimes feel remorse after spreading negative gossip (Hom & Haidt, 2002).

Fourth, gossip defines not only who is in and out of the group, but also power relationships within a group (Kurland & Pelled, 2000;

L. C. Smith et al., 1999). Gossip preserves or enhances the gossiper's social status by slyly deprecating others or by enhancing self. Hom and Haidt (2002) factor analyzed items related to social "people talk" episodes: Gossiping made participants feel more empowered and popular, and that their status was elevated when telling critical gossip.

A fifth and final function is to propagate and enforce group norms essential to group functioning. Gossip is perhaps particularly useful in monitoring and cracking down on free riders—those who receive the benefits that society gives without adequately returning in kind; too many free riders can severely limit group functioning and thus gossip performs an invaluable adaptive function (Dunbar, 2004; Foster & Rosnow, 2006). Gossip does this by "informally communicating value-laden information about members of a social setting" (Noon & Delbridge, 1993, p. 24). Norms may be communicated by commenting on people personally known (*proximate* gossip) or those probably not personally known, such as celebrities (e.g., Ben and JLo) and political figures (*distal* gossip). Gossip thus has a moral orientation; it is value-laden. It forms, maintains, enforces, or disseminates group norms. In this way gossip influences and controls attitudes and actions (Rosnow & Georgoudi, 1985). In more broad terms, gossip educates people about how to act effectively in complex social environments (Foster, 2004), especially by specific comparisons with the behavior of real or imagined others (Wert & Salovey, 2004).

CONTENT

Although gossip is important, gossip content is typically presented in a noninstrumental way by participants. That is, gossip is typically done with an apparently aimless or idle purpose or simply to pass the time (Rosnow & Georgoudi, 1985). Although it may indeed have a considered objective (trying to persuade, affiliate, exclude), it is packaged in tones of relative disinterest. In a similar way, gossip is talk about matters that are typically considered not that urgent or weighty. The content is "nonessential in the context of the exchange" (Rosnow & Georgoudi, 1985, p. 62; Michelson & Mouly, 2000). Chat about office romances, classmate peccadilloes, and family members' personality traits constitutes gossip if offered without apparent serious intent. The same topics, explored by a social psychologist in a conference paper, would not be gossip because their function would be more central to the purpose of the exchange. Again, gossip and gossiping perform central and significant functions in social life, but gossip content is typically considered less central, relevant, or important by participants.

In addition, gossip is evaluative talk—sometimes positive and sometimes negative (Foster, 2004)—although it is predominantly viewed as negative, slanderous, and derogatory (Wert & Salovey, 2004). For example, a content analysis of gossip heard by college students at a northeastern college found that 61% of it was intended to shame the gossip target; in contrast, only 2% was intended to venerate the gossipee (Walker & Struzyk, 1998). Gossip is tattle about someone— a praise or critique of their actions or attitudes (Michelson & Mouly, 2000). Tales about Joe's behavior at the office Christmas party make a statement that such behavior is laudable or laughable. Third, gossip is evaluative talk about the private and personal life of an individual rather than about a group or event (Foster, 2004). For example, middle school gossip content often includes current couple configurations ("Johnny and Jasmine are *a thing*"), personality traits ("Jackson is really nice"), sexual orientation ("Frank is homosexual"), family matters ("Brittany's mother is having an affair"), and personal histories ("George was busted for cocaine last year").

RUMOR VERSUS GOSSIP

In common usage, *rumor* and *gossip* are often used interchangeably (Rosnow, 1974; Rosnow & Fine, 1976). As previously stated, the Psyc-INFO Thesaurus currently lists *rumor* under the term *gossip*. Gossip, like rumor, is a transaction in which the hearsay is exchanged for some other commodity (Rosnow & Fine, 1976). Both have been referred to as "unofficial communication" (Kapferer, 1987/1990), "informal communication" (Michelson & Mouly, 2000), and "hearsay" (Fine, 1985).

However, rumor and gossip are not equivalent concepts; they differ in function and content. Rumor's function is to make sense of an ambiguous situation or to help people adapt to known or potential threats; gossip serves social network formation and maintenance. Put another way, rumor is intended as a hypothesis to help make sense of an unclear situation whereas gossip entertains, bonds, and normatively influences group members.

Rumor can be distinguished from gossip in three ways (Rosnow, 1974; Rosnow & Georgoudi, 1985; Rosnow & Kimmel, 2000). First, rumor is not based on solid evidence (it is unverified), whereas gossip may or may not be firmly substantiated. Second, rumor is typically about a topic of importance or significance to its participants, whereas gossip is perceived in a less urgent fashion. As Sabini and Silver (1982) put it, "Calling a story gossip and calling it rumor are both dismissive, but they dismiss in different ways. 'Rumor' attacks the speaker's claim; 'gossip' attacks its idleness" (p. 92). Third, rumor may or may not be about the private lives of individuals, but gossip is always about this topic. Ambrosini (1983) stated it this way: "Gossip focuses on the private affairs of individuals; rumor focuses on the larger sphere of human events" (p. 70). Although gossip may venerate (Foster, 2004), in conversation, at least, it is predominantly derogatory and slanderous in nature (Walker, 2003; Walker & Struzyk, 1998; Wert & Salovey, 2004; however, see Dunbar, 2004 for a contradictory finding: Less than 5% of gossip overheard in public places was derogatory).

Although rumor and gossip differ, there exist "nebulous forms" that are hard to classify (Rosnow, 2001, p. 211). For example, hearsay that the boss is embezzling funds to pay for his sizable gambling debts is unverified, is instrumentally relevant, and arises in a situation of potential threat: Embezzlement may affect company livelihood. However, such hearsay is also evaluative idle talk that might be spread by someone attempting to satisfy status or ego needs in the context of a social hierarchy. Like rumor, gossip may convey useful social information (Rosnow & Georgoudi, 1985). For example, coworkers may help one another understand the boss's motivation: "She has an absurd need for power; approach her only with requests that will make her look good to her superiors." Such a message is private information about another individual, it is entertaining, and it serves important social network formation functions, yet it is also helps make sense of an ambiguous situation and manage potential threat.

Urban, Modern, or Contemporary Legends

Urban legends are stories of unusual, humorous, or horrible events that contain themes related to the modern world; are told as something that did or may have happened, variations of which are found in numerous places and times; and contain moral implications (Cornwell & Hobbs, 1992; Fine, 1992; Kapferer, 1987/1990). The term *urban legend* is a misnomer—urban legends often involve any location, not just cities; they are more properly termed *modern* or *contemporary* legends (P. B. Mullen, 1972). The terms *urban, modern,* and *contemporary* legends are therefore used interchangeably in this discussion.

CONTEXT AND FUNCTIONS

Contemporary legends are told in a storytelling context. They have a setting, a plot, a climax, and an epilogue. For example, tourists traveling in a van in Australia hit a kangaroo and apparently killed it. They got out of the van and dressed it up in one of the tourist's jacket and took a photograph to show back home—what a laugh it would bring! But the kangaroo had the last laugh; he was merely stunned. He awoke and hopped away—jacket (which contained a wallet and a passport) and all! Moral of the story: Be kind to animals (adapted from a version circulating on the Internet in 1997, as quoted in Mikkelson, 2004a). Contemporary legends are appropriate for situations in which entertaining stories are recounted, such as in casual conversation, Internet chat episodes, and social gatherings. They serve important functions: to amuse and to propagate moral values within a culture.

First they entertain. Modern urban legends are like tall tales in their exaggeratedness (Bennett, 1985). They are interesting to listen to. Consider the story of the hitchhiker who vanished (Brunvand, 1981): Driving on a country road, a father and daughter picked up a young girl hitchhiking. She got into the backseat and told them that she lived in a house 5 miles farther on. When they arrived, the girl had vanished! Knocking on the door of the house, they discovered that a young girl, who looked like the person they had picked up, had disappeared several years ago and had last been seen hitchhiking on that very country road. And, that day was her birthday.

Second, urban legends propagate mores and values. All good stories signify a theme or meaning; in other words, there is a moral to the story. As Kapferer (1987/1990, p. 123) stated, they are "exemplary stories . . . since, like fables, their function is to set forth examples from which moral implications can be drawn." Wilkie posited that three popular contemporary legends in the 1970s circulated among Americans "to criticize and regulate the behaviors of other Americans" (1986, p. 5): Jumping up and down after sex prevents pregnancy (Don't get pregnant!); child actor Jerry Mathers—Beaver in the popular TV series *Leave it to Beaver*—died in action in the Vietnam conflict (Get out of Vietnam!); and six students high on LSD blinded themselves by staring into the sun (Don't take drugs!). The tale entitled "The Hook" criticizes teenage promiscuity. In this urban legend, a teenage couple in a parked car in the dead of night stop necking after hearing scratching noises; after they arrive home, the prosthetic hook of an escaped mental patient is found hanging on the car door handle (Brunvand, 1981). Modern legends are thus like fables that focus on "fears, warnings, threats, and promises" (Bennett, 1985, p. 223). Urban legends often contain the funny and the horrible—but the "horror often 'punishes' someone who flouts society's conventions" (Van der Linden & Chan, 2003). The story of the traveler who is lured to his apartment by a seductive woman but wakes up to discover that his kidney has been removed as part of an illegal organ-selling operation is a morality tale about one-night stands (Mikkelson, 2002). Like traditional legends, modern legends persist because they answer long-standing questions and make sense of the world; they symbolize underlying truths and values. For example, the legend of George Washington and the cherry tree symbolizes and reinforces the virtue of honesty (G. W. Allport & Postman, 1947b).

CONTENT

As in the kangaroo tale, urban legend content is first of all a narrative tale, usually complete with setting, plot, climax, and denouement. Second, these stories are unusual, horrible, or funny. They are of "notable happenings of the kind that allege 'strange but true'" (Fine, 1992, p. 2). It would be unusual, to say the least, for a Doberman to bite off and choke on the fingers of a burglar, but it could happen (Brunvand, 1984). Third, contemporary legend content contains contemporary material as opposed to traditional themes and events. The topics of the contemporary legend are "events that happened in contemporary society and depict persons, relations, organizations, and institutions, that are recognized by narrator and audience to characterize the modern world" (Fine, 1992, p. 2; although see Bennett, 1985, for a counterview). These topics include, for example, automobiles, hitchhikers, carcinogens, necking, photography, dating, and organ removal.

RUMOR VERSUS URBAN LEGENDS

Both rumor and modern legends have been seen as propositions for belief, collective processes and transactions, verbal expressions (P. B. Mullen, 1972), and unofficial news (Kapferer, 1987/1990). In addition, both consist, at their core, of beliefs, statements, or verbal expressions (P. B. Mullen, 1972). Distortion has occurred in both—in the form of inclusion of concrete details—so as to make a tale more plausible (G. W. Allport & Postman, 1947b; P. B. Mullen, 1972).

However, rumors and urban legends differ in their primary contexts, function, and content, their typical structure, and the extent to which they migrate. First, although legends may, broadly speaking, help to make sense of the world (P. B. Mullen, 1972), they often do not pertain to a particular situation. For example, they are not often proposed during company downsizings because they are of limited value in ferreting out the facts and preparing for the future. However, rumors are not set forth primarily to entertain and promote mores; rumors of low projected fourth-quarter corporate earnings are not amusing nor do they possess a moral adage. Thus, rumors tend to be about a current event or topic of discussion (Rosnow, 1974) and how these events predict the future; legends typically consist of a storylike series of events that has already occurred.

Second, rumor and contemporary legend tend to differ in structure; legends tend to be longer than rumors and to have narrative elements (P. B. Mullen, 1972). Rumors are "short, nonnarrative expressions of belief" (P. A. Turner, 1993, p. 5; Bird, 1979; Caplow, 1947; Fine, 1985). As previously noted, this distinction accrues from the differing primary functions of the two. Legends are for storytelling and amusement and therefore tend to contain a setting, plot, climax, and denouement. Rumors are for ferreting out the facts, making sense, and managing risk and thus the information tends to be received in shorter packets that are relevant to a particular situation. A narrative cannot be presented because the sense making is contemporaneous rather than post hoc.

Finally, modern legends are rumors that become migratory—they are "brought up to date" and located locally (Kapferer, 1987/1990, p. 29); thus legends are renowned for the plethora of variations in detail in different versions. For example, the K-mart snake rumor—the false story about a woman bitten by a snake when trying on clothing at a K-mart—migrated from geographic locale to locale and from K-mart to Wal-Mart. Urban legends are not anchored in time and space as rumors are (Kapferer, 1987/1990). In fact, legends have been proposed to be rumors that persisted over time, and rumors have arisen out of legends also; thus both "feed off one another" (P. B. Mullen, 1972). "Some legends may reappear occasionally embodied in the form of a rumor" (Rosnow & Fine, 1976, p. 11). Put another way, "A legend may be regarded as a solidified rumor" (D. L. Miller, 1985, p. 162). Legends, then, are rumors that, after some distortion, persist for generations (G. W. Allport & Postman, 1947b). These legends seem to touch down as rumors in a particular locale for a particular time, then disappear, only to reappear years later in another place and with the characters changed.

Empirical Evidence: Information Dimensions

So far we have sought to define and distinguish rumor, gossip, and urban legend by exploring their contexts, functions, and contents. We have in mind methodological and practical reasons for this exploration; a sharpened conceptualization of rumor will lead to more valid investigations of rumor and more valid prescriptions for handling rumor. With these objectives and concerns in mind, we investigated the question, "Do people make distinctions between pure forms of rumor, gossip, and urban legends? And if so, do they make the same distinctions that we do?" Thus far, the answer to both questions has turned out to be "yes." In the remainder of this chapter we describe a series of studies we conducted that investigated these questions.

On the basis of the knowledge we discussed earlier in this chapter, we hypothesized that classic forms of rumor, news, gossip, and urban legend would be differentially regarded along six dimensions of information: evidentiary basis, importance, extent to which content is about individuals, extent to which content is slanderous, how entertaining the information is, and how useful the information is. In specific terms, rumor should be rated low on evidentiary basis and high on importance and usefulness. News ratings should mirror these elements except for evidentiary basis, which ought to be rated highly. In contrast, gossip should be considered by participants to be low in importance and usefulness, and high in slanderous content about individuals and entertainment value. Finally, urban legends should be low in evidentiary basis, importance, and usefulness, but high in entertainment. These hypotheses are summarized in Table 1.2.

To explore these hypotheses, we generated the Information Dimensions Scale (IDS) to measure perceived dimensions of information. We presented prototypical examples of each information type to participants and they rated each on bipolar 9-point scales. We rated four information dimensions related to content: We measured evidentiary basis by rating the extent to which the information is "information that has been verified" versus "information that has not been verified," "information that you are absolutely [vs. not at all] sure is true," and "information that is [vs. is not] based on strong evidence." We measured importance of content by rating the extent to which the information is important, is significant, and will be talked about seriously. We measured content about individuals by rating the extent to which the information is about a person's private life, about individuals, and not

TABLE 1.2

Hypothesized Information Dimensions of Rumor, News, Gossip, and Urban Legend

	Evidentiary basis	Perceived importance by participants	Content about individuals	Content slanderous	Entertaining	Perceived usefulness by participants
Rumor	Low	High	L/M/H	L/M/H	L/M/H	High
News	High	High	L/M/H	L/M/H	L/M/H	High
Gossip	L/M/H	Low	High	High	High	Low
Urban legend	Low	Low	L/M/H	L/M/H	High	Low

Note. L/M/H = low, medium, or high.

about matters pertaining to the group or organization. We measured slanderous content by rating the extent to which the information discredits someone, is slanderous, and is derogatory. Participants rated one exemplar of rumor, gossip, news, or urban legend; we created two versions for each information type (see Exhibit 1.1). Fifty-nine Rochester Institute of Technology undergraduates were asked to imagine that they were at work and heard the statement from a coworker;

EXHIBIT 1.1

Rumor, Gossip, News, and Urban Legend Statements

Rumor 1: *"I heard that our department is about to be downsized."* Your supervisor has not heard anything about this but you know that the economy has not been doing that well lately.

Rumor 2: *"I heard that our department is about to be moved to another building and will be merged with another department."* Your supervisor has not heard anything about this but you know that another department was recently moved and merged because of reorganization.

Gossip 1: *"I heard that one of the managers is having an extramarital affair with his secretary."* Your supervisor has not heard anything about this but you rarely see that manager with his wife lately.

Gossip 2: *"I heard that Sally is a wild and crazy kind of girl."* (Sally works in the building but you don't know her that well.) Your supervisor has not heard anything about this but you have noticed that Sally is moderately attractive.

News 1: *"Our company must respond to a tough economy in order to survive. We will be downsizing the development department."* (You work for the development department.) Your supervisor confirms this and you know that the economy has not been doing that well lately.

News 2: *"Jim Jones, head of development, will be promoted to senior vice president of consumer relations."* (You work for the development department and Jim Jones is your supervisor.) Your supervisor confirms this and you know that he has had a long string of successes in the past 2 years.

Urban Legend 1: *"I heard this from a friend of a friend of mine: This guy was driving with a group of tourists through the Australian bush when they hit a large kangaroo. He thought, 'What a great photo opportunity! The animal stood about 6 feet tall and would really impress the pals back home.' So they propped the kangaroo up, and to add that little bit of humor, one of them put his jacket on the kangaroo. However, the kangaroo was not dead! It was only stunned and promptly hopped off into the distance complete with jacket, wallet, and passport."*

Urban Legend 2: *"I heard this from a friend of a friend of mine: A Swiss couple fled home from Hong Kong after their pet poodle, Rosa, was cooked and served to them garnished with pepper sauce and bamboo shoots at a Chinese restaurant. The couple said they took Rosa with them to the restaurant and asked a waiter to give her something to eat. The waiter had trouble understanding the couple but eventually picked up the dog and carried her to the kitchen where they thought she would be fed. Eventually the waiter returned carrying a dish. When the couple removed the silver lid they found Rosa."*

Note. Urban Legend 1 is adapted from a version circulating on the Internet in 1997, as quoted in Mikkelson (2004a); Urban Legend 2 is from a Reuters news story that circulated in August 1971, as quoted in Brunvand (1984, p. 95).

in news conditions, the statement was read from a memo from the company president. Participants then rated the statement on evidentiary basis, importance, content about individuals, and slanderous content.[3]

Content information dimension means for rumor, news, gossip, and urban legend are presented in Figure 1.1. Across the two versions, information dimension means for each type of statement were similar and were therefore collapsed. Consistent with our hypotheses, rumor and news differed only with regard to evidentiary basis, and were both rated as important, not about individuals, and not slanderous. Rumor and gossip, however, differed on every dimension except evidentiary basis (both were low). Gossip exemplars were rated as not important, about individuals, and slanderous. In addition, urban legend exemplars were rated low on evidentiary basis and importance. Therefore, our exemplars of rumor, gossip, news, and urban legend were meaningfully distinguished by content along hypothesized information dimensions.

Participants also rated functional information dimensions: the extent to which the information is entertaining and useful. The primary function of rumor and news is to make sense of an ambiguous or threatening situation. Rumor and news should therefore be useful information that may or may not be entertaining. Such information would be more likely to be discussed in a serious conversation with a boss or coworkers than at a lighthearted party. In contrast, gossip is about social-network configuration, entertainment, and communicating social norms. In a similar way, urban legends are stories told for entertainment and to convey mores. Gossip and urban legends should therefore be rated high on entertainment and low on usefulness. Gossip would be more likely to be discussed at a lighthearted party than in a serious conversation with one's boss.

To measure these information dimensions, we constructed an additional set of bipolar IDS items. We measured *entertaining* by rating the extent to which the statement was entertaining, amusing, and enjoyable; we measured *useful* by rating the extent to which the statement was "useful to you," beneficial to know, and helpful to know. A second set of Rochester Institute of Technology undergraduate participants rated one of the same eight statements on the extent to which the statement was entertaining and useful.[4] Participants also rated how likely they were to mention the statement "in a serious conversation

---

[3] Standardized alpha coefficients were as follows: evidentiary basis, .91; importance, .87; content about individuals, .70; and slanderous content, .79. This study used a between-groups design (ns = 7 or 8).

[4] Standardized alpha coefficient for each was .83; N = 50 in a between-groups design (ns = 5, 6, or 8).

FIGURE 1.1

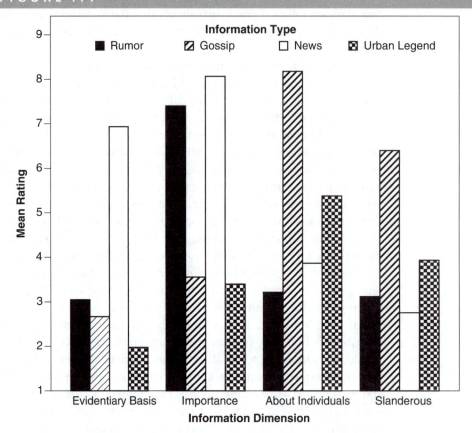

Mean information dimension ratings for exemplars of rumor, gossip, news, and urban legend: evidentiary basis, importance, about individuals, and slanderous.

with your boss," "at a party with friends where you are having a good time," and "to other coworkers within an hour after hearing it."

Mean ratings for entertaining and useful are presented in Figure 1.2; means were again similar across versions and therefore collapsed within information type. Consistent with our hypotheses, rumor and news exemplars served similar functions: Both were rated as highly useful and low on entertainment. However, gossip and urban legend were entertaining but not very useful. Thus, rumor differed from gossip and urban legend on these dimensions. Our exemplars of rumor, gossip, news, and urban legend were meaningfully distinguished by function along hypothesized information dimensions.

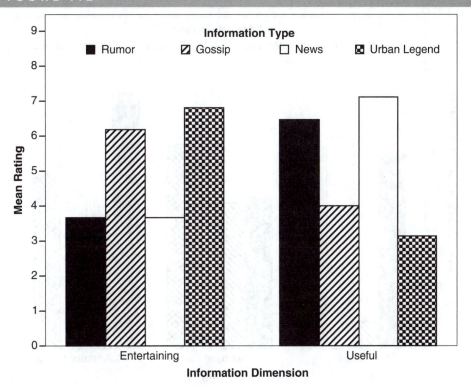

FIGURE 1.2

Mean information dimension ratings for exemplars of rumor, gossip, news, and urban legend: entertaining and useful.

Transmission likelihood means for rumor, gossip, and news exemplars also reflected hypothesized functions. Figure 1.3 presents the mean likelihood of transmitting each type of information within various settings. Rumor and news transmission likelihoods did not differ across situation, and both were more likely to be transmitted in a serious conversation with the boss or to coworkers within 1 hour than to friends having a good time at a party. These results indicate a sense-making function. In contrast, gossip and urban legend were much more likely to be shared with coworkers and within 1 hour of hearing it than in a serious conversation with the boss, which indicates the entertainment function. Once again, participants meaningfully distinguished by function between exemplars of rumor, gossip, news, and urban legend.

FIGURE 1.3

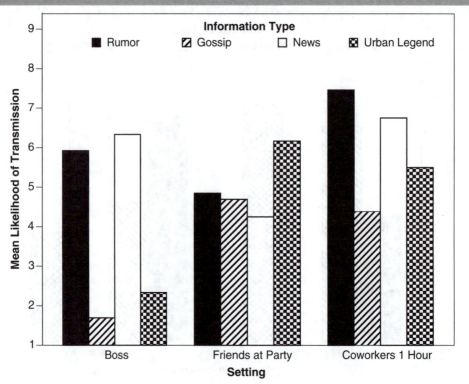

Mean likelihood of transmitting rumor, gossip, news, and urban legend in different settings. Scale anchored at 1 (*very unlikely*) to 9 (*very likely*). With boss = "in a serious conversation with your boss," friends at party = "at a party with friends where you are having a good time," and coworkers 1 hour = "to other coworkers within an hour after hearing it."

Conclusions, Implications, and Future Research

In this chapter we have defined rumor as unverified and instrumentally relevant information statements in circulation that arise in contexts of ambiguity, danger, or potential threat and that function to help people make sense and manage risk. We differentiated rumor from gossip (social chat that entertains and serves valuable social network functions) and urban legend (narrative that entertains and reinforces values). We have taken a position that these genres of communication, although sharing some similarities, exhibit meaningful distinctions. For each form of communication, we explored context, function, and content differences. In addition, we created IDSs to investigate perceptions of exemplars of rumor, gossip, news, and urban legend. Our exemplars of these information types were appropriately distinguished: We observed both content and functional differences.

What are the implications of the distinctions between rumor, gossip, and urban legend? First, it is clear that in this volume we are discussing rumors. Although the dynamics discussed in this book may apply to gossip and urban legend, they are primarily intended for rumor. Second, for rumor researchers, providing rumor exemplars (as in Exhibit 1.1) or scenarios is likely to produce responses that are pertinent to rumor rather than to gossip or urban legend. This point is important especially for rumor and gossip. In unpublished data, we have uniformly found that people do not distinguish between the terms *rumor* and *gossip*. That is, they rate them both as they would rate gossip: low in importance, slanderous, about individuals, and so on. The rumor researcher cannot simply request participants to recall rumors; rather, rumors must be defined or exemplified in such a way as to distinguish them from gossip. For example, participants could be given several exemplars of rumor and then asked to provide additional examples.[5] Profiles from the IDS may also be effectively used in content analysis to distinguish rumor from gossip and legend. These steps will help ensure that the phenomenon under consideration is truly rumor.

We note that the study presented in this chapter involved the use of pure statement forms and that these pure forms exhibited different information-dimension patterns with continuous scales. The use of continuous scales represents an advance over attempts to place a categorical label on a statement because it allows for the comparative emphasis of the statement's content, context, and function. For example, rumor may now be differentiated from gossip with comparative (e.g., rumor tends to score higher on the importance dimension than does gossip) rather than dichotomous language (e.g., rumor is considered important whereas gossip is not). Indeed, our approach easily incorporates the concept of *nebulous forms*—those statements that are difficult to classify as rumor, gossip, or urban legend. Future research could use IDSs to measure the information dimensions of nebulous forms and the extent to which they match prototypical rumor, gossip, or urban legend profiles. For example, the unverified statement about the boss's embezzlement of funds might turn out to score highly on prototypical

---

[5] We thank Charles Walker for this suggestion.

rumor and moderately on prototypical gossip. Such an approach would prove more fruitful than would attempting to categorize the statement in one or the other form, or the equally undesirable alternative of minimizing distinctions between rumor, gossip, and urban legend.

Armed with a clearer conceptualization of rumor, we turn first to a description of the phenomena. What types of rumors typically present themselves during times of uncertainty and threat? How frequently does each type of rumor occur? Do rumors cause or contribute to human attitudes and behaviors? We address these questions in the next chapter.

Forms, Frequency, and Fallout of Rumors | 2

In late August 2005, 950 people died because of a rumor. Hundreds of thousands of Shiite pilgrims had converged in Baghdad to commemorate the anniversary of Imam Musa al-Kazim's death. Pilgrims were crossing a bridge in northern Baghdad when rumors of a suicide bomber caused them to panic: "We were all chanting slogans about Imam Musa, and then people started shouting about a suicide bomber," an injured eyewitness stated. "They started crashing into each other; no one would look back or give a hand to help the ones who had fallen. People started running on top of each other, and everyone was trying to save himself."

—*Worth, 2005*

We defined rumor as collective sense making in response to uncertainty or threat. Before we approach the social and organizational processes associated with rumor, we will more fully describe the phenomena. Rumor researchers have attempted to address three descriptive questions. First, in what ways does rumor sense making manifest itself? It is obvious that rumors differ in many ways, including content, style, periodicity, and motivational goal; it will be helpful to explore what categories or forms rumor takes. Second, how often does this collective sense making occur? We once spoke with the senior vice president of PR at a large corporation who said, "I deal with rumors all the time." It is valuable to know how prevalent—how frequent—rumors are in human discourse. Third, does it matter? That is, do rumors cause or contribute to human action or attitudes in a significant way? It is surprising that this question has not often been addressed. It is frequently taken for granted—through anecdotes and intuition—that rumors affect people. Yet do they really, and if so, how strongly and to what end? Again, it is beneficial to systematically assess what the effect—the fallout—of rumor is. In the previous chapter we defined rumor; in this one we describe it.

Forms of Rumors

G. W. Allport and Postman (1947b) noted that there are many ways to classify rumors depending on the interest of the analyst: "The rumor pie may be sliced in many ways" (p. 170). Rumors may be divided according to temporal aspects such as periodicity: Some rumors (as we saw in chap. 1, this volume) are versions of long-standing urban legends that touch down from time to time and whose details adapt to the current time and locale. For example, the story that a thief, lying in wait under a woman's car that was parked in a shopping mall, slashed her ankles and stole her car surfaces periodically as a rumor about one's local shopping mall (Mikkelson, 1999). Rumors may also be segmented according to subject matter; D. L. Miller (1985) surveyed examples of product rumors (a leper had been discovered working in the Chesterfield cigarette factory), disaster rumors (a Swedish nuclear power plant leaked radiation), and atrocity rumors (a prisoner of war communicated his torture via a postage stamp). In a similar way, rumors have often been categorized by their content or theme. In this way Knopf (1975) and P. A. Turner (1993) classified rumors related to race, whereas Fine (1992) and Koenig (1985) grouped commercial rumors (see also Bird, 1979). Rumors may also be differentiated by the pattern of collective discussion surrounding them: Shibutani (1966) posited rumors arising out of low-anxiety deliberative sense-making discussions in contrast to those coming out of high-anxiety extemporaneous discussions. Extemporaneous rumor discussions are similar to Wilke's (1986) crisis rumors, which are endemic in situations in which there is a dearth of or ambiguity about information about an important topic. Kapferer (1987/1990) presented an etiological matrix of rumor based on the origin of the rumor (an ambiguous event, a hitherto-unnoticed detail, or no event) and the birth process of the rumor (did it arise spontaneously or was it deliberately set forth?).

Rumors have been cataloged according to the motivational tension that characterizes the rumor: R. H. Knapp (1944) categorized over 1,000 wartime rumors as either *dread* rumors (fearful of a negative event), *wish* rumors (hopeful of a positive event), or *wedge-driving* rumors (expressive of hostility toward a people-group). To this motivational scheme, G. W. Allport and Postman (1947b) added *curiosity* (intellectually puzzling) rumors. Knapp's classification scheme is perhaps the most popular and has been adopted or extended in a variety of contexts (Bordia & DiFonzo, 2004; Hellweg, 1987; Hershey, 1956). For example, U.S. Air Force Captain Stephanie R. Kelley categorized wartime rumors surfacing in and around Baghdad according to Knapp's scheme (S. R. Kelley, 2004). Among other interesting findings, Kelley observed a smaller percentage of wedge-driving and a greater percentage of fear rumors than did Knapp. Kelley then categorized these wedge-driving rumors according to the target of their hostility, including U.S.–Coalition forces, the Iraqi interim government, Saddam Hussein, Kurds, Shi'a, and Sunni. Finally, Kelley categorized rumors according to collective concerns of the Iraqis. A quarter of the rumors reflected apprehension regarding the emerging government and political process such as the transfer of authority to Iraq, alleged international (usually Zionist–United States) plots to rule over Iraq, and possible civil war because of sectarian strife; other concerns included quality of life, the insurgency, and security.

With Ralph Rosnow (DiFonzo, Bordia, & Rosnow, 1994), we first categorized organizational rumors recalled by company managers according to content and object of collective interest or concern, which reflected our emphasis on the sense-making function and ambiguous or threatening contexts in which rumors often arise (see chap. 1, this volume). *Turnover* rumors were about people leaving the organization and reflected employee interest in how turnover might affect job duties, advancement opportunities, and working conditions. *Pecking order* rumors were about changes in management hierarchy and reflected interest in how these changes would affect job stability and stock prices. Rumors about *job security* and *job quality* reflected concerns about employment longevity, duties, and compensation. *Costly error* rumors were about mistakes and reflected concerns about stock prices, corporate reputation, and job security. Finally, *consumer concern* rumors were about customer apprehensions and reflected concerns about sales, environmental risks, and health effects.

We also classified organizational rumors according to their *rumor public:* the people among which the rumor circulates. Some rumors are primarily internal: "those of primary interest to company personnel, suppliers, or vendors (i.e., people who are associated with the production or distribution or sale of the organization's products or services)"

(DiFonzo & Bordia, 2000, p. 176). Turnover, pecking order, job security, and job quality rumors are most likely to circulate among internal rumor publics. Some rumors are primarily external: "Those of primary interest to customers, press, stockholders, or the general public (i.e., people who purchase and use or potentially purchase and use the organization's products, services, or stocks)" (p. 176). Costly error, consumer-concern, and stock-market rumors are most likely to be external rumors. This typology reflects the likely distinctions in both content and object of collective concern in rumors circulating among different organizational constituencies.

Organizational rumors are often most populous—and troublesome—during periods of change. During a downsizing at a large hospital, we categorized internal rumors according to content and object of collective concern with regard to change (Bordia, Jones, Gallois, Callan, & DiFonzo, in press). Our organizational change rumor typology consisted of four types of rumors concerned with change: Rumors about changes to job and working conditions were about job loss, work practice changes, impacts on careers, loss of facilities, and staff reductions (e.g., "operational officers to be downsized from 300 to 100"). Rumors about the nature of the organizational change reflected concerns about changes to the structure and nature of the organization (e.g., "mental health will be collocated with geriatrics"). Rumors about poor change management were concerned with how badly change was being accomplished, such as this rumor about waste: "they are paying an extra $1 million to put an 'aesthetically pleasing' bend in the building!" Finally, some rumors were about the consequences of change for organizational performance (e.g., "there will be no oxygen available in bathrooms, only portable oxygen"). This typology again reflects the sense making and threat management functions of rumor along several different aspects of the organizational change: how well the change is being managed, and its impact on jobs, organization structure, and organizational performance.

What is to be gained from these varied attempts to parse rumors? Classifying rumors highlights the contours of the collective sense making and threat management functions of rumor: They tell us what people are concerned about. Organizational members are obviously apprehensive about changes that may affect their jobs, working conditions, and financial security; when uncertain about such issues, they will participate in the rumor mill. In addition, classification often reveals underlying attitudes and beliefs (G. W. Allport & Postman, 1947b; R. H. Knapp, 1944); dread rumors reveal an underlying fear, for example, whereas hostility rumors indicate group conflict. S. R. Kelley's (2004) observation of an entire family of rumors about alleged United States–

Zionist conspiracies to subdue Iraq revealed deep distrust and antipathy toward Israel. On a practical note, these categorization schemes prepare managers, PR officers, and opinion leaders for the types and nature of rumors they can expect.

Frequency

How often are rumors encountered? Our investigations concerning organizational rumors over a dozen years have included interviews, surveys, and lab experiments. According to anecdotal evidence, managers and communications officials often relate that they deal with rumors frequently. One manager of a software development firm undergoing downsizing quipped: "We are *swimming* in rumors" (DiFonzo & Bordia, 2006). Another complained, "I deal with rumors *all the time!*" Research into this question is scant, but what little there is characterizes rumor—contrary to our anecdotes—as less frequent than other forms of communication. Hom and Haidt found that rumors arose much less frequently than did gossip in the "social talk" of college students (Holly Hom, 2003, personal communication). Hellweg's (1987) review of grapevine research concluded that a small portion of informal network information is rumor. During 2 years of service in a regimental military unit of over 1,700 men in the Pacific during World War II, Caplow (1947) noted that rumor frequency was low; Caplow's highest count was 17 rumors in 1 month. Rumors are, of course, typically episodic in nature. In our longitudinal study of rumors in an organization undergoing radical downsizing (see the rest of this chapter and chap. 8, this volume), the average number of different rumors heard by each employee each month peaked at seven just prior to layoff announcements—a time of great uncertainty and anxiety—then receded to less than two in succeeding months. Some situations (e.g., those filled with uncertainty and anxiety) and conditions (e.g., close networks) increase rumor frequency.

Managers are sensitive to the frequency of rumors, particularly those rumors that are harmful. We investigated the frequency of harmful organizational rumors in a sample of 74 very experienced corporate PR officers (DiFonzo & Bordia, 2000). Participants were members of the Arthur W. Page Society (a prestigious group of PR professionals) or associated with the Institute for Public Relations in Gainesville, Florida. The sample consisted of senior vice presidents of PR from Fortune 500 corporations and well-known PR agency consultants. This cream-of-the-PR-crop sample averaged over 26 years of PR experience in a wide variety of industries. Participants reported that, on average, rumors that were of concern or potential concern reached their ears almost once per week.[1] Almost 90% of participants reported hearing such a rumor at least once per month. Thus, harmful or potentially harmful corporate rumors appear to be encountered frequently by PR professionals.

We also asked participants to estimate the overall proportion of harmful rumors according to our internal–external classification scheme discussed earlier (DiFonzo & Bordia, 2000). The median estimate of the percentage of primarily internal rumors encountered was 50%; for primarily external rumors, the median estimate was 30%. Thus, it appears that most harmful corporate rumors heard by PR professionals circulate among internal constituencies. Of internal rumors, the median estimates of the percentage of rumors about personnel changes, job security, and job satisfaction were 30%, 20%, and 10%, respectively. In comparison, the median estimate of the percentage of *gossip* rumors (i.e., gossip) was 15%.[2] We asked participants for examples of internal rumors that had reached their ears; what was most evident was that nearly all of them related to episodes of significant organizational change such as layoffs, mergers, outsourcing, staff changes, restructurings, and plant closings. Downsizing and restructuring, for example, led to rumors about benefit reductions and the transfer of job duties. Of the external rumors, the median estimates of the percentage of rumors about organizational reputation, stock market, and product service or quality were 30%, 18%, and 10%, respectively. As with internal rumors, perusal of the content of examples of these rumors showed that the preponderance of them related to organizational change. Impending mergers, for example, spawned stock-market rumors and rumors about the discontinuance of certain products. In organizational contexts at least, both internal and external rumors clearly become more frequent during times of change.

More recent work has focused on the frequency and flavor of internal organizational change rumors. We assessed the relative frequencies of internal organizational change rumors in the study of the hospital undergoing change mentioned earlier (Bordia et al., in press). The hospital was a hotbed of major and multiple changes taking place over several years: new hospital construction, new patient care technol-

---

[1] "$M = 5.68$, $SD = 1.15$, $n = 74$, where 5 = monthly, 6 = weekly, and 7 = daily" (DiFonzo & Bordia, 2000, p. 177; see Appendix 2.1 for the full survey instrument).

[2] Median estimates sum to less than 100% if distributions are positively skewed, as many were.

ogies, organizational restructuring, partial privatization, patient bed reduction, new use of multidisciplinary teams, and relocation. All 3,200 hospital staff members were mailed our questionnaire and 1,610 (50.3%) responded. We asked respondents, "Please describe the last rumor you heard about the changes going on at [this organization]." Of 776 responses 368 (47%) were about changes to job and working conditions; 147 (19%) concerned the nature of the organizational change; 89 (11%) concerned the management of the change; and 53 (7%) concerned how change would affect organizational performance; 10 (1%) were gossip statements; and 109 (14%) were uncodable. In addition, the overwhelming motivational tension of these rumors was fear: Of the 510 reported rumors that could be classified as either negative or positive, 479 were dread rumors and 31 were wish rumors. Again, change was a catalyst for rumors; in organizations, the nature of these rumors is sense making (amid anxiety) about how organizational change may adversely affect job and working conditions. Furthermore, the most frequent types of rumors are those concerning negative consequences to employees (e.g., loss of job). Rumor participants seem to attempt to gain a sense of control over their own situation by becoming aware of the bad things that might happen to them because of the change.

Rumor Fallout

Do rumors matter? That is, do they cause or contribute to behavior and mental processes? The answer to this question clearly is yes. Popular, business, and scientific literature is replete with instances in which rumors exerted or exacerbated powerful effects. For example, rumors during natural calamities have resulted in a number of outcomes (Prasad, 1935; Shibutani, 1966). For example, Chinese earthquake rumors spawned "panicky and fatalistic [behaviors] such as killing and eating livestock and spending savings, stockpiling food supplies, trying to leave the area, not going to work and postponing essential agricultural activities" as well as "active information seeking" (R. H. Turner, 1994, p. 252) and a revival of mystic protection rituals in traditional areas. Economic fallout of such rumors included food supply depletion and short-term inflation. Rumors have also long been implicated in precipitating ethnic riots (Horowitz, 2001; Knopf, 1975) and exacerbating racial tensions (G. W. Allport & Postman, 1947b; Fine & Turner, 2001; P. A. Turner, 1993). For example, the *Report of the American National Advisory Commission on Civil Disorders* cited rumor as responsible for inflaming racial tensions in "more than 65% of the disorders studied by the Commission" (Kerner et al., 1968, p. 173). Medical rumors are known to affect health behaviors as well (Suls & Goodkin, 1994). For example, a rumor that contraceptive use causes weakness was associated with reduced use among Egyptian women (DeClerque, Tsui, Abul-Ata, & Barcelona, 1986). A second example: False rumors that Hong Kong had been declared an area infected by severe acute respiratory syndrome (SARS) caused widespread panic there ("Teenager Arrested," 2003). Telephone networks became jammed with people spreading the rumor, which resulted in bank and supermarket runs. Rumors may even affect population rates; in one economic model, rumors that government-funded social security systems can fail because of aging populations reduce expectations about the future and lead citizens to bear fewer children (Van Groezen, Leers, & Meijdam, 2002).

Rumor effects occur even if rumors themselves are not believed. Prasad (1935) noticed that people may have disbelieved rumors circulating after the calamitous Indian earthquake of 1934, but they still acted on them. For example, trips to the Indian city of Patna were canceled on the day that a rumor predicted that Patna would cease to exist. People apparently wanted to be safe rather than sorry; that is, even though the outcomes predicted by the rumor were very unlikely, they were extremely negative. We found the same sort of inference making at work in a rumor episode we observed in 1993: the headlights hoax. This rumor was transmitted by means of a flyer resembling a safety memo; the memo spread like a contagious virus via fax machines throughout the United States (Mikkelson, 2004b). Exhibit 2.1 presents a reproduction of the fax we received in our graduate school mailboxes at Temple University (a well-meaning employee had been alarmed by the contents of the fax and had distributed it to everyone in the psychology building).

The fax urged people to not flash their car lights for anyone because of the deadly consequences that might occur. It alleged that nighttime motorists blinked their headlights at oncoming automobiles that were traveling with their headlights off as a kindly reminder to turn them on. This neighborly act resulted in the opposing motorist circling about, following the blinking motorist to his or her destination, and killing him or her—all as part of a grisly new gang initiation rite. The fax allegedly originated from the Illinois state police; when we contacted them to verify the rumor, a tired trooper stated: "We've been getting phone calls about this for 2 weeks. It never happened; it's a hoax!" After interviewing 36 people in the psychology building, we found that virtually all of them planned to abstain from headlight blinking of any sort, even after being informed of the false nature of the fax. Why? One likely explanation of these effects is prospect theory. Prospect

Headlights-Hoax Flyer

SAFETY NEWS

Date: October 15, 1993
From: Pat Duffy, Manager, Safety Department
To: All Employees and Their Families

We were made aware of the following bulletin from the Norfolk Southern police department (Virginia) and have confirmed through the New Castle County and Wilmington police departments that similar events have occurred in Los Angeles, Chicago, and Baltimore. Please take the time to read the remainder of this memo and inform your family members and friends. This awareness and precaution is important for both drivers and passengers whether at home or traveling on business or pleasure.

BULLETIN

!!!THERE IS A NEW GANG INITIATION!!!

This new initiation of "MURDER" is brought about by gang members driving around with their car lights off. When you flash your car lights to signal them that their lights are out, the gang members take it literally as "LIGHTS OUT", so they follow you to your destination and kill you!!! That's their initiation.

Two families have already fallen victim to this initiation ritual in the St. Louis and Chicago areas.

This information should be given widespread distribution on our respective territories and posted on all bulletin boards. Beware and inform your families and friends.

DO NOT FLASH YOUR CAR LIGHTS FOR ANYONE

The above information was furnished by the Illinois State police department.

theory says that people are loss-averse, that is, they tend to feel losses more intensely than they feel equivalent gains (Kahneman & Tversky, 1979). People tend to overestimate the probability of improbable negative events, perhaps because negative information is processed more thoroughly than is positive information (Baumeister, Bratslavsky, Finkenauer, & Vohs, 2001), and therefore take steps to avoid them. The consequences of blinking one's headlights, although improbable, were vividly and catastrophically negative. The net effect of this rumor: a neighborly cultural practice diminished.

Rumor effects may be classified as behavioral or attitudinal. In business settings, behavioral effects of rumor include those that affect purchase behaviors. The false rumor that Tropical Fantasy, a soft drink, was owned by the Ku Klux Klan and made Black men sterile reportedly caused sales to drop by 70% and incited attacks on delivery trucks (Freedman, 1991). Unger (1979) reported similar losses in sales resulting from false product rumors: Bubble Yum bubble gum is contaminated with spider eggs, and Pop Rocks candy, when ingested with soda pop, explodes in one's stomach. Rumors have also affected stock purchase behaviors and thus stock values (Lazar, 1973; Rose, 1951). For example, prior to publication of takeover rumors in the "Heard on the Street" column of *The Wall Street Journal*, price runups occurred, indicating that the takeover rumors pushed prices up as they diffused through the financial community (Pound & Zeckhauser, 1990); investors often "buy on the rumor." Workplace productivity has also been affected—usually negatively—by internal rumors (DiFonzo & Bordia, 2000). Tangible effects such as these are often mediated through rumor's impact on attitudes. One such attitude is reputation; clearly, rumors can wreak havoc on a company's public standing (Zingales, 1998). Koenig (1985) documented the case of Continental Bank whose reputation was besmirched by rumors of impending bankruptcy. Rumors during organizational change episodes such as restructuring and layoffs may also have damaging effects on organizational attitudes such as morale and trust (DiFonzo & Bordia, 1998; DiFonzo et al., 1994; Smeltzer & Zener, 1992). These effects are but a small sampling of the many outcomes that rumors can result in or contribute to. The remainder of this chapter summarizes systematic research from several studies conducted to investigate the scope and nature of organizational rumor effects.

EFFECTS OF RUMORS ON STOCK TRADING BEHAVIOR

Several experiments we conducted (DiFonzo & Bordia, 1997, 2002b) suggested that individual trading behavior is dramatically affected by the presence of rumors. In these studies, "investors" played a computerized stock market game in which they could buy or sell (or do neither) Goodyear stock. This microworld simulation (DiFonzo, Hantula, & Bordia, 1998) generally lasted for 60 "days" of trading; each "day" lasted 20 seconds. Stock prices started and ended at $35 per share, and each day's price change was unrelated to the next day's price change; prices rose during 30 of the 60 days and fell during the remainder. The direction of the next day's price change was thus objectively unpredictable, as it is in the actual stock market (Fama, Fisher, Jensen, & Roll, 1969; Malkiel, 1985). During each day of trading, participants were presented with the stock price for that day, the price change from the previous day, and the value of their stock and cash holdings. A sample display is reprinted in Figure 2.1. Some participants were presented with eight stock-related rumors and others received no such information. The rumors were either published in the "Heard on the Street" column of *The Wall Street Journal* or heard from an unpublished source, brother-in-law Harry (e.g., "You hear from Harry that Goodyear profits

FIGURE 2.1

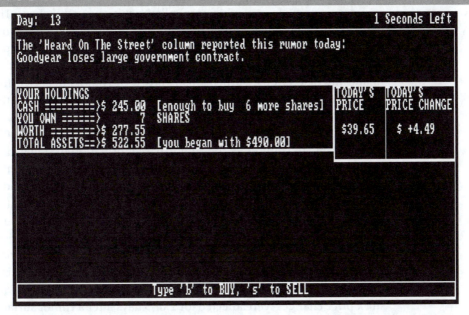

Day: 13   1 Seconds Left

The 'Heard On The Street' column reported this rumor today:
Goodyear loses large government contract.

YOUR HOLDINGS   TODAY'S   TODAY'S
CASH =========>$ 245.00 [enough to buy 6 more shares] PRICE PRICE CHANGE
YOU OWN ======>   7 SHARES
WORTH ========>$ 277.55 $39.65 $ +4.49
TOTAL ASSETS==>$ 522.55 [you began with $490.00]

                  Type 'b' to BUY, 's' to SELL

Example of a display presented on a training "day." From "Rumors and Stable Cause Attribution in Prediction and Behavior," by N. DiFonzo and P. Bordia, 2002b, *Organizational Behavior and Human Decision Processes, 88,* p. 787. Copyright 2002 by Elsevier. Reprinted with permission.

are up"). The conditions under which these rumors were heard were carefully varied: In one study, the rumor valence (whether it was a positive or negative rumor) agreed with the direction of that day's price change (up or down) 0%, 25%, 50%, 75%, or 100% of the time. The predictive validity of the rumor for tomorrow's price change was also varied. In one study, today's rumor predicted the direction of tomorrow's price change (e.g., a positive rumor would be followed by a price increase the next day); in most of the investigations, it was rigorously unrelated.

In all of these studies, participants' trading patterns were systematically affected by the presence of rumors: They tended to depart from a buy-low-sell-high trading strategy. Buying stock when the price is relatively low and selling it when it is relatively high has been dubbed a *tracking* strategy (Andreassen, 1987) and is, of course, essential to making a profit. Departing from this strategy means, for example, that participants continued to buy when the price was on the rise, or sell when the price was declining; such patterns are not very economically wise! Why did this happen? We describe the social cognitive processes involved in these studies in more detail in chapter 5 (this volume), but suffice to say that rumors led investors to attribute the causes of price changes to stable forces, which are called *stable-cause attributions*. Thus participants exposed to rumors thought that recent price trends would continue despite the fact that participants rated published and unpublished rumors as not credible, untrustworthy, and risky. The result was financially deleterious: Participants exposed to rumors departed from tracking and made significantly less profit during the simulations than did control participants.

In our most recent microworld study (DiFonzo & Bordia, 2002b) we were able to counteract the rumor-based formation of stable-cause attributions through training. In the unstable-cause training condition, participants were taught that stock-market price changes are random and unpredictable. These participants were taught to perceive that the information contained in rumors had already been incorporated into the stock price for that day—that the price efficiently reflected the aggregate opinion of the market. This *efficient market theory* (Fama et al., 1969) remains the prevailing understanding of the stock market. In the stable-cause training condition, participants were taught that stock price changes were affected for 2 or 3 days after a rumor surfaced; thus tomorrow's price change was somewhat predictable from today's rumor. Control participants received no training. Results: Investors taught to see price changes as caused by unstable forces departed less from tracking (buy low, sell high) trading strategies than did control participants or those trained to perceive stable causes. In other words, trained to perceive random variation, investors were less prone to the stable-cause attributional effects of rumor. In sum, these studies implicated stable-cause attributional mechanisms behind the systematic effects that rumors have on predictions of sequential events and on behaviors based on those predictions; these mechanisms are especially relevant to effects of rumors felt on the stock market.

EFFECTS OF CORPORATE RUMORS

In our study on the effects of corporate rumors (DiFonzo & Bordia, 2000) we presented our sample of 74 experienced PR officers with a list of 17 rumor effects (see Appendix 2.1) that we had developed from the literature and from our own previous studies (DiFonzo et al., 1994; DiFonzo & Bordia, 1998). Participants rated whether or not they had ever witnessed each effect as the result of a rumor they had personally dealt with. They also rated each effect for its average severity on a scale of small, medium, and large (we later assigned numeric values of 1, 2, and 3, respectively, to these ratings). Finally, we asked participants to give us a recent example of how a rumor caused the most serious effect(s) to occur.

Average severity rating, as well as the percentage of the sample that had ever observed the effects, is presented in Figure 2.2. Our experienced sample had observed a large majority of the effects during their long tenures; each of the top 11 effects had been witnessed by at least 78% of the sample. The most commonly experienced—90% or greater—rumor effects included detrimental consequences for employee morale, press reports, productivity, stress levels, and trust held by employees and customers. Effects were rated, overall, as moderately severe: 13 of the 17 effects were given an average severity rating between 1.50 and 2.50 (indicating medium severity). The most severe of these—those with an average rating at or above 1.75—

FIGURE 2.2

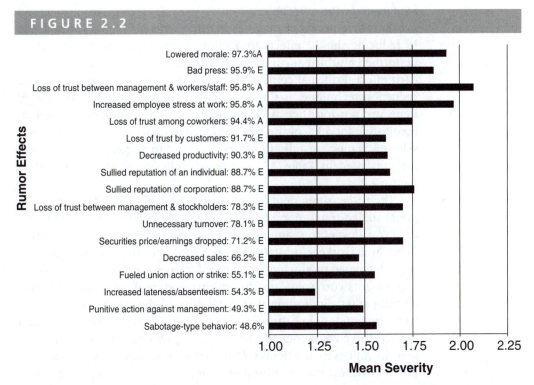

Rumor effects and mean severity ratings. Effects are in decreasing order by the percentage of respondents (*n* ranged from 66–73) who had ever observed the effect in their overall experience. Mean severity ratings are on a scale in which 1, 2, and 3 indicate small, medium, and large average effects, respectively. *E* indicates an external ramification, *A* indicates effects related to internal attitudes, and *B* indicates effects associated with internal behaviors (see text). From "How Top PR Professionals Handle Hearsay: Corporate Rumors, Their Effects, and Strategies to Manage Them," by N. DiFonzo and P. Bordia, 2000, *Public Relations Review, 26*, p. 180. Copyright 2000 by Elsevier. Reprinted with permission.

duplicated the list of most often experienced, and included a "sullied reputation of corporation" as well. Examples of how rumors caused such effects were illustrative: A rumor that the company was "up for sale" resulted in "lowered morale, resulting in loss of direction, focus, which reverberated to sales force and caused job security concerns." A rumor that "two plants in distant cities were to be closed and 4,000 people were to be terminated" had the effect of lowering morale in these plants and reducing productivity by 10%. A rumor that the corporation "would release 1998 first quarter earnings early because of losses stemming from its Asian business" caused an "intraday [stock] price dip of 2 points (price about 135) in company's common stock, which was reversed by end of day." These instances provide a glimpse of the many varieties of rumor effects that have been experienced by corporate PR officers.

Are there broader categories of rumor effects? We were interested in reducing the 17 effects to a more manageable set. We therefore performed a principal components analysis on the severity ratings for each effect. Principal components analysis, commonly used as a data reduction technique, is similar to factor analysis in which correlated items are put together as components. A three-component solution, accounting for 58% of the total variance in effect severity ratings, was selected as most meaningful. The effects and their component loadings are presented in Table 2.1; component effects are also indicated in Figure 2.2.

The three components were labeled *external ramifications* (e.g., bad press, sullied reputation of corporation, decreased sales), *internal attitudes* (e.g., loss of trust among coworkers, loss of trust between management and workers or staff, lowered morale), and *internal behaviors* (e.g., decreased productivity, increased lateness or absenteeism). These components correspond to the internal–external categorization (discussed earlier), indicating that the nature of the effect results in part from the rumor public through which the rumor recirculates.[3] We then created three component scores for each participant by averaging the severity ratings for the items within each component; thus, each participant had an external ramifications component score, an internal attitudes component score, and an internal behaviors component score. The mean of these component scores showed that external ramifications were considered to be somewhat severe, internal attitude effects were moderately severe, and internal behaviors were also somewhat

---

[3] We performed item analysis for each set of items in the three components; each was reliable (alpha coefficient for nine external ramification items was .89; for four internal attitude items, .78; and for three internal behavior items, .69).

TABLE 2.1

Rotated Factor Pattern and Final Communality Estimates From Principal Component Analysis of Rumor Effect Item Severity Ratings

Component				
External ramifications	Internal attitudes	Internal behaviors	Communality estimates	Rumor effect
77*	18	32	72	Punitive action against management
76*	1	11	59	Loss of trust by customers
73*	33	3	64	Sullied reputation of corporation
73*	15	6	55	Securities price/earnings ratio dropped
72*	21	−9	57	Loss of trust between management and stockholders
72*	−8	15	55	Bad press
69*	−9	48	71	Decreased sales
61*	22	−4	42	Fueled union action or strike
57*	29	23	46	Sullied reputation of individual
8	81*	34	78	Lowered morale
2	76*	9	59	Loss of trust among coworkers
23	66*	7	49	Loss of trust between management and workers or staff
19	65*	18	48	Increased employee stress at work
41	44	8	37	Sabotage-type behaviors
17	11	85*	76	Unnecessary turnover
8	34	74*	67	Increased lateness or absenteeism
5	44	54*	49	Decreased productivity

Note. *N* = 63. Printed values are multiplied by 100 and rounded to the nearest integer. Component loadings greater than 0.50 have been flagged by an asterisk (*). From "How Top PR Professionals Handle Hearsay: Corporate Rumors, Their Effects, and Strategies to Manage Them," by N. DiFonzo and P. Bordia, 2000, *Public Relations Review, 26*, p. 181. Copyright 2000 by Elsevier. Reprinted with permission.

severe.[4] In sum, rumors that experienced PR officers have encountered are perceived to have somewhat severe external ramifications, moderately severe effects on internal attitudes, and somewhat severe effects on internal behaviors.

EFFECTS OF NEGATIVE CHANGE RUMORS ON EMPLOYEE STRESS

It is clear that our survey of corporate PR officers found that they perceived the most serious consequences of rumor to be negative impacts on employee attitudes. We wished to further investigate this idea

---

[4] External ramifications M = 1.58, SD = .54, n = 73 (where 1, 2, and 3 indicated the effect was small, medium, and large in average severity, respectively); internal attitudes M = 1.90, SD = .58, n = 73; internal behaviors M = 1.45, SD = .52, n = 70.

by comparing the stress levels of people hearing rumors with the levels of those not hearing rumors. In the hospital study of change-related rumors introduced earlier (Bordia et al., in press), we gained a large-scale opportunity to do this.

This study was part of a broader investigation of the dynamics and effects of organizational change, and therefore change-related stress was measured. Each respondent rated how stressful the organizational changes were, using the following four dimensions taken from Terry, Tonge, and Callan (1995): (a) not at all stressful to extremely stressful; (b) not at all disruptive to extremely disruptive; (c) not at all upsetting to extremely upsetting; and (d) not at all difficult to extremely difficult. These ratings were aggregated into a single change-related stress score.[5] Now, recall that in this study, 776 of the 1,610 respondents reported the most recent change-related rumor they had heard; 834 did not report hearing a rumor. Of the 776 who heard a rumor, 479 heard negative (dread) rumors and 31 heard positive (wish) rumors. The remaining rumors (e.g., "mental health will be collocated with geriatrics") could not be classified either way and were therefore dropped from this analysis. To assess the relation between rumor and stress, we compared change-related stress scores between the negative-rumor group ($n = 479$), the positive-rumor group ($n = 31$), and the group that did not report any rumor ($n = 834$). Change-related stress was higher in the negative-rumor group than in the positive-rumor group— which is to be expected because the anticipation of a dreaded event is more stressful than that of a wished-for event—but it was also higher than in the no-rumor group. That is, employees who reported recently hearing a negative rumor were more stressed than those who didn't report hearing a rumor; ignorance may indeed be more blissful—or at least less stressful. The finding is, of course, only correlational; those who are more stressed may be more likely to hear or remember a negative rumor. Indeed, in light of the fact that uncertainty and anxiety have been linked to rumor transmission (see chap. 3, this volume), this explanation seems likely. At the very least, however, this result suggests that negative organizational rumors are associated with greater employee stress.

EFFECTS OF NEGATIVE RUMORS ON EMPLOYEE ATTITUDES, PRODUCTIVITY, AND INTENTION TO STAY

Again, our survey of corporate PR officers found that they perceived the most serious consequences of rumor to be negative impacts on

---

[5] Alpha = .92.

employee attitudes. And the cross-sectional organizational survey discussed earlier points to an association between hearing rumors and stress. We investigated these ideas in a more comprehensive and longitudinal way by measuring several well-known employee attitudes and behaviors over time in a change situation. For example, do employees who hear negative rumors over time tend to become less satisfied with their jobs? In this next study, we (and Rob Winterkorn) assessed the relationship over time between hearing negative rumors and uncertainty, anxiety, perceptions of quality of formal organizational communication, job satisfaction, organizational commitment, trust in the company, productivity, and intention to stay. We did this in a longitudinal investigation of a division of a company in Rochester, New York undergoing radical downsizing. In chapter 8 (this volume) we present the methodology of this study in greater detail and investigate the direct and moderating effects of trust on the likelihood of *rumor transmission*—defined as the likelihood of passing rumors; here, we focus on how these attitudes and behaviors are related to hearing rumors.

How might hearing rumors affect employee uncertainty, anxiety, attitudes, intentions, and productivity? It is important to note that in this study, as well as the organizational change rumor studies discussed earlier, rumors are most often dread (the division will be downsized) or wedge-driving (management has made budgetary errors) in nature. Let's begin with uncertainty, anxiety, and formal communication. As we discuss in chapter 3 (this volume), many investigations have linked anxiety and uncertainty to rumor activity; we therefore posited that uncertainty and anxiety would be associated with hearing rumors. The causal direction could go both ways, however: People who are anxious and uncertain may be more receptive to rumors (as we previously speculated), or hearing dread and wedge-driving rumors of (usually) uncontrollable events might also sustain or even heighten anxiety and uncertainty. In a similar way, formal communication quality should be negatively related to hearing rumors. Here also, causality may be bidirectional and, in addition, may be mediated by uncertainty. Poor formal communication would lead to higher uncertainty and hence greater receptivity to hearing rumors (DiFonzo & Bordia, 1998), but hearing such rumors—especially repeatedly—might lead one to conclude that formal communication efforts were poor.

Positive employee attitudes (job satisfaction, commitment to the organization, and trust in the company) and intentions to remain with the company are likely to be negatively associated with hearing negative rumors. This negative association could happen in at least three ways: Social learning (Lott & Lott, 1985) and social information processing (Salancik & Pfeffer, 1977) through negative rumors may teach employees that others feel negatively toward the company or that it is not a nice place to work. Indeed, rumors may be the quintessential vehicle by which social learning occurs. Second, equity theory (Adams, 1965) posits that employees keep account of the ratio between what they put into a job and what they get out of it, and that they compare this ratio with that of others in the company. Wedge-driving rumors seem likely to result in perceptions of inequity, and thus reduce job satisfaction, commitment, and trust. As a result, employees become more likely to think about leaving the organization. Indeed, employees are more likely to spread negative rumor about the organization when they feel that the organization has treated them unfairly (Skarlicki & Folger, 1997). Third, the law of cognitive structure activation contends that ambiguous stimuli will be encoded as consistent with the most salient schema and thereby affect relevant judgments and behaviors (Sedikides & Skowronski, 1991; also see chap. 5, this volume). Negative rumors almost certainly prime negative interpretation of ambiguous events by making negative schema salient, resulting in lower satisfaction, commitment, and trust. Again, these relations may be causally bidirectional: For example, negative rumors might reduce trust in management, but low trust in management might predispose an employee to hear—and recall—more negative rumors.

The positive employee behavior of productivity (increasing work output) might be increased or decreased by negative rumors. In our previous research, rumors of plant layoffs allegedly motivated workers to increase output (DiFonzo et al., 1994). K. Davis (1975) similarly found an average 8% increase in productivity as a result of grapevine rumors. However, anecdotal evidence suggests that engaging in rumor discussions is time consuming and distracting and thus reduces productivity (Weiss, 1982, chap. 16).

On the basis of these ideas, we hypothesized that hearing negative organizational rumors would be associated with higher levels of uncertainty and anxiety and lower levels of satisfaction with formal communication quality, job satisfaction, organizational commitment, trust in management, and intention to stay with the company; we made no prediction regarding productivity. The results of this study were consistent with these ideas.

The survey was administered once per month for 4 consecutive months to all 75 (initial) employees; response rates were high during each wave. Prior to the first and second waves, the division experienced work slowdowns and restructuring. During these periods, negative rumors—typically pertaining to dreaded layoff outcomes—abounded. After the second wave, layoff announcements occurred; 50% of the division was laid off between the third and fourth wave of the survey. Uncertainty and anxiety were measured, along with these employee attitudes: perceptions of the quality of formal organizational communication, job satisfaction, organizational commitment, and perceptions of the management as caring and trustworthy. Also, employees provided a self-rating of their recent productivity, and of their intention to stay with the company. All items were measured on a 7-point Likert-type scale and are presented in Exhibit 2.2. In addition, participants recorded the number of different rumors they had heard during the past month and rated overall how positive versus negative these rumors were. As one might expect during a time of radical downsizing, the rumors were overwhelmingly negative.[6]

Let's first examine the overall pattern of means over time for each variable. Mean numbers of rumors heard, along with uncertainty, anxiety, communication quality, job satisfaction, organizational commitment, trust, productivity, and intention to stay, are presented in Figures 2.3 and 2.4 for each wave of the survey. The number of different rumors heard spiked from the first to the second wave, then receded dramatically at Time 3 (T3) and Time 4 (T4). As the number of rumors heard increased, uncertainty and anxiety also increased, whereas job satisfaction, organizational commitment, and trust decreased. Self-rated productivity and intention to stay also decreased. These trends reversed when the number of rumors heard decreased; in addition, communication quality ratings increased. In the aggregate, then, increased numbers of negative rumors were accompanied by increased uncertainty and anxiety and more negative employee attitudes, behaviors, and intentions.

Would these same patterns obtain at the level of the individual? That is, how strongly is hearing rumors associated with each outcome? Tables 2.2 through 2.5 present correlations between the number of rumors heard during various time periods and T1, T2, T3, and T4 outcome variables. To obtain an estimate of the overall strength of these associations, we calculated average correlations.[7] A clear pattern emerged in line with predictions. First, number of rumors heard during any specified or cumulative period was strongly correlated with uncertainty ($r_{avg} = .42$ for 20 correlations) and moderately correlated with anxiety ($r_{avg} = .35$). Hearing negative rumors was thus associated with greater levels of uncertainty and anxiety. Second, moderate-sized negative correlations were observed between the number of rumors heard

---

[6] Mean rating = 2.02, $SD = 1.19$, $n = 169$ (1 = *extremely negative*, 7 = *extremely positive*).

[7] More sophisticated confidence intervals and meta-analytic combinations were not appropriate here as correlations were not independent; we simply wished to calculate a descriptive central tendency of each population of 20 correlations. Except for productivity (as discussed earlier) each set appeared to be homogeneous. In this discussion, designations of weak ($0 < r < .20$), moderate ($.20 < r < .40$), and strong ($.40 < r < .60$) correlations were guided by J. Cohen (1988, pp. 79–81).

Variables Measured in a Four-Wave Longitudinal Study of an Organization Undergoing Downsizing

Communication Quality (.66, .91, .88, .84)[a]

On the whole over the past month,
1. How well informed has the company kept you about upcoming changes? 7 = *Completely Informed*, 1 = *Completely Uninformed*.
2. How do you feel about the adequacy of communication that you receive from the company? 7 = *Completely Adequate*, 1 = *Completely Inadequate*.

Uncertainty (.77, .84, .81, .83)

On the average over the past month,
1. I was filled with questions about what current events in my company meant.
2. I was uncertain about whether friends and colleagues will lose their jobs.
3. I was uncertain about whether the company will be a good place to work.
4. I was uncertain about whether the overall quality of my job will change.
5. I was uncertain about whether I will be laid off.
6. I was filled with uncertainty related to my job and/or my company.

Anxiety (.87, .96, .88, .84)

On the average over the past month,
1. I felt anxious about possible changes that will occur in this company.
2. The thought of upcoming changes in this company worried me.

Rumors Heard

In the past month, how many different rumors have you heard related to this organization? (Write approximate number.)

Rumors Passed

Of the above number of rumors, how many did you pass on to someone else within the organization? (Write approximate number.)

Job Satisfaction (.86, .84, .88, .89)

1. In general over the past month, how well would you say your job measures up to the sort of job you hoped it would be when you took it? 7 = *Very Much Like*, 4 = *Somewhat Like*, 1 = *Not Very Much Like*.
2. All in all, how satisfied would you say you were with your job over the past month? 7 = *Extremely*, 4 = *Moderately*, 1 = *Not at All*.
3. If a good friend of yours told you he/she was interested in working in a job like yours for your employer, on average over the past month what would you have told him/her? 7 = *Definitely Recommend*, 1 = *Definitely Not Recommend*.
4. Knowing what you know now, if you had to decide all over again whether to take the job you now have, what would you have decided over the past month? 7 = *Definitely Take Same Job*, 1 = *Definitely Not Take Same Job*.

continued

EXHIBIT 2.2 *(Continued)*

Variables Measured in a Four-Wave Longitudinal Study of an Organization Undergoing Downsizing

Organizational Commitment (.82, .82, .84, .93)

On average over the past month,
1. I did not feel a strong sense of belonging to my organization. (r)
2. I felt that this organization had a great deal of personal meaning for me.
3. I felt that I would be very happy to spend the rest of my career with this organization.
4. I felt that I would enjoy discussing my organization with people outside it.
5. I did not feel like "part of the family" at this organization. (r)
6. I did not feel "emotionally attached" to this organization. (r)

Trust (.86, .87, .94, .93)

On the average over the past month,
1. I felt that the company takes advantage of its employees. (r)
2. I felt that management is concerned about employee potential and development.
3. I felt that the company is honest in its dealings with the employees.
4. I felt that the company cares about what happens to its employees.
5. I felt that the company listens to its employees.

Intention to Stay (.79, .86, .91, .96)

On the average over the past month,
1. I often thought seriously about quitting my job. (r)
2. I often had serious intentions of leaving the company. (r)

Productivity (.96, .97, .95, .95)

Over the past month,
1. How productive were you in comparison to your usual level of productivity? 7 = *Much More Than Usual*, 4 = *Same as Usual*, 1 = *Much Less Than Usual*.
2. How much work did you accomplish in comparison to what you ordinarily accomplish? 7 = *Much More Work*, 4 = *About the Same*, 1 = *Much Less Work*.

Note. Unless otherwise indicated, participants were asked to rate their level of agreement or disagreement with each statement on a 7-point scale (1 = *strongly disagree*; 4 = *neither agree nor disagree*; 7 = *strongly agree*). Measures of uncertainty, job satisfaction, and intention to stay are from Schweiger and DeNisi (1991) and previous conceptualizations of uncertainty. Communication quality, anxiety, rumors heard, rumors passed, and productivity items were generated. Trust was assessed with five items from Meglino, DeNisi, Youngblood, and Williams (as cited in Schweiger & DeNisi, 1991). Organizational commitment from the Affective Commitment Scale (McGee & Ford, 1987).
[a]Standardized alphas for time periods 1 through 4 are listed sequentially within parentheses after variable title (T1, T2, T3, T4). N = 61, 48, 40, and 29 for each successive survey administration. Items with (r) were reverse-scored.

and the following employee attitudes: trust in the company ($r_{avg} = -.29$), job satisfaction ($r_{avg} = -.26$), ratings of formal communication quality ($r_{avg} = -.26$), and—although weaker—organizational commitment ($r_{avg} = -.18$). As predicted, hearing rumors was negatively associated with key employee attitudes. Third, hearing rumors was moderately

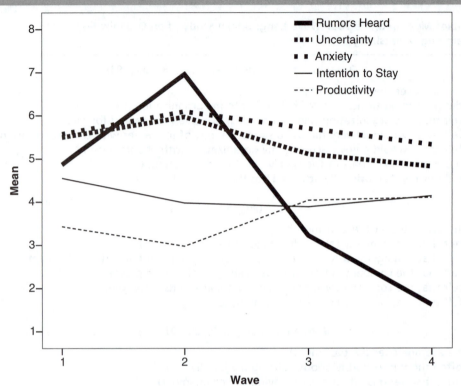

Mean number of rumors heard, employee uncertainty, anxiety, self-rated productivity, and intention to stay during an organizational downsizing.

negatively associated with the intention to stay ($r_{avg} = -.30$). Again as predicted, hearing negative rumors was associated with thoughts of leaving the company. Finally, hearing negative rumors was moderately negatively associated with productivity ($r_{avg} = -.22$), although this correlation varied widely from month to month ($r_{avg} = -.32$ for T2 and T4 outcomes, $r_{avg} = -.03$ for T1 and T3 outcomes). Hearing negative rumors was sometimes moderately negatively associated with productivity, and sometimes it was not associated with productivity.

It is important to note that these correlations obtained when the rumors were heard both during the same time period as the outcome variable and across time periods. That is, the number of rumors heard during a certain month was associated with future months' outcomes. We therefore wondered whether hearing negative rumors month after month might exert even stronger effects, and indeed there does appear to be a cumulative effect of hearing negative rumors. In general, the

FIGURE 2.4

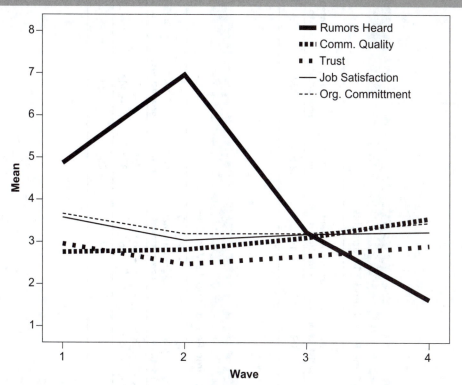

Mean number of rumors heard, perceptions of communication quality, perceptions of management as caring and trustworthy, job satisfaction, and organizational commitment during an organizational downsizing.

cumulative number of rumors heard in any given period was more (positively) associated with uncertainty and anxiety—and more (negatively) associated with job satisfaction, organizational commitment, trust, productivity, and intention to stay—than was the number of rumors heard in the most recent period only. Consider the correlations presented in Table 2.4 for T3 outcome variables. The cumulative number of rumors heard by the end of the third month was more strongly associated with every variable than was the number of rumors heard during the third month alone (correlations in the T1 + T2 + T3 row are stronger than those in the T3 row in every column). Furthermore, the pattern obtains even when one starts counting at T2: The cumulative number of rumors heard from the second through the third month was more strongly associated with every variable than was the number of rumors heard during the third month alone (correlations in the T2 + T3 row are stronger than those in the T3 row in every column).

TABLE 2.2

Correlations Between Number of Rumors Heard During Various Time Periods and T1 Variables

Time period (correlation n)	T1 uncertainty	T1 anxiety	T1 communication quality	T1 job satisfaction	T1 organizational commitment	T1 trust	T1 productivity	T1 intention to stay
T1 (60)	.20	.18	–.14	–.09	–.14	–.23^	.002	–.16

Note. ^*p* < .10.

TABLE 2.3

Correlations Between Number of Rumors Heard During Various Time Periods and T2 Variables

Time period (correlation n)	T2 uncertainty	T2 anxiety	T2 communication quality	T2 job satisfaction	T2 organizational commitment	T2 trust	T2 productivity	T2 intention to stay
T1 (47)	.37*	.29*	–.20	–.28^	–.36*	–.33*	–.35*	–.37*
T1 + T2 (48)	.45**	.27^	–.18	–.18	–.26^	–.33*	–.34*	–.34*
T2 (48)	.43**	.22	–.15	–.10	–.17	–.28^	–.25^	–.27^

Note. ^*p* < .10. *p < .05. **p < .01.

TABLE 2.4

Correlations Between Number of Rumors Heard During Various Time Periods and T3 Variables

Time period (correlation *n*)	T3 uncertainty	T3 anxiety	T3 communication quality	T3 job satisfaction	T3 organizational commitment	T3 trust	T3 productivity	T3 intention to stay
T1 (39)	.35*	.32*	–.20	–.22	–.32*	–.29^	–.08^	–.22
T1 + T2 (36)	.46**	.37*	–.38*	–.27	–.27	–.41*	–.06	–.35*
T1 + T2 + T3 (36)	.50**	.38*	–.40*	–.31^	–.30^	–.39*	–.05	–.37*
T2 (36)	.40*	.30^	–.38*	–.20	–.18	–.36*	–.01	–.31^
T2 + T3 (36)	.47**	.33*	–.40*	–.28^	–.25	–.35*	–.02	–.34*
T3 (40)	.36*	.25	–.27^	–.24	–.24	–.21	–.005	–.23

Note. ^$p < .10$. *$p < .05$. **$p < .01$.

TABLE 2.5

Correlations Between Number of Rumors Heard During Various Time Periods and T4 Variables

Time period (correlation n)	T4 uncertainty	T4 anxiety	T4 communication quality	T4 job satisfaction	T4 organizational commitment	T4 trust	T4 productivity	T4 intention to stay
T1 (29)	.18	.13	-.19	-.19	-.07	-.13	-.22	-.16
T1 + T2 (25)	.46*	.60**	-.36^	-.35^	-.10	-.30	-.36^	-.30
T1 + T2 + T3 (20)	.53*	.51*	-.40^	-.43^	-.14	-.32	-.48*	-.40^
T1 + T2 + T3 + T4 (20)	.51*	.46*	-.33	-.40^	-.18	-.34	-.41^	-.36
T2 (25)	.48*	.67**	-.30	-.28	-.04	-.29	-.28	-.30
T2 + T3 (20)	.51*	.53*	-.36	-.38^	-.12	-.31	-.43^	-.40^
T2 + T3 + T4 (20)	.48*	.45*	-.27	-.35	-.17	-.32	-.35	-.34
T3 (23)	.34	.27	-.12	-.07	.05	-.06	-.26	-.24
T3 + T4 (23)	.40^	.24	-.09	-.25	-.18	-.25	-.22	-.22
T4 (29)	.42*	.32^	-.09	-.32^	-.15	-.32^	-.26	-.24

Note. ^p < .10. *p < .05. **p < .01.

TABLE 2.6

Hierarchical Regressions Testing Predictive Power of Same-Time Rumors Heard (Step 1) Versus All Cumulative Rumors Heard (Step 2) on T4 Variables

Time period	T4 uncertainty	T4 anxiety	T4 communication quality	T4 job satisfaction	T4 organizational commitment	T4 trust	T4 productivity	T4 intention to stay
T4	.08	.04	.00	.04	.06	.07	.01	.02
T4 + T1 + T2 + T3	.28^	.28^	.23^	.19	.06	.11	.30*	.17
R^2 change	.20*	.25*	.23*	.15^	.00	.04	.29*	.14

Note. ^p < .10. *p < .05.

Similar patterns were generally observed for T2 and T4 correlational outcomes.

We also performed hierarchical regressions on these data as a stronger test of the cumulative effect for rumor; these results generally mirrored the correlational comparisons. In these analyses, we computed the variance (R^2) for each outcome variable during a time period: In step 1, we used the number of rumors heard during that same time period, and in step 2 we used the cumulative rumors heard. In each regression, the cumulative number of rumors heard almost always accounted for additional variance, and this additional variance was sometimes significant. For example, Table 2.6 presents results of hierarchical regressions for T4 outcomes; step 1 used the number of rumors heard during T4 whereas step 2 used the cumulative number of rumor heard during all 4 months. In this set of regressions, the cumulative number of rumors heard is a significantly better predictor than is the number of rumors heard in the same month for uncertainty, anxiety, communication quality, job satisfaction, and productivity. Similar, although weaker, patterns occurred for T2 and T3 outcomes, and included effects on organizational commitment, trust, and intention to stay.

These results suggest the existence of cumulative effects for rumors heard. In other words, the total number of rumors heard tends to be more strongly (positively) associated with one's current uncertainty and anxiety than does the number of rumors one has heard in the past month. Because current uncertainty and anxiety cannot affect the number of rumors heard in past months, this result suggests that negative rumors do increase uncertainty and anxiety; it is unsettling to hear a layoff rumor about one's department. Furthermore, the cumulative number of rumors heard tends to be more strongly (negatively) associated with one's current view of formal communication quality, job satisfaction, organizational commitment, trust, productivity, and intention to stay than does the number of rumors one has heard in the past month alone. Again, this result suggests that negative rumors do indeed negatively affect these job attitudes, intentions, and behaviors.

Summary

In this chapter we have examined the forms, frequency, and fallout of rumor. The way in which rumors can be categorized varies considerably; we presented recent typologies of rumor based primarily on the central function of rumor: collective sense making. Our recent typologies were therefore parsed according to thematic content, object of collective concern and locus of rumor public (internal vs. external). We also presented a typology of organizational change rumors. Although the literature presents rumor as relatively infrequent, our recent research points toward rumor as—of course—episodic in nature, and closely related to organizational change. Negative rumors seem to predominate, and harmful or potentially harmful rumors reach the ear of corporate PR officers almost once per week on average.

Rumors matter. They cause or contribute to a variety of important outcomes. Furthermore, there is evidence that these effects do not depend on belief in the rumor. Rumor effects are both intangible (including attitude and reputation) and tangible (including sales, productivity, and stock prices). We summarized a number of recent experimental studies showing that rumors systematically draw investors away from tracking trading strategies. Furthermore, we presented a number of field studies, both cross sectional and longitudinal, suggesting that rumors negatively affect a number of important organizational attitudes and behaviors: stress, job satisfaction, organizational commitment, trust, productivity, and intention to stay.

As stated in chapter 1 (this volume), rumors are never merely a private thought; rather, they are communicated. They are not simply heard, but often passed along as well. Some rumors are more often communicated than others. Why? In the next chapter we examine the psychological factors involved in rumor transmission.

Appendix 2.1
Managing Internal and External
Rumors: A Survey of Experienced
Communications Professionals

This survey[1] is being administered to a select group of communications and public relations professionals. It will assess the prevalence of different types of rumors that exist inside and outside of organizations, the effects of these rumors, and strategies used to prevent and neutralize rumors. Please answer all questions. If you wish to comment on any question or qualify your answers, please feel free to use the space in the margins or the back page. Your comments will be read and taken into account. Thank you for your help.

A *rumor* is an unverified bit of information about something of importance to a group. It is like news in every way except that it is not verified. It may or may not be true. It may be spread by word-of-mouth, fax, electronic mail, or any other communication channel. It is often introduced by the phrase "I heard that. . . ."

1. On average, about how frequently does a rumor reach your ear (i.e., you hear it or hear that it is circulating) that is of concern or potential concern to you? *(Circle one number)*: 1 *LESS THAN ONCE PER YEAR,* 2 *YEARLY,* 3 *SEMI-ANNUALLY,* 4 *QUARTERLY,* 5 *MONTHLY,* 6 *WEEKLY,* 7 *DAILY,* 8 *MORE THAN ONCE PER DAY.*

---

[1] Survey instrument from DiFonzo and Bordia (2002b).

In the next three questions, you will be asked about how prevalent different types of rumors are.

Internal rumors are of primary interest to company personnel or suppliers or vendors, that is, people who are associated with the production or distribution or sale of the organization's products or services. *External rumors* are of primary interest to customers or press or stockholders or the general public, that is, people who purchase or use or potentially purchase or use the organization's products, services, or stocks.

2. Out of all the rumors that have reached your ear, about what percentage were primarily internal rumors, primarily external rumors, or primarily both types? (*Please give approximate percentages for each type. Please keep in mind that these percentages should add up to 100%*): A. ___% WERE PRIMARILY INTERNAL, B. ___% WERE PRIMARILY EXTERNAL, C. ___% WERE PRIMARILY BOTH, D. ___% WERE PRIMARILY OTHER *(specify)*, TOTAL = 100%.

There are many types of internal rumors. Some are primarily about changes that may threaten *job security* (the loss or potential loss of jobs) or about changes that may threaten *job satisfaction*. These would typically include rumors of layoffs, downsizing, reorganization, reduced pay, or increased job responsibilities. Other internal rumors may also be primarily about *personnel changes* (changes in staffing as a result of turnover or promotion or demotion) or may be *gossip* (slander or innuendo primarily about private or personal matters).

3. Out of all the internal rumors that have reached your ear, about what percentage were primarily about job security, primarily about job satisfaction, primarily about personnel changes, primarily gossip, or primarily about some other topic? (*Please give approximate percentages for each type. Please keep in mind that these percentages should add up to 100%*): A. ___% WERE PRIMARILY JOB SECURITY, B. ___% WERE PRIMARILY JOB SATISFACTION, C. ___% WERE PRIMARILY PERSONNEL CHANGES, D. ___% WERE PRIMARILY GOSSIP, E. ___% WERE PRIMARILY OTHER *(specify)*, TOTAL = 100%.

The next question (and some others in this survey) requests an example. We have included these requests because we wish to ensure that we accurately understand your responses and we wish to obtain some sense of the rich detail that is often involved in rumor situations. Please feel free to mask any details so as to preserve the anonymity of this questionnaire.

4. Please give an example of a recent internal rumor that reached your ear and that was of concern or potential concern to you. The rumor stated:

In a similar way, there are many types of external rumors. Some are primarily about changes that would affect *stock* prices or earnings (e.g., as with potential mergers, forthcoming earnings reports, or costly management errors). Others are primarily about the *quality* of the product or service that the organization produces (e.g., that it may be unsafe). Still others are primarily about the organization's *reputation* (e.g., that the organization is in some way untrustworthy or bad).

5. Out of all the external rumors that have reached your ear, about what percentage were primarily stock market rumors, primarily product or service quality rumors, primarily organizational reputation rumors, or primarily about some other topic? *(Please give approximate percentages for each type. Please keep in mind that these percentages should add up to 100%)*: A. ____% WERE PRIMARILY STOCK MARKET, B. ____% WERE PRIMARILY PRODUCT OR SERVICE QUALITY, C. ____% WERE PRIMARILY ORGANIZATIONAL REPUTATION, D. ____% WERE PRIMARILY OTHER *(specify)*, TOTAL = 100%.

6. Please give an example of a recent external rumor that reached your ear and that was of concern or potential concern to you. The rumor stated:

Another important purpose of this study is to assess what the effects of rumors are and how severe these effects typically are.

7. On the basis of your overall experience with rumors, how severe, on average, were each of the following rumor effects? NEVER means the effect never occurred, SMALL means the effect was small, MEDIUM means the effect was moderate, and LARGE means the effect was large. Circle one word to indicate severity (if effect has never occurred, circle "NEVER"): 7.1 loss of trust between management and workers or staff, 7.2 loss of trust between management and stockholders, 7.3 loss of trust among coworkers, 7.4 loss of trust by customers, 7.5 decreased productivity, 7.6 unnecessary turnover, 7.7 decreased sales, 7.8 increased lateness or absenteeism, 7.9 lowered morale, 7.10 sullied reputation of an individual, 7.11 sullied reputation of corporation, 7.12 sabotage-type behaviors, 7.13 bad press, 7.14 securities price or earnings dropped, 7.15 punitive action against management, 7.16 increased employee stress at work, 7.17 fueled union action or strike, 7.18 other *(specify)*.

8. Of the most serious effects that have occurred, please give a recent example of how a rumor caused the effect(s) to occur (if possible, please quantify the effect in terms of % change, such as % change in productivity or information requests):

A further purpose of this study is to assess what strategies are in use to prevent or neutralize rumors and how effective these strategies are perceived to be.

9. On the basis of your overall experience with rumors, how effective, on average, were each of the following specific strategies in preventing and/or neutralizing rumors? NEVER means strategy was never used, LOW means low average effectiveness, MEDIUM means medium

average effectiveness, and HIGH means high average effectiveness. Circle one word to indicate effectiveness (if strategy was never used, circle "NEVER"): 9.1 ignore the rumor, 9.2 state "no comment," 9.3 explain why you cannot comment or give full information, 9.4 confirm the rumor, 9.5 deny rumor by company official, 9.6 deny rumor by trusted outside source, 9.7 spread counterrumors, 9.8 search for and/or seek to punish people who planted the rumor, 9.9 specifically attempt to increase trust, 9.10 encourage potentially affected parties to prepare for the worst, 9.11 set time line for official message that will contain full information, 9.12 establish committees to explore options for people affected by upcoming change, 9.13 state values that will be used to guide the upcoming changes, 9.14 state procedures by which the upcoming changes will be decided, 9.15 establish a rumor hotline, 9.16 explain how upcoming change decisions will be made, 9.17 have an employee inform you of rumors that are circulating, 9.18 other *(specify)*.

10. Please give a recent example of how one or more of these strategies was effective in preventing or neutralizing a rumor:

This next section asks questions related to the psychological and situational variables affecting the rumor. When you answer these questions, it is helpful to have a particular rumor in mind. Please think of an instance when a rumor (but not a gossip-type rumor) reached your ear that you considered harmful or potentially harmful. Please choose a rumor that has since been proven true [false] beyond a reasonable doubt (other participants are being asked for rumors that proved to be false [true]; we wish to obtain an even sampling of both kinds).

11. Please state the true [false] rumor here (it may be one you have already mentioned):

12. Please describe the situation out of which the rumor arose:

Rumors may spread through different groups of people. For the remaining questions in this section, answer with respect to one group of people who heard and/or passed the rumor. Also, rumors may change over time. For the remaining questions in this section, please answer for the point in time just prior to when the rumor was proven true.

The first question deals with how accurate or distorted the rumor became.

13. For the rumor above, how accurate or true (as opposed to distorted or false) did the rumor prove to be? 1 COMPLETELY FALSE, 2 MOSTLY FALSE, 3 HALF FALSE AND HALF TRUE, 4 MOSTLY TRUE, 5 COMPLETELY TRUE.

The next question deals with how the rumor changed over time.

14. From the time when the rumor started until when the rumor was proven true, to what extent did the rumor tend to become more accurate (as opposed to more distorted)? 1 BECAME MUCH MORE DISTORTED, 2 BECAME SOMEWHAT MORE DISTORTED, 3 STAYED

ABOUT THE SAME, 4 BECAME SOMEWHAT MORE ACCURATE, 5 BECAME MUCH MORE ACCURATE.

The next several questions deal with psychological and situational variables. As with all the questions in this section remember to answer with respect to a particular group of people who heard or passed the rumor or both.

15. Overall, how uncertain (filled with questions about what current events meant or what future events were likely to occur) were people? 1 NOT AT ALL UNCERTAIN, 2 A LITTLE UNCERTAIN, 3 SOMEWHAT UNCERTAIN, 4 MOSTLY UNCERTAIN, 5 EXTREMELY UNCERTAIN.

16. Overall, how confident were people that this rumor was true? 1 NOT AT ALL CONFIDENT, 2 A LITTLE CONFIDENT, 3 SOMEWHAT CONFIDENT, 4 MOSTLY CONFIDENT, 5 EXTREMELY CONFIDENT.

17. Overall, to what extent did people have a reduced sense of control or power over events affecting their lives? 1 NOT AT ALL REDUCED SENSE OF CONTROL, 2 A LITTLE REDUCED SENSE OF CONTROL, 3 SOMEWHAT REDUCED SENSE OF CONTROL, 4 MOSTLY REDUCED SENSE OF CONTROL, 5 EXTREMELY REDUCED SENSE OF CONTROL.

18. Overall, how important (significant, consequential) was the rumor to people? 1 NOT AT ALL IMPORTANT, 2 A LITTLE IMPORTANT, 3 SOMEWHAT IMPORTANT, 4 MOSTLY IMPORTANT, 5 EXTREMELY IMPORTANT.

19. Overall, how anxious (worried or concerned) were people? 1 NOT AT ALL ANXIOUS, 2 A LITTLE ANXIOUS, 3 SOMEWHAT ANXIOUS, 4 MOSTLY ANXIOUS, 5 EXTREMELY ANXIOUS.

These next questions continue with psychological variables. Please continue to answer with respect to a particular group of people who heard and/or passed the rumor.

20. Overall, to what extent did people desire or want the rumor to be true? 1 GREATLY DESIRED RUMOR TO BE FALSE, 2 SOMEWHAT DESIRED RUMOR TO BE FALSE, 3 NEUTRAL, 4 SOMEWHAT DESIRED RUMOR TO BE TRUE, 5 GREATLY DESIRED RUMOR TO BE TRUE.

21. Overall, to what extent did the rumor agree with or was consistent with peoples' biases (preconceived notions, attitudes, and/or prejudices)? 1 GREATLY DISAGREED WITH PEOPLES' BIASES, 2 SOMEWHAT DISAGREED WITH PEOPLES' BIASES, 3 NEITHER AGREED NOR DISAGREED, 4 SOMEWHAT AGREED WITH PEOPLES' BIASES, 5 GREATLY AGREED WITH PEOPLES' BIASES.

22. Overall, to what extent would you characterize the people as gullible (as opposed to skeptical)? 1 HIGHLY SKEPTICAL, 2 SOMEWHAT SKEPTICAL, 3 NEITHER SKEPTICAL NOR GULLIBLE, 4 SOMEWHAT GULLIBLE, 5 HIGHLY GULLIBLE.

The next several questions deal with patterns of communication.

23. When a rumor is passed from one person to another, it may involve a great deal of interaction (discussion and clarification), or it may involve very little interaction. Overall, how interactive was a typical discussion of the rumor? 1 NOT AT ALL INTERACTIVE, 2 A LITTLE INTERACTIVE, 3 SOMEWHAT INTERACTIVE, 4 MOSTLY INTERACTIVE, 5 EXTREMELY INTERACTIVE.

24. Overall, how active (frequently transmitted) was the rumor? 1 INACTIVE, 2 A LITTLE ACTIVE, 3 SOMEWHAT ACTIVE, 4 MOSTLY ACTIVE, 5 EXTREMELY ACTIVE.

25. A rumor may pass through an established communication network (e.g., an office grapevine) or through a group of people who never communicated before. Overall, how established were the communication channels of the group? 1 NOT AT ALL ESTABLISHED, 2 A LITTLE ESTABLISHED, 3 SOMEWHAT ESTABLISHED, 4 MOSTLY ESTABLISHED, 5 EXTREMELY ESTABLISHED.

26. The grapevine is an established informal communication network. To what extent could the communication network through which this rumor passed be considered a grapevine? 1 DEFINITELY NOT A GRAPEVINE, 2 A LITTLE LIKE A GRAPEVINE, 3 SOMEWHAT LIKE A GRAPEVINE, 4 MOSTLY LIKE A GRAPEVINE, 5 DEFINITELY A GRAPEVINE.

Finally, a few details about yourself for statistical purposes.

27. You are *(Circle one number)*: 1 MALE, 2 FEMALE.

28. Your present age: ___ YEARS.

29. Your current title:

30. You are a *(Circle one number)*: 1 CORPORATE COMMUNICATIONS OR PUBLIC RELATIONS OFFICER, 2 COMMUNICATIONS OR PUBLIC RELATIONS CONSULTANT, 3 OTHER *(specify)*:

31. The primary industry or industries in which you work or consult:

32. Your total years of experience in communications: ___ YEARS.

Psychological Factors in Rumor Spread

3

In the rancorous months preceding the 2004 U.S. presidential election, one of us (DiFonzo) received this false e-rumor about Senator John Kerry:

Subject: Kerry and John 16:3. The Lord has a way of revealing those of us who really know him, and those that don't! Think about it! Kerry gave a big speech last week about how his faith is so "important" to him. In this attempt to convince the American people that we should consider him for president, he announced that his favorite Bible verse is John 16:3. Of course the speech writer meant John 3:16, but nobody in the Kerry camp was familiar enough with scripture to catch the error. And do you know what John 16:3 says? John 16:3 says, "They will do such things because they have not known the Father or me." The Spirit works in strange ways.

It turns out that the same false e-rumor about President George W. Bush was being circulated at the same time.
—Mikkelson and Mikkelson, 2004

I n this chapter we identify the psychological factors underlying rumor spread. We focus on the individual-level psychological motivations involved—that is, what are people trying to accomplish when transmitting a rumor? The psychological literature on rumor has identified five variables related to rumor transmission: uncertainty, importance or outcome-relevant involvement, lack of control, anxiety, and belief (Bordia & DiFonzo, 2002; Rosnow, 1991; Walker & Blaine,

1991). We review the literature pertaining to each variable. In addition, we address the following question: "Why do these variables affect rumor transmission?" We argue that these variables represent fundamental goals in social cognition and behavior; people transmit rumors to fulfill these goals. We apply the literature on motivations in social behavior to understand the goals that motivate rumor spread. In addition, we present empirical evidence supportive of these motivational underpinnings.

This motivational approach is beneficial for at least three reasons. First, although past research has identified a collection of variables related to rumor transmission, relatively less attention has been given to theorizing why these variables predict transmission. Second, a motivation-based approach helps us connect the rumor literature with a broader social–psychological literature. For example, by considering rumor transmission as a self-enhancing activity, we are able to draw links with social identity literature and consider ways in which rumors that are derogatory to the outgroup help boost esteem associated with the ingroup. Third, the core-motivations approach notes a variety of influences on rumor spread and helps us identify research gaps in the current literature. For example, the relationship-enhancement function of rumor transmission has largely been overlooked.

What motivates any social interaction? In general, people interact with the social world to fulfill one or more of the following three goals: to act effectively, to build and maintain relationships, and to manage favorable self-impressions (Cialdini & Trost, 1998; Wood, 1999, 2000). In serving the goal of acting effectively, social interaction helps people to acquire a socially validated sense of reality and enables effective response to, and coping with, the environment. In serving the goal of building and maintaining relationships, social interaction helps build and maintain relationships that are vital for continued survival of humans as social animals. Finally, a more self-serving goal, and one that may lead to several biases in information processing, is the goal of self-enhancement. That is, in the context of social interactions, people seek to affirm their sense of the self and use the social context in various ways to boost their self-esteem.

In the context of rumor transmission, these goals are represented in three motivations: fact finding, relationship enhancement, and self-enhancement. In the following sections, we review the literature on rumor spread under the rubric of these motivations. In each section we begin by noting how the basic goal is served in social interaction and then apply the motivation to the rumor context. Following this, we discuss antecedents and consequences of these motivations for rumor transmission. Finally, with the help of results from an empirical study, we illustrate the role of these motivations in rumor transmission intentions.

Fact-Finding
Motivation

The goal of acting effectively leads to fact finding, often in a social context. Effective response and coping with the physical and social environment is necessary for our survival. This goal manifests itself in a variety of human needs such as control (Bandura, 2001); competence (White, 1959); and understanding (Fiske, 2003; Fiske, Lin, & Neuberg, 1999). To act effectively, we need valid and accurate knowledge of our circumstances. This goal thus motivates the search for—and spread of—accurate information that is essential for effective response to the situation. When motivated by the goal of acting effectively, we seek accurate information and we evaluate that information using available strategies, such as comparing it with knowledge that we already have or evaluating the credibility of its source. This information is often available in our social context (Fiske et al., 1999). Sometimes we explicitly seek information from other people. Other times, we obtain information in passive or covert ways, such as following the example of others, conforming to group norms, or complying with persuasion attempts, and generally are influenced to varying degrees by information from the social milieu (Cialdini & Trost, 1998). Indeed, in the act of establishing objective reality, validation of our experiences from significant others figures largely (Hardin & Higgins, 1996).

FACT-FINDING MOTIVATION
AND RUMOR SPREAD

Of the variables that have been identified in the rumor literature as precursors of rumor spread, the following reflect most the fact-finding motivation: uncertainty, importance, lack of control, and anxiety (we discuss belief under relationship-enhancement motivation). *Uncertainty* is defined as a psychological state of doubt about what current events mean or what future events are likely to occur (DiFonzo & Bordia, 1998). Uncertainty about issues of personal importance engenders feelings of lack of control and anxiety. For example, not knowing the precise nature and consequences of organizational restructuring and its consequences for one's job (i.e., uncertainty about a topic of high importance) leads to feelings of lack of control about how to prepare for or cope with the change and may lead to considerable anxiety among employees (Blake & Mouton, 1983; Hunsaker & Coombs, 1988; Mirvis, 1985). People are motivated to reduce uncertainty and anxiety and restore a sense of control over their circumstances (Ashford &

Black, 1996; Berger, 1987; Berger & Bradac, 1982); that is, a mix of uncertainty, importance, lack of control, and anxiety generates a need to know. In the absence of news from formal channels (e.g., management, civil administration, or news media), people turn to informal networks (e.g., office grapevine, friends, social groups) for information. The informal interpretation arising out of this collective process becomes a rumor.

The role of uncertainty and ambiguity in rumor spread was noted in some of the early theorizing on rumor spread. Belgion stated, "rumour depends upon uncertainty" (1939, p. 12). Prasad (1935) claimed that situations "of an uncommon and unfamiliar type" (p. 5) lead to rumors. G. W. Allport and Postman (1947b) similarly noted that rumor spread is directly proportional to ambiguity multiplied by the importance of the topic. Caplow (1947) observed that rumors frequently increased with uncertainty. Festinger and colleagues (1948) pointed out that rumors pertain to issues that are shrouded in cognitive unclarity. Schachter and Burdick (1955) demonstrated the effect of uncertainty in a field study. They planted a rumor in a girls' preparatory school and then exposed some students to a staged event aimed at creating uncertainty. Rumors spread in this high-uncertainty group nearly twice as much as among students who were not exposed to the staged event (low-uncertainty group). In a similar way, uncertainty was positively related to transmission among users of a suburban transit system that was facing disruption from strike action (Esposito, 1986/1987).

As noted in chapter 1 (this volume), sociological work on rumors has emphasized the role of collective sense making in situations of uncertainty (Shibutani, 1966). In the absence of information from formal channels explaining ambiguous events, group members may engage in a collective problem-solving process; that is, group members share and evaluate information that explains the ambiguous situation. In a study of group problem solving that accompanies rumor spread, we analyzed discussions of rumors on the Internet (Bordia & DiFonzo, 2004). A content analysis of over 280 rumor-related postings on Internet discussion groups revealed that a large proportion of the interaction was devoted to fact finding. Group members sought and shared information germane to the rumor, evaluated the information, and made judgments about the plausibility of the rumor. In sum, the rumor interaction served an uncertainty reduction and sense making function.

The role of topical importance (also referred to as *outcome-relevant involvement*; Rosnow, 1991) in rumor spread has also been demonstrated empirically. Rosnow, Esposito, and Gibney (1988) studied rumor transmission in the aftermath of a murder on a university campus. The proportion of people who reported transmitting rumors related to the murders was twice as high on the university campus where the murder took place (high importance) as that of another university campus in the same city (low importance). In a similar way, in Esposito's (1986/1987) study of suburban transit system users, importance of the rumor content was positively related to transmission. These findings imply that outcome relevant involvement is necessary for people to become involved in rumor spread. People are uncertain about many issues, but they pursue uncertainty reduction only on those topics that have personal relevance or threaten the goal of acting effectively.

Psychological control has also been implicated in rumor transmission in a couple of ways. As noted, situations marked by uncertainty concerning important topics are also likely to elicit feelings of lack of control (Ashford & Black, 1996; Bordia, Hobman, Jones, Gallois, & Callan, 2004) and lead to anxiety. In an analysis of circumstances leading to rumors heard by corporate public relations officers, we found that the effect of uncertainty on anxiety was mediated by feelings of lack of control (DiFonzo & Bordia, 2002a). With our colleagues (Bordia, Hunt, Paulsen, Tourish, & DiFonzo, 2004), we similarly found that the relation between uncertainty and psychological strain during a large-scale organizational change was mediated, at least in part, through feelings of lack of control.

Second, rumors have been conceived as attempts to acquire secondary control over situations marked by low primary control (Bordia & DiFonzo, 2002; Walker, 1996; Walker & Blaine, 1991). *Primary control* refers to action-focused coping responses: managing or changing one's circumstances in the desired direction. Faced with an ambiguous restructuring, for example, I may increase my productivity to increase my chances of job change survival. When primary control is not possible, people may resort to *secondary control* strategies; these involve emotion-focused coping responses such as lowering expectations, predicting the worst to avoid disappointment, attributing events to chance, and attempting to understand the meaning of events and accept them (Rothbaum, Weisz, & Snyder, 1982; Walker, 1996; Walker & Blaine, 1991). Faced with a potential layoff, for example, I may eagerly participate in water cooler rumor discussions about why and when these layoffs will occur. Walker (1996) content-analyzed 200 rumors collected on a university campus to see if they contained themes related to secondary control. All rumors contained secondary control themes, with the most common being interpretive secondary control (explaining the meaning of events; $n = 93$), followed by predictive secondary control (predicting future events; $n = 69$). These findings provide some evidence for the idea that rumors represent ways of regaining control over uncertain and uncontrollable circumstances. However, this aspect of rumor is underresearched and requires greater empirical attention.

Finally, both trait (dispositional) and state (situational) anxiety are related to rumor spread (Anthony, 1973, 1992; Rosnow, 1991). Jaeger,

Anthony, and Rosnow (1980) measured trait anxiety of students in a class with the Taylor Manifest Anxiety Scale, then planted a rumor that some students had been caught smoking marijuana during exams. High trait anxiety students spread this rumor more than did low trait anxiety students. Walker and Beckerle (1987) manipulated state anxiety. Participants were invited to help the instructor improve exam questions by answering a mock exam. While the participants waited to do this, confederates planted two rumors by saying, "I heard two rumors about what is actually going on here" (p. 356). One rumor (anxiety enhancing) claimed that the real purpose of the study was to catch cheaters; the other rumor (anxiety alleviating) claimed that the professor wanted to assess the effectiveness of classroom demonstrations. Participants in the high state anxiety condition then watched what was apparently a live event, but was in fact a videotape, in which a confederate was being rigorously questioned; those in the low state anxiety condition merely read some test questions. After a while, another confederate asked the participant, "What is going on here today?" The dependent variable was the number of prompts needed for the participant to report a rumor. Participants in the high state anxiety condition on average needed only about two prompts to repeat a rumor whereas the participants in the low state anxiety condition needed up to four prompts.[1]

It is interesting that Walker and Beckerle (1987) also found that participants in the high state anxiety condition were marginally less accurate in reporting the rumor than were participants in the low anxiety condition. This finding raises the possibility that although uncertainty about topics of high importance may induce the fact-finding motivation, anxiety may hinder fact-finding accuracy. This possibility agrees with research on the role of anxiety in information processing. Anxiety colors one's view of the world by directing cognitive resources to search for threatening stimuli (Calvo & Castillo, 1997) and overemphasize the threat from ambiguous signals (MacLeod & I. L. Cohen, 1993). An anxious individual may find the doom and gloom of dread rumors congruent with his or her emotional state and may favor the interpretation provided by these rumors. This idea may also explain why, in general, dread rumors are more widespread than are wish rumors (S. R. Kelley, 2004; R. H. Knapp, 1944). The anxiety associated with uncertain events of high personal significance biases rumor content toward negative and threatening interpretations. These rumors

---

[1] The findings should be interpreted with caution as the audiovisual stimuli in the manipulation of anxiety may have also made the rumors more salient and increased recall as compared with the control condition. Future research could replicate this study with more comparable stimuli.

also help justify the anxiety being experienced (Festinger, 1957). We return to a fuller exploration of these ideas in chapter 7 (this volume) when we discuss how rumors become more—and less—accurate.

Relationship-Enhancement Motivation

Social relationships are vital to the survival of humans and serve, enable, or enhance important goals such as mate selection, child rearing, food gathering, protection from predators, and survival during resource scarcity (Baumeister & Leary, 1995; Kenrick et al., 2002). The goal of building and maintaining relationships is reflected in a variety of everyday behaviors in the domain of interpersonal communication, such as seeking the company of others, compliance with norms and persuasive appeals to please others (Cialdini & Trost, 1998), impression management and self-presentation tactics such as ingratiation (Leary, 1995); avoidance of conversational topics that might create conflict (Knobloch & Carpenter-Theune, 2004) or hurt the conversation partner (Rawlins, 1983); use of humorous or awe-inspiring topics to hold others' attention (Guerin, 2003); and even deception (DePaulo & Kashy, 1998). For example, Tesser and Rosen (1975) demonstrated that people are reluctant to transmit bad news for fear it will generate negative affect in the recipients and the recipient may evaluate them negatively. This withholding of negative information has been labeled the *minimize unpleasant messages* (MUM) effect.

The context of the relationship influences the manner in which this goal is expressed. For example, in short-term relationships or in early stages of relationship formation, people are keen on making a good impression and pleasing others. In such circumstances, honesty may be sacrificed for other relationship-oriented goals such as generating liking or positive affect in others, and so information that helps attract or hold the attention of a desirable audience may be passed on without much care for its authenticity. However, in longer-term relationships with greater personal involvement, accurate information sharing is likely to be emphasized (Stevens & Fiske, 1995). In addition, the anthropological literature on storytelling notes how narrative content is manipulated to further interpersonal (attracting attention of the target); group (maintaining status differences); or intergroup (excluding people by making stories meaningful to only a few in the audience) goals (Sugiyama, 1996).

RELATIONSHIP-ENHANCEMENT MOTIVATION AND RUMOR SPREAD

Existing literature on rumors has paid little explicit attention to the relationship-enhancement goal[2] (cf. Guerin, 2003). One exception is research on the spread of positive versus negative rumors. Applying the MUM effect (Tesser & Rosen, 1975), Kamins, Folkes, and Perner (1997) predicted that people will refrain from passing negative rumors (compared with positive rumors), fearing that these rumors might generate negative affect in the recipient—a relationship-enhancing goal. Their results supported this prediction: Participants were more willing to transmit a positive rumor (that the ranking of their business school will rise) than a negative rumor (that the ranking of their business school will fall). However, transmitting negative rumors may also serve the cause of maintaining relationships—especially close, long-term relationships—because rumors predicting negative events can often help people cope with these events. For instance, Weenig, Groenenboom, and Wilke (2001) found that negative information was more likely to be transmitted to a friend when the information was considered useful in averting harmful consequences for the friend. Close friends are expected to share helpful information, even if it is negative. Thus, the context of the relationship can influence the sharing of negative or positive rumors.

The relationship-enhancement motivation has been invoked to explain the finding that belief in a rumor is positively related with transmission (Rosnow et al., 1988). A reputation as a credible and trustworthy source of information is vital for acceptance in social networks (Caplow, 1947; Guerin, 2003; Stevens & Fiske, 1995). One way to ensure such a reputation is to share information that is accurate and believable. Belief in rumor was strongly related to transmission among university faculty experiencing a labor dispute (Rosnow et al., 1986); among students at a university campus where a student had been murdered (Rosnow et al., 1988) or had suddenly died of meningitis (Pezzo & Beckstead, 2006); and among students at a campus in the vicinity of the Washington, D.C., sniper murders (Pezzo & Beckstead, 2006). Kimmel and Keefer (1991) noted that disbelief in the rumor

---

[2] At a mundane level, of course, following the social rules of communication (Higgins, 1981), individuals are unlikely to share a rumor with someone we know is not even remotely interested in the topic of the rumor (e.g., people might avoid conversation about work over an intimate dinner with a date).

was a reason why rumors about AIDS were not transmitted. And Rosnow (1991) reported a moderate mean effect size ($r = .30$) between belief and transmission.

Possessing and sharing valued information is also a way to heighten status and prestige in the view of others in one's social network (Brock, 1968; Fromkin, 1972; Lynn, 1991); one's higher status often leads others to like, value, or respect one more. During times of uncertainty and threat (e.g., war or natural disasters), information is even more valuable. In their eagerness to further their social standing, people may unwittingly pass on rumors. G. W. Allport and Postman (1947b) provide an example of such dissemination. A few members of an Italian American community owned transistor radios during World War II. In their desire to demonstrate their status of being "in the know," they unwittingly spread propaganda being broadcast on the radio. Being considered in the know by spreading rumors is thus one way to increase the liking, value, and respect that other people have for oneself.[3]

Self-Enhancement Motivation

The self-enhancement goal refers to the need to feel good about oneself. People seek to maintain a positive self-image and engage in cognitions that bolster self-esteem (Kunda, 1999; Steele, 1988). Self-enhancement biasing effects on thinking and judgment are well known (Kunda, 1999). For example, most people think they are better than average on a variety of skills and abilities: When people are led to believe that certain traits (e.g., extraversion) or skills (e.g., driving) are more desirable, they rate themselves more highly on these traits and are more likely to recall instances in which they behaved in this desirable manner (Kunda, 1990). A second example of self-enhancing bias: One's own characteristics, as compared with those of others, are considered more likely to lead to desirable outcomes (e.g., leadership position, happy marriage, etc.; Kunda, 1987). A third example: People are generally more resistant to information that is counter to an attitude they hold when it threatens their self-image; however, when people are feeling good about themselves (on unrelated issues), they are less

---

[3] Being considered in the know may at the same time be self-enhancing; further research is needed to tease apart these motivations (see chap. 10, this volume).

defensive in evaluating counterattitudinal information and more easily persuaded (G. L. Cohen, Aronson, & Steele, 2000).

These self-enhancing biases extend to groups people belong to or identify with. A part of our sense of self derives from the groups we belong to, such as demographic (e.g., ethnicity, gender), professional (e.g., academics, engineers), or social (e.g., hobby clubs, student associations, honor societies) groups. We derive meaning and a sense of self-worth by identifying with groups we consider high in status and prestige (Hogg & Abrams, 1988). This identification may bias our judgments so as to favor the group we are part of (the ingroup), often at a cost to the group we are not linked to (the outgroup). For example, we are more critical of negative information about the ingroup than we are of positive information about the ingroup (Dietz-Uhler, 1999). In a similar way, we readily adopt positive—but not negative—information about the ingroup as representative; in addition, we attribute outgroup success to external causes and outgroup failure to stable, internal features (Beal, Ruscher, & Schnake, 2001; Pettigrew, 1979). Negative reactions to outgroups are particularly strong when ingroup interests are threatened (Bobo & Kluegel, 1993) and outgroup derogation is a way we boost our self-esteem (Fein & Spencer, 1997). For example, negative stereotypes about Blacks (e.g., "Blacks have low intelligence") were believed more by Whites who perceived threat from Blacks than by Whites who perceived no such threat (Quist & Resendez, 2002). Negative stereotypes of outgroups serve the need to maintain favorable ingroup evaluations (Goodwin, Operario, & Fiske, 1998) or justify unfavorable outcomes for the outgroup (Quist & Resendez, 2002).

SELF-ENHANCEMENT MOTIVATION AND RUMOR SPREAD

The self-enhancing motivation can range from blatant and conscious spread of rumors for personal gain to unconscious selection and spread of self-serving rumors. In this section, we begin with an acknowledgement of conscious and motivated spread of rumors for self-gain and then discuss the role of self-enhancement in the cognitive processing of rumors.

Although this aspect is underemphasized, the rumor literature has shown that rumors may originate or spread as part of a motivated and malevolent propaganda tactic (G. W. Allport & Postman, 1947b; DiFonzo & Bordia, in press; Kapferer, 1987/1990; Rosnow, 2001; Sinha, 1955; P. A. Turner, 1993). When much is at stake (e.g., election to political office or product sales in a highly competitive consumer market), rumors afford tangible gain. In wartime, rumors are intentionally spread to demoralize enemy troops (G. W. Allport & Postman, 1947b;

Mihanovic, Jukic, & Milas, 1994). Sales agents steer consumers away from rival products and toward their own by using rumors, and rumors become the grist for the word-of-mouth advertising mill (Kapferer, 1987/1990; P. A. Turner, 1993). During elections, rumors (or "whispering campaigns"; G. W. Allport & Postman, 1947b, p. 184) sully the reputation of the opposing candidates (Kapferer, 1987/1990; Sinha, 1952). In elections in the Indian state of Madhya Pradesh, the Congress Party spread false allegations that the Indian prime minister, who belongs to the rival Bharatiya Janata Party, eats beef. Cows are sacred to Hindus and beef eating is abhorrent. The allegations created enough difficulty that the prime minister had to announce dramatically: "I would rather die than eat beef" (Verma, 2003). And Fine (2005) has suggested that malicious rumors are a way for deceivers to spread lies without actually facing the malevolent nature of their act; they take comfort in the uncertainty of rumor.

In spite of the variety of contexts in which conscious rumor spread may occur, it has generally been ignored as a variable of interest (but see Pratkanis & Aronson, 1991, 2001, as notable exceptions). One reason could be because conscious and malicious rumor spread reveals a repugnant characteristic of human nature and forms "the ugly underbelly of interpersonal life" (Leary, 1995, p. 9). Also, malicious intent in rumor birth cannot sustain rumor growth (Horowitz, 2001). For a rumor to take hold, it must find fertile ground and catch the imagination of several people; that is, it needs to serve one or more of the motivations in rumor spread. A rumor may originate or even acquire an occasional fillip from mischievous agents, but to widely circulate, the rumor needs to fulfill fact-finding, relationship-enhancing, or self-enhancing motivations. Nonetheless, we maintain that the use of rumors by conscious manipulators of public sentiments needs greater attention (see DiFonzo & Bordia, in press), particularly in the context of public education regarding rumors and their effects. Knowledge of the use of rumors by propagandists may bring about watchfulness among people and prevent their falling prey to the machinations of rumor peddlers (i.e., people must learn to distrust those who sow distrust).

A second way in which self-enhancement motivates rumor spread is as follows: Spreading rumors may boost one's self-esteem by boosting one's social identity. As discussed earlier, groups prefer interpretations that portray the ingroup in a favorable light and are derogatory of the outgroup. It is not surprising then that rumors derogating the outgroup are much more prevalent than are rumors negatively portraying the ingroup. For example, in a study conducted by R. H. Knapp (1944) during World War II, *Reader's Digest* magazine readers were invited to submit rumors they had heard. Of the 1,089 rumors collected, over 60% of the rumors were derogatory of some social group and were

labeled wedge-driving rumors because they contributed to intergroup discord.

Self-enhancement motivations are also operative when rumors are
spread to rationalize self-enhancing attitudes. When evaluating rumors,
people are more likely to favor those that support or justify existing
prejudices. Unjustified prejudice is a distasteful notion, but the prejudice acquires legitimacy through rumors that are consonant with the
prejudiced viewpoint (Van Dijk, 1987, p. 62). In other words, rumors
aid in the process of "justification construction" (Kunda, 1990, p. 483)
for the desired belief structures. G. W. Allport and Postman (1947b)
noted that "rumor rationalizes while it relieves" (p. 37), implying that
rumors derogatory of the outgroup vent the prejudice and also justify
it. For example, rumors among Whites that Blacks are overly aggressive
and violent justify discrimination. Another dramatic illustration of the
self-enhancement bias occurs when the same ambiguous event is interpreted in different but self-serving ways by different groups of people.
The race of the perpetrator of violent acts gets transposed, depending
on the race of the narrator of the rumor (Black perpetrator when the
rumor circulates in the White community, but White perpetrator when
the rumor circulates in the Black community; Rosnow, 2001). Whereas
American sources attributed the destruction of a hotel in Baghdad
during the Iraq war to a bomb planted by terrorists, the rumor among
local Iraqis was that the destruction was caused by a wayward American
missile (Shanker, 2004).

Contextual
Determinants of
Rumor-Spread
Motivations

In general, situations that threaten a goal will activate the associated
motivation. When people's ability to cope effectively with the environment is threatened, fact finding is activated: We search for accurate
information. For example, on hearing about merger talks between their
organization and a rival company, employees are likely to seek accurate
information about the consequences to the structure of their organization as a result of the merger. In a similar way, when the self or ingroup
is threatened, self-enhancement motivation may be activated and we
are likely to favor information that makes us feel good about ourselves.
In such situations, we are less likely to be concerned about the accuracy

of the rumor and more concerned about its self-enhancing value. At other times, characteristics of the person or the situation may make a particular goal (and the associated motivation) more salient. For example, a young adult keen on developing romantic relationships is likely to be driven by relationship-enhancement motivations and is likely to share a rumor that helps attract or hold the attention of his or her audience.

Sometimes, motivations work in tandem. In particular, the relationship-enhancement and self-enhancement motivations are easily served by the same rumor. Spreading a rumor that sheds positive light on the ingroup is likely to be self-enhancing (it will boost my self-esteem) and will also help form a good impression in other ingroup members (it will enhance our relationship). In a similar way, rumors that are derogatory of the outgroup are self-enhancing and also aid in the development of solidarity and cohesion (Kakar, 2005) among ingroup members. At other times, however, the motivations may compete. For example, when the recipient is an outgroup member, sharing a positive ingroup rumor may be self-enhancing but may not serve relationship-enhancement goals as well as sharing a positive outgroup rumor would.

Consider the case of a college student who hears the rumor that in the next year's ranking of colleges by *U.S. News & World Report*, his or her college is going to be ranked lower than it currently is. The rumor may create anxiety and arouse the need to ascertain its validity (i.e., the fact-finding motivation) and consequently be shared with an ingroup member. However, this rumor will reflect badly on the person and is therefore unlikely to be transmitted to an outgroup member. However, a positive rumor (that the ranking will increase next year) is self-enhancing and is therefore more likely to be transmitted to the outgroup member. What if the rumor happens to be about the outgroup (i.e., rise or fall in ranking of a rival college)? A positive rumor (rise in ranking) will likely be transmitted to a friend from the outgroup as this rumor will serve relationship enhancement. However, a negative rumor about the outgroup (fall in ranking) is more likely to be transmitted to an ingroup member as it will be self-enhancing.

To test some of these ideas, we conducted a study in which we manipulated rumor valence (negative or positive), target (rumor about the ingroup vs. about the outgroup), and recipient (an acquaintance from the ingroup vs. the outgroup). We adapted the procedure for this study from Kamins et al. (1997) but extended it in one important way: We clearly identified the recipient of the rumor as belonging to the ingroup or outgroup. The rumor referred to the rise or fall in ranking of a school in the next *U.S. News & World Report* ranking. The participants were undergraduate students from Rochester Institute of Technology

(RIT). Thus, RIT formed the ingroup. The outgroup was another school from the same city, the University of Rochester (UofR). The study had a 2 (valence: rise or fall in ranking) × 2 (target: rumor about RIT or UofR) × 2 (recipient: acquaintance from RIT or UofR) design. The participants were given a hypothetical scenario in which a friend (from RIT) tells them: "I don't know if this is true, but I heard that RIT's [or UofR's] ranking in *U.S. News & World Report* will fall [or rise] by four positions next year."

They then were asked to imagine that they happen to meet an acquaintance, another student from RIT [or UofR]. With the following two items, the participants were asked how likely they were to share the rumor with this acquaintance (i.e., likelihood of transmission): "How likely are you to tell the student the statement about the *U.S. News & World Report* ranking?" and "Is this statement something that you would mention to other—similar—acquaintances?" The two items were strongly related (*r* = .90) and were combined as a measure of likelihood of transmission. To explore the role of motivations underlying the intention to transmit, we also measured fact-finding motivation ("rate the extent to which you were motivated to figure out whether or not this statement was true or false" and "rate the extent to which you were motivated by a desire to see if the acquaintance knew if it was true or false"; *r* = .53), relationship-enhancement motivation ("rate how you think the acquaintance will feel about you if you tell him or her this statement" and "rate how you think the acquaintance's level of respect for you will change if you tell him or her this"; *r* = .65), and self-enhancement motivation ("you were motivated to say something that would make yourself feel good, not bad" and "you were motivated to create a pleasant mood—and not an unpleasant mood—in yourself"; *r* = .71). All ratings were on a 9-point scale.

Figures 3.1 to 3.3 present the results for fact-finding, relationship-enhancing, and self-enhancing motivations. Overall, the patterns of motivations were as expected. The fact-finding motivation was highest in the case of a negative rumor about the ingroup when the recipient was also from the ingroup (see Figure 3.1). The relationship-enhancement motivation was highest for the condition in which the rumor was positive and about the outgroup, and the recipient was an outgroup member (see Figure 3.2). Finally, the self-enhancement motivation was highest when the rumor was positive and about the ingroup, and the recipient was from the outgroup (see Figure 3.3). Motivational strength varied as a function of rumor valence, rumor target, and rumor recipient.

The results for the likelihood of transmission are presented in Figure 3.4. Several interesting patterns are visible. First, rumors about the ingroup were more likely to be transmitted to ingroup recipients. In

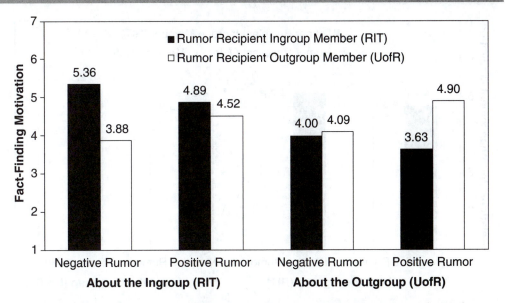

FIGURE 3.1

Fact-finding motivation in conditions of positive versus negative rumor about the ingroup or the outgroup when the recipient is from the ingroup or the outgroup. RIT = Rochester Institute of Technology; UofR = University of Rochester.

general, the ingroup audience was the preferred target in all conditions, except when the rumor was positive in valence and about the outgroup. Second, contrary to the MUM effect, when the rumor was about the ingroup and the recipient was a member of the ingroup, both positive and negative rumors were equally likely to be transmitted. In other words, participants did not hesitate to transmit negative rumor to an ingroup recipient. We expected the fact-finding motivation to underlie this effect. To test this idea, we conducted a mediation analysis that tested the effect of rumor recipient (ingroup vs. outgroup) on likelihood of transmission, when the rumor was negative and about the ingroup. We predicted that participants were more likely to transmit a negative rumor about the ingroup to ingroup recipients (as compared with outgroup recipients) because they wanted to know if the rumor was true. Our prediction was partly supported: The effect of rumor recipient on likelihood of transmission was partially mediated by the fact-finding motivation.[4]

---

[4] The standardized regression weight of the relationship between rumor recipient and the likelihood of transmission dropped from −.57 to −.41 after the mediator was

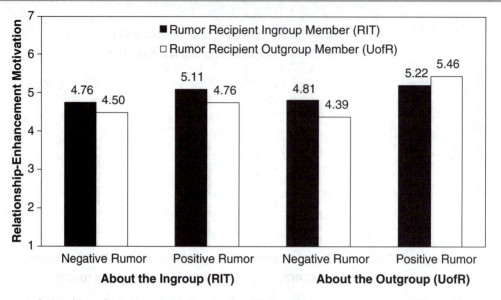

FIGURE 3.2

Relationship-enhancing motivation in conditions of positive versus negative rumor about the ingroup or the outgroup when the recipient is from the ingroup or the outgroup. RIT = Rochester Institute of Technology; UofR = University of Rochester.

Third, when the outgroup was the recipient of the rumor, the MUM effect did operate; that is, positive rumors (compared with negative rumors) were more likely to be transmitted to outgroup recipients. We expected the relationship-enhancement motivation to underlie this effect: That is, positive rumors (compared with negative rumors) were transmitted to outgroup members in the hope that the positive rumors would generate liking for the narrator. Once again, we tested the mediating effect of the relationship-enhancement motivation on the effect of valence (positive vs. negative) on the likelihood of transmission to an outgroup member. Results supported our prediction.[5]

controlled for; however, it remained significant. The Sobel test (R. M. Baron & Kenny, 1986) for the indirect effect of the independent variable through the mediator was significant ($Z = -.205$; $p = .04$).

[5] The effect of valence on likelihood of transmission (.31) became nonsignificant (.17) when relationship-enhancement motivation was in the equation. Moreover, the Sobel test for the indirect effect through the mediator was significant ($Z = 2.69$; $p = .007$).

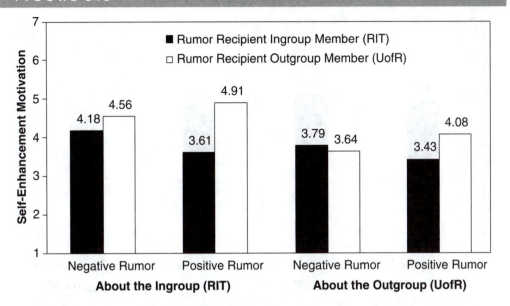

FIGURE 3.3

Self-enhancement motivation in conditions of positive versus negative rumor about the ingroup or the outgroup when the recipient is from the ingroup or the outgroup. RIT = Rochester Institute of Technology; UofR = University of Rochester.

Finally, we took a look at conditions in which motivations might compete. Consider the situation in which the outgroup member is the recipient of the rumor. Positive rumors about the ingroup might be more likely to be communicated to this outgroup member for self-enhancement reasons. However, relationship-enhancement motivation would be better served by the transmission of a positive rumor about the outgroup. The patterns of means for the likelihood of transmission, self-enhancement motivation, and relationship-enhancement motivation for the two conditions (positive rumor about the outgroup vs. the ingroup) when the recipient is in the outgroup condition are shown in Figure 3.5. As the figure shows, the self- and relationship-enhancement patterns go in opposite directions. However, likelihood of transmission is in the same direction as relationship-enhancement, which suggests that, in the context presented in the current study, relationship-enhancement motivation was more influential. To test this idea we conducted a mediation analysis; relationship-enhancement motivation did indeed mediate the effects of rumor target (about

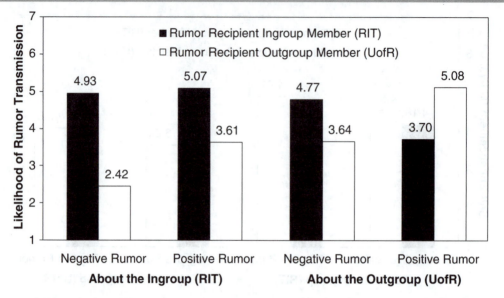

FIGURE 3.4

Likelihood of positive versus negative rumor transmission about the ingroup or the outgroup when the recipient is from the ingroup or the outgroup. RIT = Rochester Institute of Technology; UofR = University of Rochester.

ingroup vs. outgroup) on likelihood of transmission to an outgroup member.[6]

Conclusion

Rumors serve several goals. At times they are part of a search for valid information. Other times rumor interactions help in forming or strengthening relationships. Still other times, rumors assuage a threatened sense of self-worth or prop a prejudicial viewpoint by derogating an outgroup. The strength and influence of a motivation depend on several contextual features, including characteristics of the narrator,

---

[6] The relationship between rumor target (ingroup vs. outgroup) and likelihood of transmission became nonsignificant after the relationship-enhancement motivation was controlled for. Also, the indirect effect was marginally significant (Sobel test $Z = 1.89$; $p = .057$).

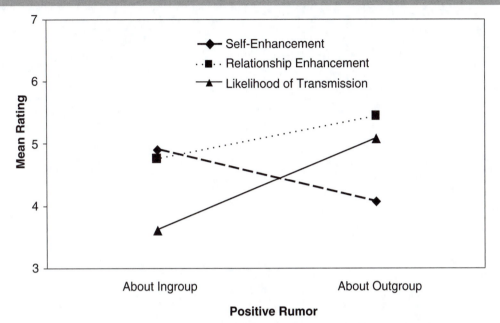

Self-enhancement motivation, relationship-enhancement motivation, and likelihood of transmission to an outgroup member of positive rumor about the ingroup versus the outgroup.

the recipient, the relationship between them, the content of the rumor, and so on. In this chapter, we have described the origins of the motivations in rumor transmission and reviewed rumor literature pertaining to each motivation. We also presented some empirical evidence regarding the role of these motivations in transmission intention.

We began by considering conceptual and descriptive issues related to rumor. In this chapter we provided a motivational framework for understanding rumor transmission. Next we turn to processes underlying belief in rumor.

Factors Associated With Belief in Rumor

4

In 2003, Ali Karim and Hussein Ali, both residents of Fallujah, Iraq, were quite angry. Karim had heard that "US President George W. Bush wants the US Army to kick everyone out of their homes [and] force them to live in tents" (Slackman, 2003, p. F1); furthermore, Fallujah would become a military camp. Ali, a coffee shop owner, heard that the United States plans to install a king to rule Iraq. Other Fallujians heard equally inflammatory negative rumors about the United States: American soldiers were spying on Muslim women with night-vision goggles and handing out pornography to children. To Americans, rumors such as these seem strange, yet to Fallujah residents in 2003, they were believable.

Rumors of all shapes and sizes often enter by way of the auditory canal, exit through the oral cavity, and make an important stop along the way: the cerebrum. These anatomical locations conveniently symbolize three broad steps thought to be involved in the life of a rumor (DiFonzo, Bordia, & Rosnow, 1994; Rosnow, 1988, 1991). In the generation stage, participants become motivated to receive rumor in an attempt to relieve anxiety or dispel uncertainty. In the transmission period, rumors are communicated through social interchanges. Between these periods is the evaluation phase, in which a rumor's likelihood of being true is assessed.

This assessment has implications for the life of any rumor. As noted in the previous chapter, people are more inclined to pass along a rumor they believe is true than one they believe is false (Rosnow, Yost, & Esposito, 1986). It has been theorized that disinclination to share a rumor perceived as false stems from a relationship-enhancement motive: penalties will be exacted from any false messenger. If the rumor describes a pipe dream (R. H. Knapp, 1944) the messenger risks becoming a source of disappointment. If the rumor excites fears, the messenger becomes a stimulus for undue anxiety. Either way, the reputation of one who raises false hopes or triggers false alarms is tarnished. Therefore, relationship-enhancement reasons sometimes coincide with fact-finding motivations, and people are desirous of accurately evaluating the rumor's credibility or veracity.

Although inclined to discern the truth, people are sometimes notoriously bad at the task. False or fabulous rumors often enjoy widespread acceptance. Consider these examples: Some Iraqis believe the United States plans to install a king in Iraq. The false rumor that the Procter & Gamble Corporation tithed to the Church of Satan generated 15,000 calls per month to the besieged corporation as well as a threat of product boycotts (Austin & Brumfield, 1991; Blumenfeld, 1991; Cato, 1982; Marty, 1982); many people believed this rumor. And more than one third of a sample of African American church members believed the rumor that "the AIDS virus was produced in a germ warfare laboratory to be a form of genocide against Black people"; another third were "unsure" about it ("Black Beliefs," 1995, p. B1).

Probabilistic Mental Models: Using Cues to Assess Authenticity

It is easy to see how people might impute credence to a plausible rumor, but widespread belief in such incredible ones as these begs explanation. In broader terms, how do individuals engaged in social exchange infer authenticity of rumors? Because a thorough literature search (as described later) yielded neither an explicit theory pertaining to belief in rumors nor a review of this topic, we examined the literature on belief in comparable entities. A relevant theory was proposed by Gigerenzer, Hoffrage, and Kleinbölting (1991; cf. Day, 1986). These authors proposed probabilistic mental models (PMMs) to explain how people arrive at judgments of confidence in statements of general knowledge. *Confi-*

dence judgments are subjective estimates of the probability that a proposition is true, and are conceptually similar to strength of belief ratings in a rumor.

PMM theory is a form of Egon Brunswik's *lens model* of judgment (1952). Brunswik's lens model posits that people infer judgments on the basis of cues. We judge a person's age, for example, on the basis of cues such as presence or absence of facial wrinkles, hair, and age marks. These cues form the lens through which we perceive distal attributes (e.g., age). In PMM theory, cues are variables through which we infer a statement's veracity. For example, recipients of a persuasive message on the effectiveness of pesticides are more persuaded by a chemist than a chemistry student (Rajecki, 1990); here the cue is source expertise. In a similar way, persons may express high confidence in the statement "Buffalo has over a million people" presumably because Buffalo has a football team in the National Football League (NFL) and populations in NFL cities usually exceed 1 million; here the cue is the presence or absence of an NFL team (Gigerenzer et al., 1991).

Certain cues may work well in some situations and poorly in others (Gigerenzer et al., 1991). If the front page of the newspaper states "Dewey Wins," then one may (incorrectly) infer that Dewey, and not Truman, has won the 1948 U.S. Presidential election; the cue here is "I read it in the newspaper." Of course, not everything one reads in the newspaper is true; journalists and pollsters sometimes err. The extent to which they are in error will affect how often the use of the "read it in the newspaper" cue will result in a flawed inference.

Within the general structure of PMM theory, the question of how rumor veracity is assessed may be framed as follows: What cues are used by recipients of rumor to assess its truthfulness? We address this question by first reviewing and meta-analyzing literature considering factors associated with belief in rumors. We set forth these factors in propositions about what elements of a rumor lead to its acceptance, and then we interpret these elements as cues that recipients use to assess veracity. We then present results from a set of interviews conducted with brokers in which these cues were explored.

Literature Search and Meta-Analytic Methods

We began the search by generating literature from 20 major academic electronic indexes. In light of rumor's conceptual ambiguity (see chap. 1, this volume), the following search terms were used: *rumor**, *rumour*, grapevine, bruited about, gossip*, hearsay, whispering campaign*, mudslinging, scandal, and scuttlebutt* (S. D. Knapp, 1993; asterisks indicate any letter combination, for example, rumor* will search for rumors, rumoring, and rumored). All articles relevant to the topic of rumor were retained and the reference sections of each were culled to obtain additional studies. This procedure produced over 170 manuscripts on the topic of rumor, 37 of which bore directly on the subject of belief in rumor. Where sufficient statistical information was reported, product–moment correlations (*r*s) were calculated for effect sizes (see B. Mullen, 1989, chap. 6; R. Rosenthal & Rosnow, 1991, chap. 22; Shadish & Haddock, 1994) for factors thought to influence belief. Eighteen separate effect size *r*s were computed from 10 independent investigations, all of which measured belief.[1]

Consistency With Attitudes

A substantial quantity of descriptive and correlational research points toward belief in rumors that are consistent with the hearer's currently held attitudes. These conclusions are intuitively appealing. If a rumor supports or accords with what the actor already holds to be true, it is plausible that the actor would assign greater credence to it. These conclusions also dovetail with a long line of attitude research findings showing the effects of attitude on judgment. For example, attitudes affect judgments of information that is relevant to the attitude (Pratkanis & Greenwald, 1989). In a similar way, partisan identification—an attitude—has been shown to bias the evaluation of arguments on a political issue (Lord, Lepper, & Ross, 1979), and judgment of the veracity of the Clinton–Lewinsky scandal allegations was strongly predicted by one's prior Clinton approval rating (Fischle, 2000). It is a short step to therefore state that attitudes also affect belief judgments about rumors. Before we consider the evidence for this, however, it is important to clarify how the term *attitude* is used here.

Although attitudes have been conceptualized as having three separate components (affect, cognition, and behavior; see Rajecki, 1990,

---

[1] For example, Jaeger, Anthony, and Rosnow (1980) asked subjects to rate their belief in a planted rumor on a 4-point scale ranging from 0 (*no-confidence*) to 3 (*complete confidence*). The number of belief scale alternatives varied from two (e.g., *believe* vs. *do-not-believe*; Goggins, 1979) to 11 (e.g., 0 = *no confidence in truth of rumor* to 11 = *strong confidence in truth of rumor*; Esposito, 1986/1987; Kimmel & Keefer, 1991).

chap. 2), few attitude component distinctions were explicitly made in the rumor literature. However, affective or cognitive attitudinal components were implicitly indicated from the context. For example, the "Eleanor Club" rumors we referred to in chapter 1 (this volume) are consistent with anti-African-American and anti-Roosevelt sentiment and the fear of inversion of status, which are affective in nature (G. W. Allport & Postman, 1947b, p. 175). However, those who considered wartime rationing programs to be unfair or unnecessary believed World War II rumors of waste and special privilege more than did those who considered them fair or necessary (F. H. Allport & Lepkin, 1945); consideration is a cognitive activity. Perhaps this approach stemmed directly from consistency theory; even the *cognitive* of Festinger's (1957) *cognitive dissonance* seems to include affect as well (Rajecki, 1990). Furthermore, although G. W. Allport and Postman (1947b) differentiated between the "intellectual and emotional contexts" in which rumors are transmitted, they maintained that these contexts are "indistinguishably blended" (p. 100). In this discussion, then, attitude is conceptualized primarily in terms of its cognitive and affective components.[2]

Descriptive evidence consisted mainly of case studies and collections of rumors. These rumors are presented in Table 4.1, along with the attitudes with which the rumors are presumed to be consistent. Perhaps the most exemplary set of speculations comes from the benchmark work on prejudicial rumors by Gordon W. Allport and Leo Postman (1947a, 1947b). These researchers asserted that racial stereotypes and animosities lay behind the prevalence of racist rumors. In a similar way, Robert H. Knapp speculated that widespread inconvenience and political or prejudicial sentiment produced the disproportionate percentage (65.9%) of World War II wedge-driving rumors in the United States (e.g., "the Catholics in America are trying to evade the draft," Knapp, 1944, p. 24).

Some attitudes are so deeply rooted in a group that they are more rightly considered as culture. One of R. H. Knapp's (1944) characteristics of a thriving rumor was that it accorded with the cultural traditions of the group. Prasad (1935) noted that rumors gained currency when they were consistent with local superstitions. In a later (1950) study, he characterized rumor as a picture completion task, with attitude (largely made up of cultural traditions) painting the picture. London and London (1975) similarly speculated that widespread false variations of a rumor that President Nixon had stolen a teacup from Chairman Mao during his visit to China sprang from elements of Chinese national

---

[2] In chapter 10 (this volume) we propose how future researchers may fruitfully distinguish these components.

TABLE 4.1

Descriptive Evidence for Belief in Attitude-Consistent Rumors

Reference	Rumor(s)	Attitude with which rumor is consistent
Abalakina-Paap & Stephan (1999)	Conspiracy rumors (e.g., AIDS is a plot to wipe out minority groups, the government is storing information in computer files to against its citizens, and fluoridating drinking water will hurt people).	Authoritarianism, anomie, and powerlessness.
G. W. Allport & Postman (1947a, 1947b)	Rumors of incidents of "the Negro's criminal and disloyal tendencies . . . Negro stupidity, gullibility, and laziness, [and] . . . myriad tales of Negro sexual aggression" (1947b, p. 177).	White supremacy. For example, "What can we do with a black man who is disloyal, criminal, clownish, stupid, menacing, and immoral—except to keep him in his place just as we are now doing?" (1947b, p. 177).
G. W. Allport & Postman (1947a, 1947b)	"Eleanor Club"[a] rumors circulating in southern states in 1943; the theme of these rumors was that large numbers of African American women were banding together to reverse the social order (e.g., "A White woman was away for a while, and when she returned she found her colored maid sitting at her dresser combing her hair with her comb," 1947b, p. 175).	Anti-African American and anti-Roosevelt sentiment and fear of inversion of status. "White rumor spreaders find their feelings of economic and social insecurity to some extent explained and relieved by these stories" (1947b, p. 176).
G. W. Allport & Postman (1947a, 1947b)	Rumors of incidents of Black men having sexual relations with unwilling White women.	Self-vindication with regard to sexual morality. For example, "Even if we are not blameless, yet his misdeeds (as recounted in rumor) are overt and worse than ours. We need not feel guilt at our peccadilloes" (1947b, p. 179).
G. W. Allport & Postman (1947b)	World War II wedge-driving rumors (e.g., "The Jews get the cushiest jobs in the Army").	Religious and racial prejudice.
Ambrosini (1983) Case 1	A psychiatric hospital patient "had sexual relations with a man on the ward and . . . would suffocate herself while in the hospital" (p. 76).	Internal aggressive and sexual conflicts. The rumors allowed patients and psychologists to rationalize their own sexual and aggressive impulses.

(continued)

TABLE 4.1 *(Continued)*

Descriptive Evidence for Belief in Attitude-Consistent Rumors

Reference	Rumor(s)	Attitude with which rumor is consistent
Ambrosini (1983) Case 2	Recurrent rumors that "the clinical psychology department of a prestigious university was about to be disbanded" (p. 77).	Internal sense of separation and anxiety. The rumor meshed well with new graduate students' sense of disillusionment and depression after their initial elation at being accepted into the program (e.g., "This program isn't so great after all").
Ambrosini (1983) Case 3	A therapy group's co-leader (a psychiatrist) was "imminently departing from the group" (p. 78).	Internal sense of separation and loss. The rumor meshed well with group members' belief that the group would eventually disband.
Festinger et al. (1948)	A researcher who was stimulating community activities in a tenant's association was an avowed communist.	Opposition to the project and anti-communist sentiment.
Hicks (1990)	Satanic rumor panics that are believed and propagated by police.	The "satanic model that has emerged at conferences of therapists, police, and cult survivors . . . obtained 'through hours of networking' between the various professionals" (p. 383).
Jung (1959)	Recurrent rumors of flying saucers.	The collective archetypes of the self, the masculine–feminine antithesis, the antithesis of what is "above and below," the antithesis of "unity and quaternity," and the antithesis concerning the "enigmatic higher world and the ordinary human world" (p. 16).
Kelley (2004)	Iraqi hostility rumors.	Ethnic and political sentiment (e.g., Anti-U.S./Coalition, Anti-Israel, Anti-Sunni, Anti-Saddam, Anti-Shiite, Anti-Turk attitudes).
R. H. Knapp (1944)	Wedge-driving rumors.	Religious and racial prejudice.
Knopf (1975)	Rumors circulating during 20th-century race riots.	Racial hostilities.

(continued)

TABLE 4.1 (Continued)

Descriptive Evidence for Belief in Attitude-Consistent Rumors

Reference	Rumor(s)	Attitude with which rumor is consistent
London & London (1975)	Variations of a widespread rumor that President Nixon visited China because he needed Chairman Mao's praise to be re-elected, that he had stolen a valuable "nine-dragon" teacup and denied it, and that a magician had deftly or cleverly retrieved the cup from Nixon.	Elements of Chinese national character: "superiority and face saving." For example, "Nixon visited China because he needed Mao's support" (China is superior); "we retrieved the cup" (superiority) "without embarrassing him" (face saving).
Nkpa (1977)	Rumors of mass poisoning collected in Biafra in a period encompassing the Nigerian civil war (1967–1970).	Biafran religious belief that those killed by poison would not be reincarnated. Nkpa speculated that this belief was responsible for the low percentage of poison rumors in comparison with other types of rumors.
Prasad (1950)	Rumors collected after a massive Indian landslide that contained recurrent themes such as the disappearance of rivers, eclipses and planets, the destruction of a capital town, a rain of blood, strange animals, and the end of the world.	Myths and legends. For example, the "rain of blood is mentioned in the great epics of Valmiki, Ramayana, and Mahabharata" (p. 140).
M. Rosenthal (1971)	Racial rumor circulating in Detroit, Michigan, in 1967 through 1968, falsely alleged that a child using a shopping mall lavatory was castrated by a gang of teenage boys.	Racial stereotypes. When repeated in the White community, the gang was said to be Black and the victim White. When told in the Black community, the gang was said to be White and the victim Black.[b]

(continued)

character. Finally, Jung (1959) ventured beyond culture as the mold in which some rumors are cast; he viewed rumor generation as a kind of projective mechanism giving evidence of presuppositions that are handed down from our ancestors through a *collective unconscious*.

Correlational evidence for attitudes that bear specifically on the rumor in question is consistent with these ideas. Studies in which belief in rumor was related to attitudes are presented in Table 4.2. One investigation in this set was performed by Floyd H. Allport and Milton Lepkin (1945) during World War II. A rationing program caused shortages of many commodities and inconvenienced many citizens to one

TABLE 4.1 (Continued)

Descriptive Evidence for Belief in Attitude-Consistent Rumors

Reference	Rumor(s)	Attitude with which rumor is consistent
Scheper–Hughes (1990)	Brazilian shantytown children are routinely abducted and mutilated by American or Japanese agents to obtain profitable body organs for transplants.	Class conflict attitudes, such as that the poor are given inadequate medical treatment and are unfairly treated, and that children of the poor are prey to an unscrupulous "baby trade."
Victor (1989)	Rumor panic about dangerous satanic cults alleging ritual meetings, animal sacrifice, blood drinking, and the planned kidnapping of a blond-haired, blue-eyed virgin.	Dissatisfaction with changing societal values, as well as fear of the effect of "dangerous new influences" (p. 39) on children.

Note. [a]Named after Eleanor Roosevelt, "Eleanor Club" rumors fused anti-Roosevelt and anti-African American themes. [b]Belief was not measured. We assume that the presence of a rumor indicates some belief as well. For example, the absence (in the White community) of the rumor that the teenage castrators were White is taken to mean that this rumor was not believed in that community.

degree or another. Of concern to government officials were certain wedge-driving rumors that commodities were being wasted or were freely accessible to those of higher status (e.g., "A certain prominent government official has 3 cars and a large underground storage tank filled with gasoline for his own use," p. 5). Because these allegations were either false or unsubstantiated, Allport and Lepkin wondered what caused people to believe in these rumors of waste and special privilege. Among other variables, they measured strength of belief in each of 12 rumors as well as attitudes that Allport and Lepkin posited might cause belief.

The relations in Table 4.2 are arranged in order of ascending strength within each study; correlations vary widely. The strongest associations between belief and attitudes are for those attitudes that are highly specific to the rumors. For example, belief in rumors of waste and special privilege was more highly correlated with unfavorable attitudes toward the rationing program than with adverse attitudes toward the Roosevelt administration (F. H. Allport & Lepkin, 1945). That is, the attitude that "the rationing program is unfair or unnecessary" is highly specific to such rumors as "A certain prominent government official has 3 cars and a large underground storage tank filled with gasoline for his own use." We note that the Pearson-*r* correlation for this relationship was weak to moderate (.19). A similar attitude–specificity relationship increase occurred in the DeClerque et al. (1986)

TABLE 4.2

Correlational Evidence for Belief in Attitude-Consistent Rumors

Rumor	Attitude–belief relationship	Effect size[a]
12 World War II rumors of waste and special privilege (F. H. Allport & Lepkin, 1945).	*Attitude of being greatly inconvenienced or personally frustrated.* Those inconvenienced by the scarcity of goods and by the rationing program (in a moderate number of commodities) believed rumors more than did those who did not feel so inconvenienced (after controls).	Not estimable
	Adverse attitudes toward the national administration. Those not "satisfied that we have the best men now in office for leading positions of the national government and the army" believed rumors more than did those "satisfied."	$r = .03$, $p = .10$, $t = 1.30$, $N = 1,956$[b]
	Emotional distance from the war. Those with a relative or personal friend serving in the armed forces in this country believed rumors more than did those with a relative or friend serving overseas (after controls).	$r = .05$, $p = .06$, $t = 1.53$, $N = 1,044$[b]
	Lack of faith in fellow Americans. Those who thought that "not all classes and occupations of Americans are working as hard as could be expected in the War effort" believed rumors more than did those who thought that all classes are working hard (after controls).	$r = .06$, $p = .04$, $t = 1.75$, $N = 948$[b]
	Attitude of being moderately inconvenienced or personally frustrated. Those inconvenienced by the scarcity of goods and by the rationing program (in a moderate number of commodities) believed rumors more than did those who did not feel so inconvenienced (after controls).	$r = .11$, $p = .0006$, $t = 3.26$, $N = 948$[b]
	Adverse attitudes toward rationing program. Those who considered the rationing program to be unfair or unnecessary (as a whole or in part) believed rumors more than did those who considered it fair or necessary (after controls).	$r = .19$, $p = 1.43E-6$, $t = 4.68$, $N = 600$[b]

A rumor circulating in 1980 among Egyptians that oral contraceptive use causes weakness (DeClerque et al., 1986).	Attitude that the pill is "unreliable" (as opposed to not having this attitude).	$r = .06$, $p = .0057$, $\chi^2(1) = 7.63$, $N = 2,120$
A rumor circulating in 1980 among Egyptians that oral contraceptive use causes weakness (DeClerque et al., 1986).	Attitude that the pill is "very harmful" (as opposed to not having this attitude).	$r = .17$, $p = 4.98E - 15$, $\chi^2(1) = 61.27$, $N = 2,120$
13 pro- and 13 anti-Soviet news-type statements presented to subjects as rumors (G. H. Smith, 1947).	Attitude toward Soviets. Subjects were classified as pro-Soviet, neutral, and anti-Soviet. Mean belief ratings in pro-Soviet rumors increased from the anti- to neutral to pro-Soviet groups. Mean belief ratings for anti-Soviet rumors exhibited the opposite ordering.	Not estimable

Note. [a]Estimable effect sizes (*r*s) were based on secondary analysis of data (Rosenthal & Rosnow, 1991) and measured the effect of association between strength of belief in the rumor and strength of agreement with the attitude. All *p*s were one-tailed in the direction of relationship. Where effect sizes were not estimable, the study reported finding a statistically significant result. [b]*N*s for F. H. Allport and Lepkin statistics are for responses, not subjects, violating the independence-of-observations assumption. Therefore, study results are presented here but should be viewed as suggestive rather than conclusive. An estimate of the number of subjects involved for each hypothesis may be obtained by dividing the *N* by 12 because each subject rated 12 rumors (1945, p. 22).

study: Having the attitude that the pill is "very harmful" was similarly associated ($r = .17$) with the rumor circulating among Egyptians that oral contraceptive use causes weakness. The corresponding increase in belief rate in a Binomial Effect Size Display (R. Rosenthal & Rosnow, 1991, pp. 280–283) between people possessing attitudes consistent with the rumor and those not possessing such attitudes is 17%—an important practical effect.[3]

These results suggest an association between belief in rumor and attitudes specifically consistent with that belief (Proposition 1). No studies offered evidence that attitudes caused belief in particular rumors, although almost all implied such a conclusion. This conclusion is plausible, given that the attitudes described and measured seem more stable than do the beliefs in rumor (implying temporal precedence). It is also plausible, however, that rumors influence attitudes. This association was hypothesized in only the DeClerque et al. (1986) study; these researchers posited that an Egyptian rumor that the birth control pill causes weakness (loss of physical strength) had led to negative perceptions of the pill.

Rumor Source Credibility

A long line of research in persuasion has shown that source credibility is linked to attitude formation and change (Hovland & Weiss, 1951; Petty & Cacioppo, 1981). In a similar way, it is likely that rumors heard from more credible, authoritative, or well-positioned sources (e.g., layoff rumors heard from a manager) would tend to be more strongly believed than would rumors heard from less credible, authoritative, or well-positioned sources (e.g., layoff rumors from a fellow worker). And indeed, the evidence supported this idea. To begin with, researchers assembling collections of rumors have consistently observed that attri-

---

[3] An r-value of .17 is typically considered weak to moderate (J. Cohen, 1988), but even weak effect sizes may indicate important effects (R. Rosenthal & Rosnow, 1991; see also R. Rosenthal, 1991, pp. 132–136). For example, the effect of aspirin on reducing heart attacks is $r = .034$ (Steering Committee of the Physicians Health Study Research Group, as cited in R. Rosenthal & Rosnow, 1991). Although this correlation accounts for only 0.11% of the variance, the result is of great practical importance, as the increase in the percentage of lives saved by taking one aspirin per day versus not taking aspirin is 3.4% (i.e., over three lives per hundred treated). With regard to DeClerque's investigation, an effect size r of .17 accounts for "only" 2.89% of the variance, yet a 17% increase in the belief rate is hardly inconsequential.

bution to a credible source is part of the typical rumor formulation (e.g., Bird, 1979; Blake, McFaul, & Porter, 1974; R. H. Knapp, 1944). After compiling and cataloging 1,089 World War II rumors in September 1942, Knapp (1944) concluded that "successful" (flourishing) rumors tended to be attributed to authoritative sources: "From whatever humble beginning a rumor may spring, it is soon attributed to a high authoritative source. This gives the rumor . . . the appearance of veracity" (p. 30). In a similar way, folklorist Donald Allport Bird (1979) amassed and analyzed the stylistic characteristics of an immense collection of rumors from printed sources, archives, and student questionnaires, and found that rumors are frequently ascribed to a high-status community member or someone "in the know" (chap. 2). Blake et al. (1974) posited and found evidence that, under normal conditions (i.e., low collective excitement), rumors gained plausibility by the addition of an authoritative citation and a media source from which the rumor was supposedly heard. When questioned about a rumor that a hatchet murderer "would kill several coeds at a small college in Ohio" (p. 7), 94% of respondents attributed the source of the rumor to Jeane Dixon[4] and 51% stated this prediction was published in newspaper or radio media (Blake et al., 1974).

The only direct investigation measuring rumor source credibility and rumor belief fully accords with these conclusions. Porter (1984) found that rumor communicator credibility was moderately to strongly related to belief in negative rumors about birth control in the Dominican Republic ($r = .40$; pp. 27, 29). Taken all together, these findings imply an association between credibility of source and belief in rumor (Proposition 2).

Hearing Repeatedly

Persuasive circumstantial evidence points toward the proposition that repetition (the number of times a rumor is heard) is associated with belief. A series of experiments investigated the confidence placed in responses to questions that are repeated. The original study in this series was by Hasher, Goldstein, and Toppino (1977). On three separate occasions, they asked subjects to answer true–false items of general knowledge and rate their confidence in their responses. Some of the

---

[4] We suppose that in the domain of prophetic statements, reference to self-proclaimed seer Jeane Dixon may be considered an authoritative citation, although in fact her record of accurate prophecies is abysmal (Donnelly, 1983).

items were repeated over the three occasions. The researchers found that subjects placed increasing confidence in their responses to repeated items only and concluded that "If people are told something often enough, they'll believe it" (p. 112). Later research replicated this *illusory truth* effect (Bacon, 1979; Begg, Anas, & Farinacci, 1992; Boehm, 1994). If being presented with and responding to a true–false item increases confidence in the response to that item, then perhaps hearing and evaluating a rumor repeatedly may increase belief in the rumor.

Direct evidence is also supportive. Weinberg et al. (1980) found that undergraduates tended to receive a rumor about a campus hit-and-run accident two or three times before passing it on. F. H. Allport and Lepkin (1945) found that those who had previously heard the rumors presented in their survey believed them more than did those who had not previously heard them.[5] These findings mesh well with R. H. Knapp's (1944) intuition regarding the effect of rumors on public opinion: "Once rumors are current, they have a way of carrying the public with them. Somehow, the more a rumor is told, the greater is its plausibility" (p. 27). In other words, rumors, when repeated, seem more believable. All together, the available evidence implies a third proposition: There is an association between repetition (the number of times a rumor is heard) and belief (Proposition 3).

Rumor Rebuttal

In light of rumor's long-standing ignominy as a saboteur of morale and reputation (summary in Bird, 1979, chap. 1), it is not surprising that a number of studies have explored how to effectively combat rumor. Effect sizes for studies that have investigated how rebuttal affects belief in a rumor are presented in Table 4.3. Earlier studies used a between-groups design in which all subjects received rumor, but some also then received a rebuttal of the rumor; belief was then measured and compared between the rebuttal and no-rebuttal groups. Our own investigations used a within-groups design in which belief in the rumor would be measured both prior to and after the rebuttal. Results from eight rebuttal studies[6] were meta-analytically combined (R. Rosenthal & Rosnow, 1991, p. 505), yielding an N-weighted $r_{avg.} = .33$—a moderate

---

[5] $t(5216) = 21.5$, $p_{1\text{-tailed}} = 1.29\text{E-}98$, $r = .29$; see Table 4.2, note b.

[6] The studies in Table 4.3 were used, excluding F. H. Allport and Lepkin's (1945) results because they violate the independence-of-observation assumption (see Table 4.2, Note b).

effect.[7] Caution is in order, however, because these eight effect sizes were quite heterogeneous,[8] although in light of the variation in rebuttal sources and study methodology, heterogeneity is to be expected.

It is important to note that we have been discussing the effect of rebuttal overall and have not considered moderating variables; these may be quite important in enhancing or negating the effect of rebuttal on belief (indeed, the heterogeneity of our meta-analysis points toward this). For example, Koller (1992) found mixed evidence for an interaction between method of rebuttal (positive advertising, denial, or no-comments) and prior knowledge of the rumor. Iyer and Debevec (1991) found that conciliatory rebuttals were more effective than were inflammatory ones. They also found that credibility of the rebuttal source interacted with the origin of the rumor (positive, neutral, or negative stakeholder). In our own research we found that appropriate (Bordia, DiFonzo, & Travers, 1998), honest (Bordia, DiFonzo, & Schulz, 2000), and high-credibility (Bordia, DiFonzo, Haines, & Chaseling, 2005) rebuttal sources enhance rebuttal effectiveness. We review in more detail the moderators of denial effectiveness—on belief and other outcomes—in chapter 9 (this volume). Overall, however, these results lead to a fourth proposition, that there is an inverse association between belief in rumor and the presence of a rebuttal (Proposition 4).

Other Factors

A small potpourri of other factors associated with belief appeared in our review of the literature. Kimmel and Keefer (1991) reported a jumbo-sized association ($r = .70$) between importance and belief; they posited importance to be a mediating variable between belief and transmission. F. H. Allport and Lepkin (1945) reported a nonsignificant relation between education and belief, but Kapferer (1989) reported a moderate negative ($r = -.32$) relationship. We turn now to recent empirical evidence of factors associated with belief.

---

[7] The corresponding decrease in belief rate in a Binomial Effect Size Display (R. Rosenthal & Rosnow, 1991, pp. 280–283) caused by rebuttal is 33%. With R. Rosenthal's (1979) file drawer analysis, 341 unpublished studies averaging null results would have to exist to bring the overall $p_{1\text{-tailed}} = .0003$ (based on $z_{avg.} = 3.42$) to a "just significant" $p = .05$ level.

[8] $\chi^2(7) = 46.44$, $p = 7.19E-8$ (see R. Rosenthal & Rosnow, 1991, pp. 500–501).

TABLE 4.3

Effect of Rebuttal on Reduction in Belief

Reference	Rumor	Effect size[a] of rebuttal on reducing belief
Jaeger et al. (1980)	Several students had smoked marijuana during a final exam.	$r = .28$, $p = .0007$, $F(1,146) = 11.94$, $N = 148$
G. W. Allport & Postman (1947b, p. 5)	Damage from the World War II Pearl Harbor bombing was worse than reported.	$r = .19$[b], $p = .0072$, $\chi^2(1) = 7.22$, $N = 200$
Iyer & Debebec (1991)	Environmental tobacco smoke is harmful to nonsmokers.	$r = .15$[c], $p = .0217$, $t(175) = 2.03$, $N = 187$
F. H. Allport & Lepkin (1945)	Twelve World War II rumors of waste and special privilege.	$r = .08$[d,e], $p = .0023$, $t(1258) = 2.83$, $N = 1{,}260$
Bordia, DiFonzo, & Travers (1998)	Psychology students will need to have a specific grade point average to enroll in second-year subjects.	$r = .56$[f], $p = 3.00E - 9$, $F(1,93) = 43.03$, $N = 94$
Bordia et al. (2000)	"The undergraduate library is being closed down."	$r = .18$[g], $p = .05$, $t(86) = 1.68$, $N = 87$
Bordia, DiFonzo, Haines, & Chaseling (2005, Study 1, Condition 1)	A computer virus with the subject line "Good Times" will rewrite your hard drive.	$r = .77$[h], $p = .0002$, $t(14) = 4.53$, $N = 15$
Bordia, DiFonzo, Haines, & Chaseling (2005, Study 2)	A computer virus with the subject line "Good Times" will rewrite your hard drive.	$r = .61$[i], $p = 4.08E - 10$, $t(79) = 6.98$, $N = 80$

| Bordia, DiFonzo, Haines, & Chaseling (2005, Study 3) | A computer virus with the subject line "Good Times" will rewrite your hard drive. | $r = .60^i$, $p = 4.48E - 9$, $t(76) = 6.46$, $N = 77$ |

Note. [a]Estimable effect sizes (*r*s) were based on secondary analysis of data (Rosenthal & Rosnow, 1991) and measured the effect of rumor rebuttal on belief in rumor. All *p*s were one-tailed in the direction of relationship. [b]G. W. Allport and Postman (1947b) imply that a majority of the subjects heard Roosevelt's February 23, 1943, rebuttal but do not give an exact proportion. We calculated possible effect sizes corresponding to various majority proportions. The effect size reported here is the smallest of these and is based on the conservative estimate that 190 out of 200 subjects heard the rebuttal; smaller majorities result in much higher *r*s. [c]Calculated over all 12 cells of a 3 (rumor origin) × 4 (rumor-quelling strategy) factorial design. Contrast weights for each level of rumor origin (negative, neutral, and positive stakeholder) were −1, −1, −1, and +3 for low credibility conciliatory, low credibility inflammatory, neutral source, and no rebuttal, respectively, so as to compare the average belief rating in cells in which rebuttal had been given with cells in which no rebuttal had been given. [d]*N*s for F. H. Allport and Lepkin statistics are for responses, not subjects, violating the independence-of-observations assumption (see Table 4.2, Note b). [e]Based on the credence-index (an aggregate index of belief) difference between those who read the rebuttals in the "Rumor Clinic" column of the *Syracuse Post-Standard*. Only responses of subjects who had heard the rumor before (prior hearers) were included in the comparison. [f]Based on an overall dependent-groups comparison of belief in the rumor before denial and after denial; rumor was denied in four between conditions: a fellow student, a lecturer, the head of department, or the vice-chancellor (president of the university). [g]Based on an overall dependent-groups comparison of belief in the rumor before denial and after denial; rumor was denied in three between conditions: a library staff member at the loans desk, the librarian, or the vice chancellor (president of the university). [h]Based on a dependent-groups comparison of belief in the rumor before denial and after denial; rumor was denied by the Computer Incident Advisory Capability, a computer security watchdog group run by the U.S. Department of Energy. [i]Based on an overall dependent-groups comparison of belief in the rumor before denial and after denial (Study 2); rumor was denied in four conditions in a 2 (high–low quality denial) × 2 (high–low credibility denial source).

Field Interviews
With Brokers

To explore cues used to infer veracity in field settings, we conducted field interviews with a sample of 10 stockbrokers in Philadelphia, Princeton, and New York who were willing to be interviewed (DiFonzo, 1994, Study 2). Subjects were contacted via personal acquaintance and snowball sampling (participants were asked if other brokers they knew would provide additional interviews). All were employed in several major investment firms and typically possessed 8 to 12 years of experience. A critical incident technique (Flanagan, 1954) was used to query subjects about actual instances of rumors: Participants were asked, "Think of a rumor that you have heard that is relevant to a security that is important to you" and "What was the source of the rumor?" To assess belief, we asked participants, "On a scale of 0 to 10 where 0 means 'no confidence' and 10 means 'complete confidence,' how confident were you, at about the time you first heard it, that this rumor was true?" To explore what cues were being used to arrive at that confidence judgment, we asked participants, "How did you arrive at that judgment?" To assess the repetition cue, we asked, "From how many independent sources did you hear this rumor?" To assess the source credibility cue, we asked the participants to identify the source of the rumor. We assessed cue validity of the source of the rumor by asking participants, "In general, what percentage of rumors that you hear from [the source of this rumor] are true?" A total of 18 separate rumors were discussed; these are presented in Table 4.4. Although takeover rumors were most numerous, the set deals with a diverse range of content areas (e.g., staff changes, crop-planting patterns, cover-up attempts). Most of the rumors were recent; 64% of the rumors had been heard within 8 months prior to the interview. Brokers were also asked if the rumor had proven true; the set was roughly evenly divided between the three possibilities of true ($n = 8$), false ($n = 5$), or uncertain ($n = 5$).

Cues used fell into seven fairly distinct categories, three of which matched our propositions. First, investors used consistency with hearer's attitude. For example, one trader inferred some degree of likelihood to admittedly "radical" and "extreme" rumors that then-U.S. President Clinton wanted to devalue the dollar (as compared with the yen) so as to reduce the apparent United States–Japanese trade deficit. Such a rumor meshed with the broker's attitude that the government likes to take the "shabby, easy way out" of difficult problems. Second, investors

TABLE 4.4

Broker Field Interview Rumors and Cues Used to Infer Belief

Rumor ID[a]	Rumor	Cue(s) used	Source of rumor	Source cue validity	No. of sources	Belief[b]
1.1	President of Company X just flew somewhere to fix a major problem.	1. Fit the pattern: Past instances had occurred in which this president traveled and fixed major problems. 2. Source credibility[c]: Source had nothing to gain by spreading rumor, was trusted, and was close to the situation.	Acquaintance close to situation.	1. 95% for rumors for which source is close to situation. 2. 65% for rumors for which source is not close to situation.	1	9
1.2	Small-company product *p* will be purchased by large Company X.	Source credibility[c]: Source had something to gain by spreading rumor.	Investor associated with company prior to its public sale of stock.	"small %"[d]	1	2
1.3	Company X will obtain new contracts.	Price changes in accord with rumor.	Can't remember exact source.	Can't remember.	<5	9
2.1	Company X is "frying the books" (using illegal accounting procedures).	Analyst opinion that rumor was false.	Can't remember.	Can't remember.	1	3–4.5
2.2	John Sculley is leaving Spectrum Technologies.	Low confidence in source[c] (views Dorfman as "incompetent").	Dan Dorfman (CNN).	20%–30%	1	2–3
3.1	Vince Foster had committed suicide in a location different than what official accounts noted (negative implications for White House staff).	Not plausible that White House staff involved in homicide.	*Johnson-Smick Report* (a financial news service).	75%	3 (and lots of related stories)	Began at 2–3; rose to 5.
3.2	Large Industrial Firm X lost $2.5 billion.	Fit the pattern: Trading behavior of persons associated with the firm was unusual and made the rumor very plausible.	Traders, then news media.	20%	10	9

continued

TABLE 4.4 (Continued)

Broker Field Interview Rumors and Cues Used to Infer Belief

Rumor ID[a]	Rumor	Cue(s) used	Source of rumor	Source cue validity	No. of sources	Belief[b]
4.1	Japanese banks are bankrupt and are selling off assets. Ministry of Finance is helping them through this crisis. Clinton wants to push yen a lot higher to reduce apparent trade deficit.	1. Fit the pattern: "It explained unusual things I saw" (e.g., why is the yen so high?). 2. Compatible with attitude that Clinton administration would be likely to take a politically easy solution (government likes to take the "shabby, easy way out").	Other marketplace participants.	30%–40%	3–4	Began at 3–4; rose to 7–8.
4.2	There will be massive planting of corn over beans.	1. Meshes with Clinton policy. 2. There are "other reasons" why it is plausible.	Another trader.	Unknown	1	Began: 1–2; rose to 5.
5.1	Checkers drive-in fast-food restaurant chain will be bought out by Pepsi-Cola.	Fit the pattern: Stock is in industry that is consolidating.	Another broker.	50%	2	4
5.2	Baltimore Bank Corp. will be taken over.	1. Fit a trend: Super-regional commercial banks are buying small banks. 2. Saw increased insider trading. 3. Saw price increasing. 4. Possible merger was featured in a financial report.	Another broker.	50%	2	5–6
5.3	Bank South will be taken over.	Fit a trend: Super-regional commercial banks are buying small banks.	A money manager.	10%–15%	4–5	5–6
6.1	Germantown Savings Bank will be taken over.	Low confidence in source[c] but fit a trend: Super-regional commercial banks are buying small banks.	"The grapevine" (brokers, clients).	2%	1–3	1–2

Rumor ID	Rumor		Source			
6.2	Baltimore Bank Corp. will be taken over.	1. Low confidence in source.[c] 2. Possible merger was featured in a financial report. 3. Fit a trend: Super-regional commercial banks are buying small banks.	"The grapevine" (brokers, clients).	2%	>2	3–4
7.1	John Sculley will become CEO of Spectrum Technologies.	"Seemed possible to people familiar with Apple and Spectrum."	Don't remember.	25%	1–2	5
7.2	For each share of stock purchased in St. Joe's Paper Co., you are buying one tenth acre of land in Florida.	Knew something about company that "made rumor seem likely."	*Dick Davis Digest* (financial newsletter).	33%–40%	1	8–9
8.1	Federal government will not permit AT&T merger with McCaw Cellular because of anti-trust laws.	Didn't fit the pattern (i.e., Clinton economic mandates).	Analysts and portfolio managers.	<10%	4–5 brokers and several analysts	1
9.1	Company X's earnings would be 6 cents per share when only 1 cent per share was expected.	1. Frequency: testimony of nine brokers. 2. Fit the pattern: Recent acquisitions of two companies generated revenues. 3. Credible sources.[c]	Several brokerage firms.	50%	2	8.5
10.1	Purposely unaware of rumors and doesn't trade on rumors because they are unreliable.			50%		

Note. [a]*Rumor ID* is composed of *broker rumor* (e.g., 5.2 signifies broker number 5, rumor number 2). [b]Strength of belief is measured on a 1 (*no confidence*) to 10 (*complete confidence*) scale. [c]Indicates one of the six cases in which source credibility cue was used. [d]15% was estimated in the calculation of *r* between cue validity and strength of belief (see text).

used credibility of rumor source as a veracity cue. One investor felt the rumor source was credible because "he [the source] was close to the president [of the company]." Most sources were word-of-mouth tips from market participants less highly positioned. It is not surprising that published sources, such as the *Dick Davis Digest*, the *Johnson-Smick Report*, and the "Heard on the Street" column, were generally assigned greater credibility than were nonpublished sources. Source credibility was used in six cases; a Pearson-r calculated between cue validity and strength of belief for this small a number of cases can be viewed only as suggestive, but it was very large ($r = .88$).[9] Third, there was anecdotal evidence that frequency of hearing related to belief in the rumor. One investor was initially doubtful about false rumors implicating White House involvement in former staff member Vince Foster's suicide; on hearing the rumor "lots and lots" of times, he adopted a "let's-wait-and-see attitude." In a similar way, a Pearson-r calculated between number of sources and strength of belief was moderate but not significantly different from zero ($r = .24$).[10]

Fourth, one investor used stakeholder status as a veracity cue. Tips from tippers with "something to gain by spreading the rumor" were viewed skeptically; rumors from disinterested sources were viewed more favorably. Fifth, rumors that "fit the pattern" tended to be perceived as veridical. The pattern referred to here could be a larger trend exemplified in the rumor. Larger trends exemplified in specific rumors included the following: super-regional commercial banks are buying small banks, fast-food industry is consolidating, Clinton economic policy favors expansion of communications industry, acquisitions of smaller companies increase revenues, and problems get fixed when president of Company X flies to problem site. The pattern could also refer to the configuration of unusual and unexplained events that the rumor attempts to explain. Instances of such unexplained configurations included unusual trading behavior of persons associated with a large industrial firm and the unusually high valuation of the yen. Sixth, investors used consistency with emerging data—in this case, congruent price changes—to infer veracity. One broker stated that a rumor that Company X would obtain lucrative contracts "had to be true [because] the price kept doubling." Other investors typically heard a rumor and then monitored price changes to verify the rumor. Seventh, brokers used expert consensus to infer veracity. Rumors "spurred research," caused an investor "to talk with the people familiar with Apple and

---

[9] $p_{\text{1-tailed}} = .01$, $n = 6$.

[10] $p_{\text{1-tailed}} = .17$, $n = 18$.

Spectrum," and spawned "phone calls to my colleagues to see what they thought." Analysts' opinions were also highly valued.

Finally, it is important to note the influence of cues that changed over time. Although all cues could, theoretically, change over time, repetition or congruent price changes seemed prone to change the most quickly. A rumor could be repeated throughout the course of a trading period; prices, obviously, can change. In some instances judgments changed under the influence of these cues.

Summary

Taken as a whole, the literature and our interviews with brokers suggest that rumors are believed to the extent that they (a) agree with recipients' attitudes (especially rumor-specific attitudes), (b) come from a credible source, (c) are heard or read several times, and (d) are not accompanied by a rebuttal. Cues follow naturally from these propositions: How well does the rumor accord with the hearer's attitude? How credible is the source perceived to be? How often has the hearer heard the rumor? Has the hearer not been exposed to the rumor's rebuttal? These cues should lead to greater acceptance of the rumor. In addition, other cues have been suggested, including the extent to which (e) the denial source has nothing to gain from the rebuttal, (f) the rumor fits a pattern already in place, (g) the rumor is consistent with emerging data, and (h) the rumor agrees with expert consensus. Overall, the results shed light on the process of rumor evaluation and are consistent with a probabilistic mental model framework. Would-be believers "hear it on the street" but also listen for cues to guide them in their assessment.

In this chapter we have explored factors associated with belief using a lens model of judgment. In the next chapter, we use social–cognitive models to explore how groups make sense using rumors.

Rumor as Sense Making 5

In mid-1991 a rumor claimed that Prodigy, an Internet service provider, might be tapping the hard drives of its subscribers' computers. In early May of that year, someone posted the following to an online discussion group: "I've heard that Prodigy subscribers can have their hard drives tapped when they're logged onto the service. . . . Has anyone else heard of this?" Over the next week, the group members discussed the rumor's plausibility, shared personal experiences and information (including media coverage on CNN and *The Wall Street Journal*; M. W. Miller, 1991), expressed belief and disbelief, and analyzed the technical details that might allow Prodigy access to information on the hard drives. The group discussion vividly demonstrated the sense making that accompanies the emergence and spread of rumors.

Rumors help people to make sense of the world. Rumor does this at at least two levels: individually and collectively. Individual sense making involves how people make sense of the world within their own minds, and has much to do with individual cognition. Collective sense making has to do with how people make sense of the world by interacting with others, and has much to do with group processes. In this chapter we explore rumor sense making at both levels. To link rumor and individual sense making, we explore connections between rumor and explanation theory, causal attribution, illusory association, and prediction. To link rumor and collective sense making, we consider the content, functions, and flow of rumor discussions.

Rumor and Individual Sense Making

Individuals use rumors to make sense. In this section we explore this idea by discussing how rumor affects explanation processes and, in particular, causal attribution; we also explore the significance of these effects for certain classes of judgments and behaviors. Rumors draw attention to events, set forth initial explanations, activate knowledge structures with which to interpret events, and motivate the examination of an explanation. Stable-cause attribution is especially involved in these processes. As a consequence, rumors often lead to associations that are in fact illusory, and rumors also engender systematic biases in prediction.

RUMORS AND THE EXPLANATION PROCESS

Anderson, Krull, and Weiner (1996; see also Krull & Anderson, 1997) proposed a model of explanation integrating a number of cognitive processes that are undoubtedly affected by rumors. In this model, an event is an occurrence or characteristic for which a person seeks understanding or predictive meaning. In the beginning stages, the event must be noticed and interpreted, and an initial explanation is set forth; these stages involve relatively automatic processes. A person must first notice the event and its potential causes; the noticeability of these causes influences the likelihood that they will be adopted as explanations. Factors influencing noticeability include novelty, visual dominance, relevance to one's goals, and temporary or chronic activation of particular categories (Hilton & Slugoski, 1986). The event is then interpreted. The event itself and prior expectations (e.g., stereotypes, primed or chronically accessible categories, contextual cues) are factors affecting interpretation. These activities are successful if they produce an initial explanation. The person may then, if so motivated and if not constrained by time or cognitive resources, engage in more effortful processes that iteratively test and ultimately select a final explanation.

Each stage within Anderson et al.'s (1996) explanation theory is guided by the activation of *knowledge structures*, which are mental representations of an object, event, or construct. Examples include category representations, scripts, procedures, episodic memories, and understandings of specific persons. Knowledge structures are conceptually similar to "explanation kernels" (Abelson & Lalljee, 1988), "cognitive structures" (Sedikides & Skowronski, 1991), "causal mental models" (Jungermann & Thüring, 1993), and "causal schemas" (H. H. Kelley, 1973). Knowledge structures must first be activated before they are used in accomplishing explanation tasks such as noticing and interpreting an event and evaluating and selecting a proposed explanation. Activation of a knowledge structure depends "upon salience, availability, or accessibility" or similarity (Anderson & Slusher, 1986, p. 272). Changing the structure, then, will change the subsequent outcome of the explanation task and result in the *law of cognitive structure activation*: Ambiguous stimuli will be encoded as consistent with the most salient knowledge structure and thereby affect relevant judgments and behaviors (Sedikides & Skowronski, 1991).

Rumors influence this explanation process at several junctures. First, rumors make people notice an event. False rumors of Continental Bank's impending bankruptcy because of large loans to underdeveloped nations (Koenig, 1985) informed people of these considerable debts. Second, rumors offer an initial explanation for noticed events. The false rumor that the soft drink Tropical Fantasy contained a substance that would make Black men sterile provided an explanation as to why the soda was sold primarily in minority neighborhoods (Freedman, 1991). Rumors often perform both of these functions synonymously. False rumors that Procter & Gamble Corporation donates to the Church of Satan may have drawn attention to celestial components in the company's logo at the time and encouraged their interpretation as Satanic (Marty, 1982). Third, rumors activate knowledge structures that direct the search for further information. For example, rumors of an impending loss in company profits may compel a review of next-day stock-price changes (DiFonzo & Bordia, 1997, 2002b). Fourth, rumors often convey anxiety-provoking information that may sustain motivation to prolong the examination of explanations. The rumor that Prodigy (an Internet service provider) taps users' hard drives for marketing purposes was proposed, evaluated, and debated on an electronic bulletin board discussion; it was apparent that anxiety propelled the discussion over several days (Bordia & Rosnow, 1998). Thus, rumors may materially affect the explanation process at several stages.

At each stage, rumors inform or activate knowledge structures that determine the course of explanation throughout the process. One knowledge structure that seems central in this regard as it pertains to rumor is causal attribution.

RUMOR AND STABLE CAUSE ATTRIBUTIONS

Rumors help people make sense of the world because they are often embedded with ready-made attributions of stable causes for events. Some causal attributions are derived from ready-made explanations available from knowledge structures about why Person A slapped Person B) or nonperson (Pop Rocks candy exploded in Mikey's stomach) events occur. Put another way, causal attributions are explanations about why events occur.[1] In this discussion then, the term *explanation* is used synonymously for causal attribution.

The question of whether and how often people engage in effortful causal analyses to arrive at explanations has received attention (Fiske & Taylor, 1991; E. R. Smith, 1994). The explanation process proceeds differently depending on whether or not one has knowledge of a pertinent and specific domain (Hilton & Slugoski, 1986). This prior knowledge may automatically yield explanations, dictate the search for further information (Trope & Thompson, 1997), or suggest particular explanations for evaluation (Anderson et al., 1996; Hilton & Slugoski, 1986). If no knowledge is present, then simple rules of causality are used (e.g., those of H. H. Kelley, 1973, analysis of variance model; cf. Einhorn & Hogarth, 1986). An alternative that has received little attention, however, is that people may simply adopt a ready-made explanation that becomes available to them in a social milieu. The explanation may come to them, as it were, prepackaged. As Fiske and Taylor (1991) put it, "While one may argue that social contact is a vehicle for filling out missing information in an attributional search . . . it is also evident that sometimes the motive is simply to acquire a ready-made causal explanation from someone who is better informed" (p. 63). We suggest here that rumor may be the quintessential ready-made explanation in the attributional process.

Many rumors are obviously causal attributions, that is, they are explanations of why a person or nonperson event occurred. For example, "I heard that Manny was being laid off because he was working too quickly on the assembly line and making the rest of us look bad." Now consider an example of a nonperson event explanation: "Goodyear stock plummeted today; I heard it was because Goodyear profits are down." These rumors offer explanations for phenomena. Some rumors do not explain, of course; they simply offer information:

---

[1] Although attribution theorists have traditionally been concerned about how people interpret their own or others' actions (B. Harris & Harvey, 1981; Heider, 1958; Jones & Davis, 1965), the focus of attribution has broadened to include causation in general (E. R. Smith, 1994; cf. Antaki & Fielding, 1981).

"I heard that Manager X is resigning, the plant is being shut down, Prodigy taps hard drives, Michael Jordan is returning to basketball, and Tropical Fantasy causes sterility in Black men." However, even these information statements tend to possess an explanatory flavor in that they are causal attributions in the process of being constructed or they explain one's own feelings (Festinger, 1957). Here is an example of the former: The rumor "I heard that Manager X is resigning" is quickly replied to with "Really? That's interesting! I wonder why. Perhaps he wants to start his own business." The rumor quickly evolves into a causal explanation: "Manager X is resigning because he wants to start his own business." Here is an example of a rumor explaining one's own feelings: "I feel anxious and suspicious [these feelings are unstated]; it must be because Prodigy [a large corporation] is tapping into my hard drive!" In a similar way, as we noted in chapter 4 (this volume), racist rumors can explain one's own feelings of being threatened: "I feel threatened; it must be because "an [out-group] man castrated an [ingroup] boy in a shopping mall lavatory and left him in a pool of blood" (M. Rosenthal, 1971). These observations are not new (although they are more fully elaborated here); G. W. Allport and Postman (1947b) stated that rumors contain causal attributions: "In ordinary rumor we find a marked tendency for the agent to attribute *causes* to events, *motives* to characters, a *raison d'etre* to the episode in question" [italics in original] (p. 121).

An important aspect of causal attribution is how stable versus unstable the cause of an event is judged to be (Anderson et al., 1996; Weiner, 1985). A stable cause, such as one's disposition, is relatively permanent. An unstable cause, such as chance, is relatively temporary. A fruitful line of research into depression, for example, has discovered attributional differences between individuals with depression and those without depression (Seligman, Abramson, Semmel, & von Baeyer, 1979). Stable-cause attributions in the face of a failure event ("I got a D on the midterm because I'm stupid") are part of a depressive and pessimistic explanatory style; however, unstable-cause attributions ("I got a D because I didn't study") form part of an optimistic explanatory style (Struthers, Menec, Schonwetter, & Perry, 1996).

We speculate that most of the causal attributions conveyed by rumors are stable in character. That rumors contain stable-cause explanations can first be inferred from Heider's (1958) observation that people prefer stable causal explanations because they need to see the world as understandable and predictable. As discussed in chapter 1 (this volume), rumors fulfill this need for understanding and predictability. We reason that rumors wouldn't be very successful at enhancing understanding and predictability if they didn't possess stable-cause attributions. Second, a perusal of rumors collected from a variety of investigations suggests that causal explanations embedded in rumors are almost always stable (e.g., dispositional, unchanging), rather than unstable (e.g., random, chance-like), in character. Racist rumors among Whites often included the notion that African American men possessed excessive (stable) sexual and aggressive desires (G. W. Allport & Postman, 1947b). Rumors about government—such as that government officials had unfair access to rationed commodities during World War II—proposed that this was so because of (stable) negative dispositional qualities such as greed (F. H. Allport & Lepkin, 1945). Rumors of downsizing because of (stable) declining profits (DiFonzo & Bordia, 1998), rumors of CEO turnover because of their (stable) desire for autonomy (DiFonzo, Bordia, & Rosnow, 1994), and rumors of Internet provider's illegal tapping of user hard drives because of (stable) corporate marketing incentives and (stable) corporate avariciousness (Bordia, DiFonzo, & Chang, 1999; Bordia & Rosnow, 1998) are representative examples from our own research. However, we are hard-pressed to think of an unstable-cause attribution set in a rumor. Even rumors of random acts of gang violence contain the stable-cause dispositional attribution that gang members are evil (Vigoda, 1993).

Experimental evidence also supports this idea (DiFonzo & Bordia, 1997, 2002b): "Investors" playing the computerized stock-market games described in chapter 2 (this volume) were exposed to rumors that were not predictive of daily stock-price changes, yet they strongly attributed price changes to these rumors. For example, the rumor that "Goodyear profits are up" was judged to be the cause of stock-price increases on the day the rumor appeared and the next day also; the cause was stable enough to last at least 2 days. The interview study of brokers described in chapter 4 (this volume) also qualitatively supported this idea. Brokers unanimously felt that the effect of real stock-market rumors lasted for 2 to 3 days (DiFonzo, 1994, Study 2). Put another way, real brokers judged rumors to be the cause of stock-price changes, not just that day, but the day after and the day after that as well. Thus, some—perhaps most—rumors are embedded with stable-cause attributions.

Stable-cause attributions have been implicated in a number of systematic judgment biases. We explore two of these here: illusory association and antiregressive prediction.

RUMOR AND ILLUSORY ASSOCIATION

Stable-cause attributions have produced *illusory associations*: erroneous judgments that two characteristics are associated (Jennings, Amabile,

& Ross, 1982). Undergraduates and clinicians, after viewing random pairings of Draw-A-Person test drawings and a psychological diagnosis, thought that an emphasis on the eyes (in the drawing) covaried with paranoia; this result occurred even though the diagnosis of paranoia was not associated with large or salient eyes in drawing (Chapman & Chapman, 1969). Why then did participants associate the two? A stable-cause attribution—drawing large eyes is caused by a paranoid sensitivity to being watched—led subjects to associate these variables. Stable-cause attribution leads people to see relationships even when they don't exist.

In a similar way, rumors lead people to see relationships even if they are nonexistent; that is, stable-cause attributions embedded in many rumors lead to illusory associations. For example, rumor has long been associated with the formation and maintenance of racial stereotypes (G. W. Allport & Postman, 1947b; R. H. Knapp, 1944; Knopf, 1975; P. A. Turner, 1993). Rumors embedded with stable-cause race-characteristic attributions encourage these illusory associations. Children hearing multiple variations of such rumors as "I heard that Johnny Black stole a car" (because Blacks are thieves) or "I heard that Officer White beat him unnecessarily with his billy club" (because Whites are brutal) will be led to associate African Americans with theft and European Americans with aggression. Experimental evidence accords with these ideas. The investors in the computerized stock-market simulation game described earlier were exposed to price changes that were uncorrelated with rumors yet they thought that these price changes were associated with rumors (DiFonzo & Bordia, 2002b). Investors perceived relationships that were nonexistent.

RUMOR AND ANTIREGRESSIVE PREDICTION

Stable-cause attributions have also produced systematic errors in prediction of categories (e.g., Is this person an engineer or a lawyer?) and sequential events (e.g., How likely is it that football team x will win their next game?). In these prediction situations, people tend to rely on causal information to the neglect of often more predictively valid *base-rate information* (Ajzen, 1977). Base-rate information is typically the proportion of specified outcomes in a possible population of events. For example, when presented with a fictitious name ostensibly sampled randomly from a population in which 70% of the people are lawyers and 30% are engineers, control subjects tend to use the engineer base rate—30%—when predicting how likely it is that the person is an engineer. However, when given additional causal information in the form of a character sketch of the person (e.g., "He has a need for order and clarity, and for neat and tidy systems"; Kahneman & Tversky, 1973, p. 238), subjects abandon these base rates, rely on the character sketch, and predict that the person is an engineer. They reason that a stable dispositional cause—the need for order—manifests itself in the desire to become an engineer and hence they estimate a higher probability of being an engineer.

Causal attribution effects have also been found for predictions about events in a sequence (Kahneman & Tversky, 1982; Matthews & Sanders, 1984). Given a stable cause for recent events in a sequence (e.g., stock prices are decreasing because of poor management), people tend to predict that the next event in the sequence will reflect the recent trend (continued decrease) rather than the often more predictively valid base rate of past outcomes. Predictions that the recent trend will continue are necessarily not regressive toward the central tendency of previous events and are therefore called *nonregressive* or even *antiregressive* predictions. For example, subjects presented with both the long-term average proportion of football team game wins—say, 50%—and the recent sequence of team outcomes—win-loss-win-win-win-win-win—would tend to predict that the team would win at their next game, presumably because their recent wins are because of a stable cause (e.g., team talent, or the team is "hot"; Gilovich, Vallone, & Tversky, 1985). However, the base rate—50% in this example—would be more predictive.

In a similar way, stable-cause attributions in rumors lead to nonregressive predictions. Aggregate-level studies of the effect of rumor on stock trading have shown that rumors are responsible for nonregressive deviations from randomness in stock prices (Lazar, 1973; Pound & Zeckhauser, 1990; Rose, 1951). Simply stated, rumors affect stock prices' changes in a nonregressive fashion. Individual-level experiments also agree with this. Hearing the rumor "Goodyear profits are up" led investors to predict that tomorrow's Goodyear stock price will rise and to abandon more predictively valid base-rate information about tomorrow's price change (DiFonzo & Bordia, 1997, 2002b). In the stock simulation research described earlier, investors seized on causal information embedded in rumors and ignored more predictively valid base-rate information when trading stock. They did so despite rating the rumors as noncredible, untrustworthy, and unbelievable. In other words, rumors did not have to be believed or trusted to powerfully affect trading; they simply had to make sense. As a consequence, investors exposed to rumors engaged in less profitable trading strategies than did those who received no rumors. If stock-market price changes are indeed unpredictable (Fama, Fisher, Jensen, & Roll, 1969; Malkiel, 1985), then hearing rumors may be bad for one's portfolio!

Rumors and Collective
Sense Making

Groups also use rumors to make collective sense. In this section we explore this idea by examining the content, functions, and flow of statements made during rumor discussions on the Internet; this species of rumor has much to tell us about rumor discussions in general (Fisher, 1998). We show that these rumor discussions are rich conversations in which a variety of statements are uttered, most of which are related to or concerned with the task of sense making. To fulfill the functions necessary to make sense, people adopt transient roles during rumor discussions, and the rumor episode typically passes through a multistage group sense-making process ordered around the assessment of rumor veracity and meaning.

In this section, we draw heavily from our quantitative content analysis of 14 rumor discussions on the Internet (Bordia & DiFonzo, 2004; see also Bordia & Rosnow, 1998). In this study, we gathered rumor interaction episodes (RIEs) by searching archived discussions on computer networks and by observing ongoing computer discussion groups. Each rumor discussion had to contain five or more postings spread over at least 2 days and reflect some earnestness on the part of participants. The rumors touched on a variety of domains, including health ("Ibuprofen increases susceptibility to flesh-eating bacteria," "Smallpox-infested blankets were distributed in Indian reservations"), information technology ("A virus titled 'Good Times' is being spread by an electronic mail message," "Certain features will be included on Windows 95," "Prodigy taps hard drives of its subscribers' computers"), conspiracy ("Republican party was involved in the explosion of the space shuttle"), and sports ("Michael Jordan is returning to professional basketball"; Bordia & DiFonzo, 2004, p. 38).

CONTENT OF RUMOR DISCUSSION STATEMENTS

What types of statements constitute rumor discussions and what is their relative prevalence in a typical rumor episode? To address these questions, we, along with our colleagues, developed a coding system—the Rumor Interaction Analysis System (RIAS; Bordia & DiFonzo, 2004; Bordia & Rosnow, 1998)—and used it to content analyze each RIE in the sample. We began by parsing all text into thought units using guidelines provided by Wheelan, Verdi, and McKeage (1994). Often these statements were in the form of simple sentences, such as "I am not sure if this is true or not," "It happened in 1968," and "I hope this happens." The reliability of this unitizing procedure was assessed by an independent judge and was very high (93.07% agreement). The development of the RIAS was guided by the conceptualization of rumor as a collective problem-solving process as described in chapter 1 (this volume). That is, in conditions of ambiguity, rumors are working hypotheses of the group that attempt to make sense, manage threat, and restore a sense of predictive or interpretive control; they are *improvised news*. This more sociological perspective emphasizes the collective sense-making function of rumor.

We identified 14 types of statements: prudent, apprehensive, authenticating, interrogatory, providing-information, belief, disbelief, sense making, directive, sarcastic, wish, personal-involvement, digressive, and uncodable. The RIAS, along with the overall percentage of each statement type, is presented in Table 5.1. Table 5.1 shows that these rumor discussions overall were composed of statements that were directly or indirectly useful to the group as they attempted to make sense of their situation. The most frequent type of statement was in fact sense making (29.4%), by which discussion participants directly attempted to solve the problem of whether or not the rumor was true. In other words, rumor discussants devoted a plurality of statements to interpretation, analysis, and inference. In addition, most of the remaining statements were indirectly related to sense making. Participants provided information, asked questions, authenticated credentials and information, shared relevant personal experience, expressed belief and disbelief, and attempted to persuade others. All of these activities support the collective goal of sense making. Thus, the content of these diverse Internet rumor discussions was a rich social sense-making interplay involving an exchange of hypotheses, opinions, views, proposals, arguments, and emotions.

CONTENT AND COMMUNICATIVE POSTURES OF CONTRIBUTIONS

In any discussion, people take turns communicating; one person contributes a set of statements, then another provides an additional set of statements. Discussions can be thought of as serial contributions of statement sets; understanding the content and function of such statement sets affords a better understanding of the nature of the discussion. Rumor discussions are no different. For example, a rumor discussant may contribute a statement that provides information (Pi) then, still holding the microphone, propose a sense-making explanation (Sm).

TABLE 5.1

Rumor Interaction Analysis System Statement Types and Overall Percentage of Statements in 14 Rumor Interaction Episodes[a]

Statement type (abbreviation)	Definition	Examples	Overall % of statements[b]
Prudent (Pr)	Cautionary statements used to qualify what follows as being "hearsay."	"I am not sure if this is true or not"; "This may or may not be true."	3.5
Apprehensive (Ap)	Statements expressing rumor-related fear, dread, anxiety, or apprehension, or a sense of feeling "threatened."	"I gave this Prodigy thing a little thought and promptly scared myself."	2.8
Authenticating (Au)	Statements expressing the speaker's attempt to add credibility to what he or she was saying.	"I read it in the *Wall Street Journal*"; "I, as a programmer . . ."	4.8
Interrogatory (I)	Questions seeking information (not including sarcastic remarks or persuasion attempts).	"What does this stage.dat file do?"	2.9
Providing information (Pi)	Statements providing information relevant to the rumor being discussed.	"It happened in 1968."	16.7
Belief (B)	Statements indicating belief in the rumor.	"It's true."	2.2
Disbelief (Di)	Statements indicating disbelief in the rumor.	"It's too farfetched."	3.8
Sense making (Sm)	Statements reflecting attempts to solve the problem of whether or not the rumor is true; that is, statements that analyze, dispute, disagree with, or draw inferences from what someone else has said; statements that justify one's own views, actions, and beliefs; and statements describing decision rules and heuristics.	"What could be happening is . . ."; "I think the way it works is . . ."	29.4

continued

Rumor Interaction Analysis System Statement Types and Overall Percentage of Statements in 14 Rumor Interaction Episodes[a]

Statement type (abbreviation)	Definition	Examples	Overall % of statements[b]
Directive (Dr)	Statements suggesting a course of action.	"We should stop using this product"; "This discussion has gone on long enough; let's move on."	2.7
Sarcastic (S)	Statements ridiculing someone else's beliefs or comments.	"Please write about something you know anything about next time."	3.4
Wish (Wi)	Statements conveying a hope or wish for a desired object or consequence.	"I hope this happens."	0.7
Personal involvement (P)	Statements describing experiences of the speaker in the context of the rumor.	"My child had the same symptoms."	3.9
Digressive (Dg)	Statements not directly relevant to the original rumor.	Narratives and information seeking not relevant to the rumor.	18.6
Uncodable (U)	Statements not able to be categorized, usually because of ambiguity.		4.6

Note. [a]All material in this table from "Problem Solving in Social Interactions on the Internet: Rumor as Social Cognition," by P. Bordia and N. DiFonzo, 2004, *Social Psychology Quarterly, 67,* pp. 39–43. Copyright 2004 by American Sociological Association. Adapted with permission. [b]Percentages based on a total of 2,881 statements.

To better understand the nature of rumor discussion, we asked, "What is the content of statement set contributions during a rumor discussion?" That is, what typical combinations of statement sets are presented during turns taken by rumor discussants? We were interested in the make-up of participants' turns because they reveal the function of each contribution at that point in the rumor discussion; we have dubbed these functions *communicative postures* (Bordia & DiFonzo, 2004).

Communicative postures are conceptually similar to the "communication roles" or "communication styles" posited by Shibutani (1966) such as the "*messenger,* the person who brings a pertinent item of information to the group" and the "*interpreter,* the person who tries to place the news in context, evaluating it in the light of past events and speculating on implications for the future" [italics in original] (1966, p. 15; see also R. H. Turner & Killian, 1972). Each role performs some function in the context of the discussion (e.g., bringing information, interpreting data). We coined the term *posture,* however, to better reflect Shibutani's idea that these roles are transient in nature: A speaker's posture seems less permanent than his or her role or style. For example, in an Internet discussion I may post a message that brings information to the discussion; it therefore performs an information-delivering function (and I have exhibited an information-delivering posture)—but later I may post a skeptical message that performs a disbelieving function (and it displays a disbelieving posture). Postures can change during the course of a discussion. We wished to empirically explore these ideas and generate a more definite conceptualization of the transient contributions—the postures—made to rumor discussions.

In our Internet rumor study, rumor discussion contributions consisted of 281 message postings from the 14 Internet RIEs (Bordia & DiFonzo, 2004). To identify common patterns of statement sets in each posting, we performed a hierarchical cluster analysis on these postings. Cluster analysis groups cases on the basis of their similarity along various dimensions; in this investigation, we grouped postings according to their similarity on RIAS statements (these groupings are called *clusters*). In other words, we used cluster analysis to discover categories of participant postings to the discussion that had similar RIAS statement profiles. Thus, the unit of analysis here is the postings submitted to the rumor discussion—a higher level than the RIAS statements in the previous section, but a lower level than the individuals who composed the postings.

Eleven clusters were identified; each had a statement profile consisting of the average number of RIAS statement types (Pr, Ap, Au, etc.) contained in postings belonging to the cluster. We used these profiles to interpret the communicative posture of that cluster. For example, Cluster 1 exhibited a high average number of prudent (Pr) and providing-information (Pi) statements but low means for all other types of statements; we interpreted this cluster as an explanation-delivering posture whose function was to present the rumor. Cluster 2 displayed a very high mean number of sense-making (Sm) statements relative to all other statement types; we interpreted this cluster as an explanation-evaluating posture whose function was to interpret the rumor. Statement profiles for all 11 clusters are presented in Table 5.2 along with our interpretation of their associated communicative postures.

We were guided here in part by Anderson et al.'s (1996) explanation theory. As discussed at the beginning of this chapter, an event is noticed, an initial explanation is generated, and—depending on the motivation to engage in effortful processing—the explanation is iteratively tested. We adapted this cognitive model to a collective framework, and the fit was quite natural. Groups seeking to explain events must perform similar sense-making activities: They must notice the event, generate initial explanations, test explanations, decide whether or not to continue searching for alternate explanations, and direct the gathering of information. The 11 identified clusters naturally displayed these types of activities. To wit, in addition to explanation presenting and explanation evaluating, two additional postures functioned to analyze the rumor and voice agreement (explanation verifying) and disagreement (explanation falsifying); a fifth posture simply voiced acceptance of the rumor (explanation accepting). Two postures performed information-sharing (information reporting) and questioning (information-seeking) functions. One posture contributed information and suggested courses of action (directing). Two postures functioned to sustain motivation by voicing hopes (motivating by considering gains) and fears (motivating by considering losses). Finally, one posture displayed noninvolvement in sense making (casual participation). Thus, during the turns taken in Internet rumor episodes, participants typically contribute to the discussion in 1 of 11 ways, and most of these ways can be understood in relation to collective sense making.

DYNAMICS OF RUMOR DISCUSSION STATEMENTS

How do rumor discussions flow over their lifetimes? In more specific terms, how do postures and statement types change over the course of the discussion? These questions concern the dynamics of RIEs.

Once again using the 14 RIEs (Bordia & DiFonzo, 2004), we explored these questions in a couple of ways. First, we divided each RIE into "quarters" by dividing the number of postings chronologically by 4; the type and number of postures during each quarter were then analyzed. Clear posture trends—in line with collective sense making—were observed: Explanation-delivering and directing postures were

TABLE 5.2

Content and Communicative Postures of Postings to Internet Rumor Discussions

Communicative posture of posting	Posture description (and example)	Statement profile (mean number of statement types in posting)												
		Pr	Ap	Au	I	Pi	B	Di	Sm	Dr	S	W	P	Dg
1. Explanation delivering	Presents brief explanation—the rumor—to the group ("Here is an explanation that I heard; I am not sure if it is true.")	2.3	0.0	0.6	0.2	3.4	0.0	0.0	1.6	0.1	0.2	0.0	0.6	0.1
2. Explanation evaluating	Analyzes and interprets the explanation ("Here's a possible explanation.")	0.9	4.2	2.0	0.2	0.6	3.1	0.0	17.3	0.1	0.2	0.0	0.1	0.5
3. Explanation verifying	Analyzes and agrees with explanation ("Here's an explanation that I believe for the following reasons.")	1.0	0.0	6.0	0.0	0.4	3.4	0.0	6.4	0.0	0.0	0.0	0.0	0.0
4. Explanation falsifying	Analyzes and disagrees with the explanation ("Here's why I don't believe the explanation.")	0.4	0.0	1.0	0.3	1.0	0.1	3.5	4.4	0.4	0.6	0.0	0.1	0.2
5. Explanation accepting	Accepts the explanation ("I believe the explanation.")	0.0	0.0	0.0	0.0	0.0	1.7	0.0	0.3	0.3	0.0	0.0	0.0	0.0

continued

TABLE 5.2 (Continued)

Content and Communicative Postures of Postings to Internet Rumor Discussions

Communicative posture of posting	Posture description (and example)	Statement profile (mean number of statement types in posting)												
		Pr	Ap	Au	I	Pi	B	Di	Sm	Dr	S	W	P	Dg
6. Information reporting	Shares information and personal experiences ("Here's what I know related to the explanation.")	0.2	0.4	0.2	0.2	2.5	0.1	0.1	1.2	0.5	0.2	0.0	3.5	0.6
7. Information seeking	Seeks information ("Here's what is needed to be known to generate or evaluate an explanation.")	0.4	0.1	0.6	3.0	0.8	0.0	0.0	1.4	0.0	0.2	0.0	0.1	0.3
8. Directing	Provides information and suggests a course of action ("Here's what I know and someone should do XYZ to gather more information.")	0.6	0.2	0.2	0.5	2.8	0.1	0.1	2.0	3.4	0.0	0.0	1.0	0.5
9. Motivating by considering gains	Justifies explanation, hoping for certain consequences or things ("Here's a hoped–for consequence of this explanation, which is why we should continue to evaluate it.")	0.0	0.0	0.0	1.5	0.0	0.0	0.0	2.0	0.0	0.0	2.5	0.0	0.0

10. Motivating by considering losses	Posture reflects concern and fear of the rumor or its consequences ("Here's a feared consequence of this explanation, which is why we should continue to evaluate it.")	0.0	2.4	0.4	0.2	0.6	0.0	0.0	0.8	0.2	0.0	0.0	0.4	*1.8*
11. Casual participating	Easily distracted, indulges a little in problem solving.	0.0	0.1	0.2	0.0	1.8	0.0	0.0	2.6	0.1	0.4	0.1	0.0	*3.1*

Note. The 11 clusters were derived from 276 postings (5 were uncodable) to 14 Internet rumor interaction episodes and represent communicative postures (see text). See Table 5.1 for key to statement type abbreviations. Higher means of statement types in each cluster are italicized and were used in labeling (Column 1) and describing (Column 2) the posture. From "Problem Solving in Social Interactions on the Internet: Rumor as Social Cognition," by P. Bordia and N. DiFonzo, 2004, *Social Psychology Quarterly, 67,* pp. 44–46. Copyright 2004 by American Sociological Association. Adapted with permission.

more common in the first quarter of rumor interaction, explanation evaluation peaked during the third quarter, and casual participation peaked at the end. In other words, the discussion first centered on presenting the rumor and directing efforts to make sense of the rumor, then proceeded to sifting and analyzing the rumor; sense making then subsided as people lost interest. A second quarterly analysis—this time of the incidence of common RIAS statement types—accorded with this interpretation. Interrogatory statements peaked during the first quarter, disbelief in the second, sense making during the third, and casual participation during the fourth. Providing-information statements were frequent in all but the third quarter. Thus, collective Internet rumor sense making seems to proceed in a multistage process of bringing the rumor to the attention of the group (Stage 1), sharing information (Stage 2), evaluating explanations (Stage 3), and then resolving problems (Stage 4).

GENERALIZABILITY TO FACE-TO-FACE RUMOR INTERACTION EPISODES

It is important to remember that our conclusions regarding collective sense making stem mainly from our analysis of Internet rumor episodes. These computer-mediated types of RIEs may differ in substantial ways from face-to-face episodes. First, we selected only RIEs in which participants displayed some earnest interest in the discussion and thus importance was probably high; other computer-mediated or face-to-face episodes may not be so involving. Second, the nature of computer-mediated networks means that each discussion contribution was potentially read by every person in the group; in other words the group was closely—rather than diffusely—connected. These characteristics seem to encourage what H. Taylor Buckner (1965) dubbed "multiple interaction": the process by which a rumor is actively recirculated within the same group of people (see chap. 7, this volume). Less important rumors transmitted through more diffuse social networks may not exhibit the content, postures, and dynamics we observed in computer-mediated episodes (see chap. 6, this volume, for a similar discussion of the differences between serially transmitted and collaborative rumor activity).

Conclusions

In this chapter we explored the sense-making function of rumor from both social–cognitive and collective levels of analysis. Rumor affects the individual's attempt to explain events at a variety of junctures such as noticing the event, providing an initial explanation, motivating further exploration, and activating cognitive structures with which to interpret the event. We considered how rumors are often embedded with stable-cause attributions and how the activation of these types of cognitive structures may lead to illusory associations and nonregressive prediction. Rumors also influence the collective sense-making process. We explored the content of statements that are made during rumor episodes, as well as the content, functions, and flow of the contributions made to rumor discussions.

We've considered here the sense-making processes—both individual and interpersonal—involved in rumor activity. How efficacious are people at this important task? We consider this question next.

Rumor Accuracy: Patterns of Content Change, Conceptualization, and Overall Accuracy

6

Negative rumors abounded among the 75 employees in a division of a large corporation near Rochester, New York, in the late 1990s (see chaps. 2 and 8, this volume). The division was a tight-knit community of professionals who had heard that drastic layoffs were in the offing. Indeed, fully half of the division was eventually let go. One week prior to the official announcement of who would be laid off, workers circulated a rumor listing the names of targeted persons. Remarkably, the rumor was 100% accurate.

During the American Civil War, telegraph cables strung across trees in the manner of an agricultural grapevine carried intelligence messages (K. Davis, 1972). Today, the "intelligence" efforts of organizational members often rely heavily on rumors passed through the communications grapevine (Burlew, Pederson, & Bradley, 1994; K. Davis, 1972; Harcourt, Richerson, & Wattier, 1991; Newstrom, Monczka, & Reif, 1974; Smeltzer & Zener, 1992; Walton, 1961; Zaremba, 1989). Indeed, substantial portions of a national sample of middle managers in a recent survey "rated the grapevine as superior to formal communication" and as the best source of information for certain topics such as promotion opportunities, company future plans, departmental future plans, and salaries and raises (Harcourt et al., 1991, p. 357; see also Modic, 1989).

How effective are these informal intelligence efforts? That is, how well do groups fare in ferreting out the facts? The question is of both academic and practical interest. As was seen in chapter 2 (this volume), some organizational rumors have disrupted productivity, sullied reputations, and eroded trust (K. Davis, 1975; DiFonzo, Bordia, & Rosnow, 1994; Zaremba, 1988). When rumors are false or distorted, such effects are sadly unwarranted. In addition, from the "rumor consumer's" point of view, normative questions of how much credence ought to be placed in any bit of information carried by a channel of communication hinge on the overall validity of that channel. If rumors are generally accurate, then it would seem that they are worthy of belief. However, if rumors are usually inaccurate, they ought not to be trusted.

This chapter and the next address several questions related to accuracy. First, we review patterns of change in rumor content. Next, we explore the concept of accuracy and its measurement. Third, we assess the overall accuracy of rumors, with a special focus on organizational rumors. In the next chapter, we will examine the mechanisms by which rumors become more (or less) accurate. Finally, we will address how such mechanisms are likely to operate in organizational contexts. At several points we introduce our own recent empirical research bearing on accuracy.

Patterns of Rumor Content Change

It is instructive to review theory and research on overall change patterns in rumor content. In general, four types of changes have been identified: *leveling, sharpening, adding,* and *assimilation.* As we show later, the main controversy in this corpus of literature is whether leveling or adding occurs in everyday rumor activity. The debate stems partly from differences in *serial transmission* (ST) versus *collaborative* (COL) approaches to studying and conceptualizing rumor and whether both approaches generalize to real-life rumor situations. With this in mind, we review patterns of rumor content change here with special attention to ST versus COL conceptual and methodological issues.

FOUR PATTERNS OF RUMOR CONTENT CHANGE

How does rumor content change over time? For example, does the corpus of details grow larger or smaller? Does the content of the rumor become more or less exaggerated? Does the rumor begin to conform to widely held ideas? Researchers have addressed these questions and identified four patterns of rumor content change: leveling, adding, sharpening, and assimilation.

Leveling

Leveling refers to the loss of detail and the reduction in length at each successive transmission so that the rumor is more easily grasped, especially during early transmissions. Rumors are leveled to "short concise statement[s]" (G. W. Allport & Postman, 1947b, p. 81) in the sense that complex buildings are leveled to simple and small heaps. Kirkpatrick (1932) called the process "condensation." For example, of 20 detailed statements in an original stimulus description, 15 may be leveled and only 5 remain.

Adding

Adding is our term for addition to rumor content in the form of new material or additional details. Adding has been referred to as "snowballing" (Rosnow, 1991), invention and elaboration (G. W. Allport & Postman, 1947b), "compounding" (Peterson & Gist, 1951), "embroidering" (G. W. Allport & Postman, 1947b), and "fabrication" (Sinha, 1952). For example, after observing a photograph of a mob of people without weapons, clubs were supplied to that mob in successive serial retellings of the details of that photograph (G. W. Allport & Postman, 1947b, pp. 116–121). Peterson and Gist (1951) also found that new themes were added—not leveled—in a set of rumors about a murder. Rosnow (1991) described the snowballing of the false "Paul McCartney is dead" rumor. Note that adding is to leveling as addition is to subtraction.

Sharpening

Sharpening refers to the accenting and highlighting of certain details in the rumor message. This accenting may occur as a result of leveling; certain details are brought into sharpened focus necessarily by the clearing away of other details. For example, the odd term *remonstrated* was retained—presumably because it was an odd term—throughout serial retellings of a certain tale that became successively shorter (G. W. Allport & Postman, 1947b); the term was thus emphasized. Sharpening may also occur as a result of changes such as exaggeration (e.g., as when one Negro became four Negroes; G. W. Allport & Postman, 1947b); the idea "a Negro was present" was therefore highlighted (see also Firth, 1956; R. H. Turner & Killian, 1972).

Assimilation

Assimilation refers to the shaping of rumor content—through leveling, adding, and sharpening—so as to be in greater accord with personal cognitive schemas. Assimilation may be a relatively cool (i.e., cognitive) process, such as when details are leveled, added, or sharpened so as to make the rumor more thematically coherent and plausible (e.g., an ambulance became a Red Cross station to fit a battle theme; see also Kirkpatrick, 1932), to complete incomplete data (e.g., *Gene Antry* became *Gene Autry*), to simplify a complex stimulus (e.g., a set of subway posters became *lots of advertising*), and to fit our expectations and linguistic conventions (e.g., *kilometers* on a road sign was changed to *miles* by Harvard students; G. W. Allport & Postman, 1947b, pp. 99–104). Assimilation may also be a relatively hot (i.e., defensive or motivated) process, such as when rumor change occurs because of personal interests (e.g., details about clothing or occupation predominated among subjects interested in clothing or occupation, respectively), self-interest (e.g., a group of police officers focused favorably on the police officer in a story), and prejudice (e.g., hostile behavior was imputed to minority figures; pp. 105–115).

Whereas leveling, adding, and sharpening are more elemental patterns of content change, assimilation is akin to overall pattern fitting. Assimilation is thus a more holistic and higher level pattern of change. It is the guiding of these subpatterns of change so as to be in accord with personal schemas.

GENERALIZABILITY OF PATTERNS

Consistent evidence points to sharpening in the service of assimilation in real-life rumor situations (Buckner, 1965; Peterson & Gist, 1951; Rosnow, 1991; Shibutani, 1966; R. H. Turner, 1964, 1994; R. H. Turner & Killian, 1972). However, disagreement persists regarding the extent of leveling versus adding in real-life rumor situations (Rosnow, 1991; Shibutani, 1966; Turner & Killian, 1972). Leveling, rather than adding, has tended to occur in ST laboratory situations and in planted-rumor field study situations characterized by ST-like passing of information. Our position is that leveling occurs mostly in some real-life rumor episodes marked by low ambiguity and in which a group is primarily engaged in ST-like information diffusion (i.e., simply passing along the information). However, adding, rather than leveling, has occurred mostly in field observation studies with high ambiguity and high-importance contexts such as catastrophes and murders. It occurs in real-life ambiguous situations of importance in which the group is quite interactive and collaborative. We explore these findings and our position more fully first by examining ST and COL approaches to the study of rumor, and then by considering evidence and arguments for the generalizability of both leveling and adding.

Serial Transmission and Collaborative Approaches

If we conceive of rumors as being serially transmitted, then distortions occur at each transmission node, at each telling of the rumor down the line (Shibutani, 1966). This approach tends to highlight the changes that occur during transmission as a result of cognitive (e.g., narrowing of attention, limits to memory, perceptual biases) and motivational (e.g., fact-finding, relationship-enhancement, and self-enhancement) factors at work in the individuals involved at each node (these factors are discussed in chap. 7, this volume). The ST framework has been primarily, although not exclusively, used in the laboratory setting. Laboratory studies in this vein have reported a three-part embedding process; *embedding* refers to leveling and sharpening guided by assimilation (G. W. Allport & Postman, 1947b[1]; Bartlett, 1932; Higham, 1951; Kirkpatrick, 1932; McAdam, 1962). In particular, leveling—not adding—occurred in these studies. In fundamental terms, such studies are mostly about passing information along, and they generalize to real-life rumor situations that are mostly characterized by some type of ST.

If we conceive of rumors as the tentative and changing hypotheses produced as persons in a group collaborate more actively in an ambiguous situation, then the focus tends to shift to group, network, and situational features (also discussed in chap. 7, this volume). This framework assumes that rumor is a collaborative, not a serial, activity; that is, each person makes a collaborative rather than additive contribution (Shibutani, 1966). For example, persons A and B discuss a rumor about impending downsizing and who will be laid off; A and B compare notes on the basis of information they each bring to this discussion and they quickly modify the rumor. Out of this collaboration, a predominant interpretation of an ambiguous situation arises. The COL framework

---

[1] G. W. Allport and Postman (1947b) also discussed invention and elaboration, but felt that these were so infrequent as to presumably be not part of the embedding process.

has used primarily field observational settings. These studies have garnered support for sharpening, assimilation, and especially adding—but
not leveling (Peterson & Gist, 1951; Shibutani, 1966; R. H. Turner,
1964; R. H. Turner & Killian, 1972). Studies investigating this type of
rumor activity are fundamentally about interactively collaborating in
an ambiguous and important situation and generalize to real-life rumor
situations that are characterized by collaborative sense making.

We note that both types of real-life rumor episodes—those characterized by ST-like transmission and those best described as COL-type
activity—involve sense making. However, ST-like transmission tends
to produce leveling whereas COL-type activity tends to produce adding.
Let's consider evidence and arguments for the generalizability of each.

Generalizability of Leveling

G. W. Allport and Postman (1947b, pp. 134–138) argued that the
embedding process (which includes leveling) is representative of what
happens with everyday rumor. To support this statement, they offer
the example of a rumor arising from an incident that occurred in Maine
in 1945 shortly before the surrender of the Japanese: A Chinese teacher
on vacation asked for directions to a scenic outlook. Within short order,
an assimilated rumor was being actively transmitted in the community:
"a Japanese spy had ascended the hill to take pictures of the region" [italics
in original] (p. 134). They state that this story had been leveled and
sharpened according to a dominant interpretive schema (i.e., the Japanese spy motif). G. W. Allport and Postman (1947b) also supported the
generalizability of the embedding process by pointing to the similarity of
their ST results with that of Gestalt memory studies on geometric shapes
and projective test studies (memories and projections are similarly leveled and sharpened in the service of assimilation).

But the argument that leveling was observed in ST, Gestalt memory,
and projective test studies indicates only that the results of each type
of study were similar, not whether ST study results can be generalized
to all (or some) everyday rumor episodes. In addition, ST research has
been criticized as not being *mundane realistic* (i.e., the lab experience
does not match real-life experience in key ways; DiFonzo, Hantula, &
Bordia, 1998; Rosnow, 1980) in such a way as to predispose leveling
(Bordia, 1996; Shibutani, 1966; R. H. Turner & Killian, 1972). At least
three main arguments in this vein have been raised; we present each
here and critically examine them.

First, Buckner (1965) posited that distortion in ST occurs mostly
because of memory limitations: "In Allport and Postman's experiments,
the words are leveled out because of the difficulty of remembering
twenty or so new and discrete items of information" (p. 59). G. W.

Allport and Postman (1947b) themselves noticed that ST participants are instructed to be accurate and would therefore be prone to not relay statements of which they are the least bit unsure (p. 76). Laboratory ST subjects similarly have no opportunity for questioning, challenging, and probing and may thus be prone to encoding failure. However, subsequent laboratory ST experiments that allowed discussion at each transmission node—ST plus interaction—exhibited less distortion (see chap. 7, this volume), but leveling still occurred (Leavitt & Mueller, 1951; McAdam, 1962); that is, statements became shorter and more easily grasped. Such "ST plus interaction" situations are more mundane realistic and thus more generalizable than are pure laboratory ST procedures.

Second, ST participants are much less emotionally involved (and therefore not motivated to speculate) than are real-life rumor participants (Shibutani, 1966; R. H. Turner, 1964). Although ST laboratory experiments that did use more involving rumors found greater transmission accuracy (see chap. 7, this volume), leveling still occurred (Higham, 1951).

Third, R. H. Turner (1964) stressed that ST cannot accommodate the invention stage of everyday rumor. Invention occurs when people create hypotheses to explain an ambiguous situation; it is then that rumor often snowballs. Laboratory ST studies and field studies in which *formed* rumors have been planted therefore preclude invention by not supplying the requisite undefined situation. Ambiguity in a situation of importance does seem to lead to invention. Published stock-market takeover rumors, for example, seem to "derive from market professionals' interpretations of unusual firm-specific trading activity" (Pound & Zeckhauser, 1990, p. 306). "Seldom does the rumor . . . precede the unusual price and volume activity. Usually rumors follow this activity as market observers seek to explain its cause" (Pound & Zeckhauser, 1990, p. 306). Thus, according to Turner's crisis model, (a) a crisis occurs and people seek information; (b) information is lacking or the sources of formal information are not trusted, and therefore people feel frustrated and seek information from informal channels; and (c) if no information available, people engage in *affirmative rumoring*, that is, they speculate on the basis of whatever evidence and framework of understanding they possess; invention occurs at this stage.

There is evidence supporting Turner's objection. Most field studies reporting leveling tend to be planted-rumor studies that do not seem to involve ambiguous and important situations. One such study is self-labeled "a community diffusion experiment" (De Fleur, 1962, p. 51). Seventeen percent of 249 households were told the slogan "Gold Shield Coffee—Good as Gold." Then 30,000 leaflets were airdropped on the community. These leaflets stated that every house would be interviewed and free coffee would be given to those who knew the slogan. Leveling (as well as sharpening and assimilation) occurred after two tellings of the information. A second example follows: W. L. Davis and O'Connor (1977) planted information in an academic department that Davis's wife was pregnant; the information contained a number of details (e.g., the doctor's name, the child's possible name) that were leveled. Here is a third, more recent, example: A planted rumor condensed around the main fact that "next year's T-shirt may cost the students money" (Sedivec, 1987, p. 37). The point is that situations involving coffee slogans, office birth announcements, and student T-shirt costs seem to be far less ambiguous and involving than, say, situations that threaten safety, health, job, or well-being.

However, this objection (that invention is precluded) presupposes that all real-life rumor episodes are highly and interactively collaborative; they do not address the possibility that some real-life rumor episodes are ST-like in their transmission pattern. Some leveling clearly has occurred in field observational situations as a result of ST-like transmission. Scanlon (1977) traced a single rumor in a disaster situation through a serial chain. Although he found clear evidence of adding more detail—as we would predict in a COL situation—he also found some evidence of leveling (some details were lost in the transmission). In addition, most rumors in Caplow's (1947) field study tended toward "simplification" (p. 301); Caplow noted that most rumors contained three statements, many contained one or two, and few contained more than three. This simplification is a form of leveling. Furthermore, Nkpa (1977) reported a pipe-dream wartime rumor that underwent leveling as it spread: A detailed story about how Northern Nigerian General Gowon had been killed by Nigerian rulers dissatisfied with his performance became "I heard that Gowon has died in Kaduna" (p. 32). Again, some leveling occurs in real-life rumor transmission; this may happen simply because some portion of rumor transmission is serially transmitted.

Generalizability of Adding

Most field studies about high-ambiguity and high-interest rumor episodes show adding rather than leveling (Peterson, unpublished, cited in De Fleur, 1962; Peterson & Gist, 1951; Schachter & Burdick, 1955). In Peterson and Gist's (1951) field study of rumors surrounding a very high interest baby-sitter murder, the central theme was not distorted, but was compounded with additional speculations. That is, in this high-ambiguity rumor episode, details and variations proliferated rather than leveled out. Rumors following public disclosure of the scandalous loan practices of an important bank were "completed and enriched" (Roux-Dufort & Pauchant, 1993, p. 238). Again, adding occurred in this high-ambiguity episode.

Although adamant that snowballing is a "misconception," even G. W. Allport and Postman (1947b, p. 153) observed some invention (i.e., adding) in their laboratory ST demonstrations and offered one possible situation in which rumors might snowball: After highly emotionally straining events, people may tend to perseverate, "mull it over, talk about it endlessly, [and] explore in fantasy all possible consequences" (p. 154). Furthermore, Schachter and Burdick's (1955) field experiment strongly supports this idea. This study manipulated importance while creating a highly ambiguous situation: The percentage of girls reporting new rumors in the high-importance conditions was much higher (70%) than in the low-importance conditions (15%). In addition, the diversity of rumors was also much greater in the high-importance conditions (average of 12 different rumors in each condition vs. average of 1.5 different rumors in the low-importance conditions). The high-importance condition groups were composed of friends of the girls who had been suddenly removed from a classroom setting; these friends were undoubtedly earnestly and interactively collaborating about the event and thus prone to invention. The low-importance groups were composed of girls who were not acquainted with the accomplices; these girls were presumably passing along (serially transmitting) interesting bits of information. Again, adding seems to occur in real-life situations that are interactively collaborative in character.

CONCLUSIONS

In sum, what can we say about patterns of content change? First, certain real-life field situations, particularly those possessing high-ambiguity and high-interest contexts, predispose adding. These rumor episodes are about making sense of an important and ambiguous situation. Other real-life situations, particularly those characterized by low-ambiguity and low-interest contexts in which the rumor is simply being transmitted, seem to engender leveling. These rumor episodes are about serial diffusion of a message. Of course, even some high-importance–high-ambiguity situations may involve ST ("There is a fire in the building! Leave now!" will probably be passed along quickly without discussion, interaction, or collaboration), but we speculate that ST-like situations are less frequent in real life than are COL-type situations. Second, in addition to adding or leveling, sharpening also occurs. Finally, all three types of changes occur in service of assimilation.

Thus far we have considered broad categories of rumor content change. We next examine patterns of changes in rumor accuracy. We begin by more clearly conceptualizing the term *rumor accuracy*.

Accuracy Conceptualization and Measurement

What exactly do we mean when we say that a rumor is accurate? In this section, we sharpen the conceptualization of accuracy and discuss how accuracy is measured.

RUMOR VERITY AND RUMOR PRECISION

Two senses of the construct *rumor accuracy* bear exploration. One refers to the degree to which a rumor corresponds with fact, reality, and truth. When we say a rumor is accurate in this sense, we mean that it corresponds to the facts. We term this sense of accuracy *rumor verity*. The opposite of accuracy here is falsehood. Both true and false rumors may be generated, sifted, and evaluated when groups attempt to define ambiguous situations. A veritable rumor circulated in the aftermath of the Hiroshima bombing: The devastation was caused by energy released when small particles were split (D. L. Miller, 1985). This true rumor circulated along with many other false ones as people attempted to comprehend what had happened. R. H. Turner and Killian (1972) described rumors generated as a crowd milled after discovering the body of a man in a car parked near a hotel. The original rumor generated and accepted by the group (that the man had been murdered by the owner of the vehicle) turned out to be false; the veritable one (that he died of alcohol poisoning) was proposed but rejected. Sinha (1952) categorized rumors circulating after a landslide as truth, exaggerations, or "outright falsehoods"; accuracy in the sense of verity is the dimension that incorporates the first and last of these characterizations. Accuracy here is akin to the concept of validity in psychometrics: Does the rumor faithfully represent some real state of affairs?

The second sense of *accuracy* refers to the degree to which the rumor corresponds with an original perception or message. When we say a rumor is accurate in this sense, we mean that it corresponds closely to some original version. We call this sense of accuracy *rumor precision*. The opposite of accuracy in this sense is distortion, which refers to the degradation of or reduction in quality of some original message during transmission. G. W. Allport and Postman (1947b) reported rumor distortion as rumors were serially transmitted in their laboratory studies; the terminal reports invariably differed from the original stimuli. All 96 girls in a girls' school reported hearing an undistorted version of a planted rumor in Schachter and Burdick's (1955) field experiment; note that the rumor was false to begin with, although accurate in the sense of being precisely transmitted. In Sinha's (1952) three-part classification scheme, accuracy in this sense is the dimension that incorporates the term *exaggeration* (an exaggeration contains distortions in the direction of greater quantity or quality). Accuracy here is akin to the concept of reliability in psychometrics; how consistent is the rumor with its original version?

It is useful to momentarily consider six of the possible combinations of these senses of accuracy, which are presented in Table 6.1. Some rumors are true and were precisely transmitted; these *stars* seem unaffected by potential forces of distortion and change. Other rumors are false and were precisely transmitted; these *counterfeits* began false and don't change (like counterfeit coins). Some rumors are true but were not precisely transmitted; they are either *converts* that changed for the better during their lifetime or *grainies* that became slightly distorted (as a grainy photograph). Finally, certain rumors are false and were distorted during transmission; some are *fallen stars* that started well but ended badly and others are *hopefuls* that started false but show signs of slight improvement. This categorization sketches the careers by which true and false rumors obtain and frames some of the questions pertinent to rumor accuracy. First, both veritable and false rumors can be generated, but how is verity measured, how often does it occur, and what processes are involved in such generation? Second, rumors can change,

TABLE 6.1

Verity–Precision Rumor Categories

Rumor verity	Rumor precision		
	Precise	**Distorted toward truth**	**Distorted toward falsehood**
True	**Stars:** True rumors that were precisely transmitted	**Converts:** True rumors that were distorted (toward veracity) in transmission	**Grainies:** True rumors that were distorted (toward falsehood) in transmission
False	**Counterfeits:** False rumors that were precisely transmitted	**Hopefuls:** False rumors that were distorted (toward veracity) in transmission	**Fallen Stars:** False rumors that were distorted (toward falsehood) in transmission

and they can change toward or away from verity. How is such change measured, how often does it occur, and what processes are involved in such change? We begin with measurement.

MEASUREMENT OF VERITY AND PRECISION

Rumor verity accuracy has tended to be measured in field studies approaching rumor from a collaborative (COL) perspective. These investigations typically involved collecting rumors or variations of a rumor within a particular field setting and assessing what percentage of these rumors was true. For example, verity accuracy in organizational grapevine research was measured as the percentage of communication bits in a rumor or set of rumors that were true (K. Davis, 1972; Marting, 1969; Rudolph, 1973; Walton, 1961; Weinberg & Eich, 1978). The percentage of takeover rumors published in *The Wall Street Journal* that proved true (Pound & Zeckhauser, 1990) assessed verity. More qualitative measures of verity include Sinha's (1952) three-part categorization and Caplow's (1947) global recollection of the overall truth of military rumors.

Rumor precision accuracy has tended to be measured in research using variants of the ST paradigm in a lab or field-experiment setting. Lab studies typically involve observing an original stimulus (e.g., a drawing, photograph, or videotape) and transmitting a description of that stimulus through a chain of participants without discussion. In field settings the original stimulus is a planted rumor in an actual organization; transmission here, of course, involves discussion. Rumor precision accuracy is the percentage of the final report that corresponds to the original stimulus. G. W. Allport and Postman's (1947b) classroom demonstration studies exemplify this approach in the laboratory (see also Higham, 1951; Lyons & Kashima, 2001; Werner, 1976). Other laboratory studies allowed discussion during transmission (Leavitt & Mueller, 1951; McAdam, 1962).

Field studies using planted rumors have also tended to measure rumor precision rather than verity: All 96 girls in Schachter and Burdick's (1955) study reported an undistorted version of a planted rumor. Accuracy was the extent to which the planted rumor had resisted distortion rather than the quality of the groups' efforts to make sense of the situation. This point is underscored by the fact that many new rumors arose, some quite bizarre. Accuracy was not measured as the percentage of rumors that corresponded to the actual facts (the sudden removal of girls from the classroom was part of a psychological experiment) or even the planted rumor (the girls had been removed on suspicion of stealing tests). Precision accuracy has also been measured as a continuous and a dichotomous variable. Sedivec (1987) first measured accuracy as the percentage of items that participants recalled out of an original set of seven parts of a planted rumor in a student organization; missing, distorted, and added lines each counted as inaccurate statements. Using the same data, he also measured the accuracy of recalled statements as either containing or not containing the one main fact.

Although researchers—especially those in the laboratory ST tradition—may have measured rumor precision, rumor verity is what all rumor researchers have been ultimately interested in. ST researchers measuring precision accuracy tended to assume that rumor precision was synonymous with rumor verity in real-life situations because they used their results to explain why rumors were often false. For example, G. W. Allport and Postman (1947b) concluded that "so great are the distortions . . . that it is never under any circumstances safe to accept rumor as a valid guide for belief or conduct" (p. 148). Like our rumor researcher forebears, we are likewise interested in rumor verity. We are concerned with rumor precision to the extent that it sheds light on some of the processes involved in rumor verity. Therefore, unless otherwise specified, we use the term *accuracy* to refer to rumor verity.

How Accurate Are Rumors Overall?

The term *rumor* connotes inaccuracy. Subjects in our studies typically stated that they would risk far less money on rumors than on news and viewed them as neither credible nor trustworthy; these ratings applied to both unpublished and published rumors (DiFonzo & Bordia, 1997; see also G. H. Smith, 1947). Rumor clearly has a bad name, but is this reputation deserved? We address this question by first presenting results of empirical investigations of rumor accuracy in the literature and from our own recent unpublished studies.

RUMOR ACCURACY LITERATURE

A handful of studies have gauged rumor accuracy in field settings; these are summarized in Table 6.2. These investigations typically involved collecting rumors or variations of a rumor and assessing what percentage of these rumors (or rumor components) was true. Table 6.2 summarizes the rumor samples collected and arranges them in descending order of accuracy percentage (the percentage of each sample that was true). We conclude from these summaries that rumor accuracy varied substantially, but certain field settings seemed to produce accurate

TABLE 6.2

Summary of Accuracy Studies

Reference	Rumor sample and setting	N subjects	Accuracy %[a]	N rumors
Caplow (1947, p. 301)	Grapevine rumors in military.	nr	Almost 100%	nr
Marting (1969, p. 123)	Grapevine rumors in a vertical segment of management and non-management employees in a mid-sized electronics manufacturing firm.	451	98.42%	15
Rudolph (1971, p. 187; 1973)	Grapevine rumors in a public utility.	124	96%	nr
Davis (1972, p. 263)	Grapevine information in industry for noncontroversial company information.	nr	80–99%[b]	nr
Walton (1961, p. 48)	Information attributed to the grapevine at the Naval Ordinance Test Station, China Lake, CA.	<101	82%[c]	12
Pound & Zeckhauser (1990, p. 293)	Financial takeover rumors published in *The Wall Street Journal* "Heard on the Street" column.	na	43%	42
Weinberg & Eich (1978, p. 30)	Rumors collected on a hotline during a university strike by graduate students.	nr	16.2%	nr
Prasad (1935, pp. 1–4)	Rumors collected after a catastrophic flood.	nr	9%[d]	23
Sinha (1952)	Rumors collected after a catastrophic landslide.	nr	Very low	nr

Note. nr = not reported. na = not applicable. [a]Refers to the overall percentage of communication details that could be assessed as true or false, which were true in a rumor or set of rumors. [b]Refers to Davis's summarization of his own research (i.e., several studies). [c]Refers to the percentage of correct responses of those attributed to grapevine information on a 12-question quiz administered to employees. Choices included a "don't know" option, however, which garnered between 35% and 77% per question (*M* = 52%), thus limiting the 82% accuracy figure to those responses for which the employees felt "reasonably" certain of their answers (Walton, 1961, pp. 48–49). [d]Prasad (1935) presented a "representative set" of 30 rumors, 23 of which were verifiable (i.e., dealt with empirical as opposed to metaphysical events).

rumors. We consider these factors later, but note here that rumors within established organizational settings, especially those characterized as grapevine rumors, tended to be very accurate. This finding accords with Hellweg's (1987) conclusion in her literature review of organizational grapevine research: Grapevine information (including rumor) tends to be accurate, although incomplete.

Our own, more recent empirical studies are consistent with this conclusion. We report here three studies we conducted to investigate questions related to rumor accuracy in organizations. The first was a set of field interviews with organizational communications personnel; the others were questionnaire studies with samples of employed students. All three sets of results are consistent with the conclusion that rumor accuracy varies widely, but rumors within organizations tend to be accurate.

1996 FIELD INTERVIEWS

The first study—herein referred to as the 1996 Field Interviews—used an in-depth critical-incident methodology (Flanagan, 1954) in organizational settings. This method asks participants to recall a specific event—the *critical incident*—that exemplifies the phenomenon under investigation and then answer questions about that incident. In 1996 we conducted field interviews with organizational communications personnel from several corporations in the metropolitan area of a U.S. city as part of a multistage study investigating the harmful effects of organizational rumors and how managers dealt with them. These personnel were typically directors of communication or vice presidents of public relations. Each interviewee was asked to recall a specific incident of a harmful or potentially harmful rumor that he or she had responded to. Of the 18 largest publicly traded corporations contacted (as listed in a local trade publication), 6 consented to an in-depth interview (the remainder refused for a variety of reasons including a reluctance to discuss the organization's rumors and managerial time constraints). Most of the organizations represented in this sample were multinational in scope as well as recognizable household names. Each interview was audiotaped, transcribed, and analyzed with respect to various hypotheses related to accuracy. Accuracy was determined by asking participants to estimate the percentage of the rumor (or rumors) that was (or were) true.

Table 6.3 presents the rumors, their publics (the groups within which they circulated), and their accuracy percentages in descending order. All of the rumors but one (brittle reactor vessel) circulated within an established organizational setting. All but the last two had survived over a period of time (see table notes). An inspection of the findings shows that rumor accuracy varied widely, but like the rumor studies within organizational settings reported in the literature, these organizational rumors tended to be accurate. It is important to note that organizational communications personnel were not asked to provide true rumors; however, most did. Furthermore, if we consider only those rumors that survived over time, overall accuracy was even greater.

TABLE 6.3

1996 Field Interviews Accuracy Data

Rumor	Rumor public	Accuracy percentage
Two manufacturing centers would consolidate operations.	Employees at each plant	100
Two manufacturing plants would consolidate operations.	Managers at each plant	100
Subsidiary company would be sold.	Subsidiary employees	100
A large operations center would be closed.	Employees at targeted center	80
University president was secretly working for government agency.	University faculty and staff	60
Company would be taken over.[a]	Company employees	0
Utility had a brittle reactor vessel in danger of cracking.[b]	News media	0

Note. [a]This rumor was quickly squelched during group interaction. [b]Squelched when news media contacted utility to verify.

STUDENT RUMOR SURVEY 1

A second investigation collected workplace rumors from employed students in 1996; this investigation is herein called Student Survey 1. Fifty-six students in two upper level psychology courses were administered a questionnaire (see Appendix 6.1). Rumor was first defined as "an unverified bit of information about something of importance to a group." Participants were asked to "Think of an instance when a rumor occurred in a workplace setting. You may have simply heard/read the rumor or you may have also passed it along to coworkers." To calculate an accuracy percentage, we directed students to "Choose a rumor that has since been proven true or false beyond a reasonable shade of doubt; we are not interested in rumors that are still uncertain." In an open-ended question, students were asked to "State the rumor." *Rumor accuracy* was assessed by asking: "How accurate (true) did the rumor prove to be?" *Rumor accuracy trend* was assessed by asking: "From the time when the rumor started until when the rumor was proven true or false, to what extent did the rumor tend to become more accurate?"

Fifty-four usable questionnaires were obtained; 12 of these were discarded because they described incidents of gossip rather than rumor (e.g., "Two employees were having an affair").[2] The final sample of 42 workplace rumors is presented in Table 6.4. Accuracy ratings were bimodal—as expected given the request for true or false rumors— and negatively skewed, indicating that, as a whole, workplace rumors tended to be very accurate. Most were 100% or nearly 100% true.[3] This finding is again consistent with the literature review and results from the 1996 Field Interviews. Accuracy trend ratings were also negatively skewed, indicating that workplace rumors tended to become more accurate over their lifetimes.[4] Overall, then, workplace rumor participants tend to be fairly good at ferreting out the facts of a situation.

Dummy coding represents each range of scores in a distribution with a categorical or ordinal value (e.g., see note to Figure 6.1). By dummy coding the accuracy and accuracy trend variables for this sample, we assessed the frequency of the verity–precision combinations presented in Table 6.1. These frequencies are presented in Figure 6.1 and identified in Table 6.4. By far, most of the rumors in this sample resembled converts; they proved all or mostly true and also became more accurate during their lifetime. Some were stars in that they proved true but had changed very little. And some proved all or mostly true but had been distorted; these were grainies. Of those that proved false, most resembled fallen stars in that they tended to become more degraded. A handful were counterfeits because they proved false but had changed very little. Very few were hopefuls (false rumors that had become more accurate). In summary, the clear central tendency of this workplace rumor sample was toward accuracy.

STUDENT RUMOR SURVEY 2

A third investigation collected workplace rumors from employed U.S. college students from 1997 to 1998; this investigation is herein called Student Survey 2. One hundred eighty-five students in lower- and upper-level psychology courses were administered a questionnaire similar to Student Survey 1. Rumor was first defined as "an unverified bit of information about something of importance to a group. It is like news in every way except that it is unverified." In an attempt to weed out gossip, we instructed the participants that "Gossip, however, is usually about something personal or private, and is usually meant

---

[2] The final sample (*M* age = 22.56 years, *SD* = 3.32) was composed of 14 females and 27 males (1 did not report sex).

[3] Mean accuracy = 7.29 on a scale of 1 to 9, *SD* = 2.64, *N* = 42.

[4] Mean accuracy trend = 6.21 on a scale of 1 to 9, *SD* = 2.34, *N* = 42.

TABLE 6.4

Workplace Rumors From Student Survey 1

Type	Rumor summary
CF	The stolen petty cash was an inside job and the thief was a certain employee.
CF	Kris is going to leave the company.
CV	The candidates for a position of chairman at a college or department [will be so-and-so].
CV	Person A [of our group] gets paid the highest salary.
CV	We would be getting new computers at work.
CV	Bill Parcells is leaving the New England Patriots after the season to coach the New York Jets.
CV	A certain department would be laid off.
CV	A coworker was fired.
CV	A coworker was injured the night before.
CV	Several coworkers were going to be fired, but no one knew who.
CV	The supervisor was going to be fired and replaced.
CV	[University] administrators have $287 million in undesignated funds but refuse to spend it on student community because they are tightwads.
CV	A coming lay-off of many workers in my company.
CV	A fellow co-op student was fired from an automobile factory for taking a nap inside a car in one of the test facilities.
CV	Someone was leaving.
CV	We will get to choose our work schedules for next quarter instead of having them decided for us.
CV	Someone [a coworker] was going to get fired.
CV	A few of my sorority members were getting prank phone calls.
CV	A rumor that I would be named battalion commander.
CV	A really good cook was returning to work with us.
CV	Coworker got fired for shoplifting from the bulk department.
CV	Mary is leaving the company.
CV	Certain persons were breaking into our restaurant and getting to our liquor.
CV	The upstairs balcony of my fraternity house will be [turned] into a lounge.
CV	Michelle is being let go.
CV	There are going to be significant cutbacks (40%).

continued

TABLE 6.4 (Continued)

Workplace Rumors From Student Survey 1

Type	Rumor summary
FS	A coworker never shows up for meetings.
FS	Our company was going to buy a division of another company.
FS	A certain coworker slashed my coworker's tires.
FS	A coworker is getting fired.
FS	Students who used a business course as an engineering elective will not graduate on time because the course won't be counted.
GN	All workers will have to take 2 weeks off without pay so that the company will be able to report better profits.
GN	Boss cheats on taxes.
GN	A female coworker was being stalked by a male coworker and harassment charges were filed leading to termination.
GN	The photography department was going to be cut by 50%.
GN	Several persons would be "on their way out."
HP	There was a rumor that I was quitting.
ST	Coworker was demoted from a management position for leaving a cashbox sitting out.
ST	A coworker was taking scrap metal (that was still usable) and recycling it for cash.
ST	Some people in higher management will quit their jobs.
ST	A fellow worker sold drugs.
ST	Rick, who just had an accident, is coming back to work.

Note. N = 42; CF = counterfeits; CV = converts; FS = fallen stars; GN = grainies; HP = hopefuls; ST = stars.

primarily to convey social standards or to entertain." Participants were asked to "Think of an instance when a rumor (not gossip) occurred in a workplace setting. You may have simply heard/read the rumor or you may have also passed it along to coworkers." To sample equally from rumors that had proven true and those that had proven false, we asked students to recall a rumor that had proven true and then one that had proven false (the order of the request was alternated).

The 185 questionnaires could have yielded a possible set of 370 rumors (two per questionnaire). Of these 370, 94 were gossip, 2 were missing accuracy and accuracy trend ratings, and 30 did not describe the rumor. The final sample consisted of 146 subjects—48 of whom contributed one rumor and 98 contributed two rumors—for a total N

FIGURE 6.1

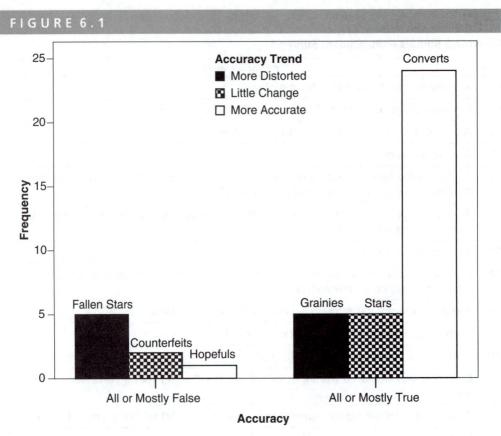

Verity–precision combination frequencies (Student Survey 1). N = 42; Accuracy dummy = proved all or mostly false if accuracy < 4; = proved all or mostly true if accuracy > 6 (no values = 4, 5, or 6); accuracy trend dummy = more distorted if accuracy trend < 4; = more accurate if accuracy trend > 6; otherwise = little change.

of 244 rumors.[5] One hundred thirty-seven rumors were true; 107 were false. To assess more closely the types of change occurring in true and false rumors, we computed the frequency of the verity–precision combinations for this sample; these are presented in Figure 6.2. The results are very similar to those of Student Survey 1. We first observe that the overwhelming majority of rumors were all or mostly true or false; there appeared to be little middle ground for rumors that had since been proven true or false. Of the all or mostly true rumors recalled, most by far resembled converts. Of those that proved all or mostly

[5] The final subject sample (M age = 24.96 years, SD = 7.64, 15 did not report age) was composed of 118 females and 113 males (13 did not report sex).

FIGURE 6.2

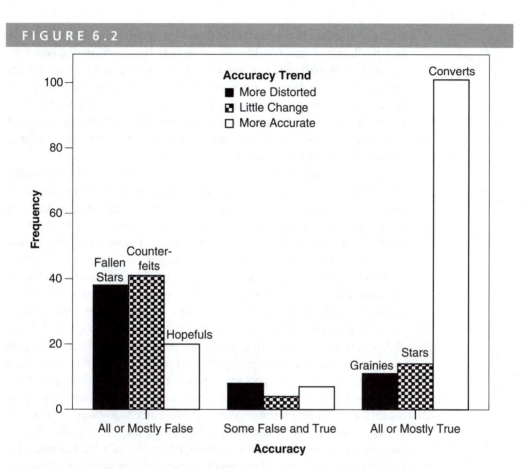

Verity–precision combination frequencies (Student Survey 2). *N* = 244. Accuracy dummy = proved all or mostly false if accuracy = 1, 2, or 3; = some false and true if accuracy = 4 or 5; = proved all or mostly true if accuracy = 6, 7, or 8. Accuracy trend dummy = more distorted if accuracy trend = 1, 2, or 3; = little change if accuracy trend = 4 or 5; = more accurate if accuracy trend = 6, 7, or 8. Both scales ranged from 1 to 8.

false, most resembled either fallen stars or counterfeits. In summary, rumors tended to change toward or away from verity. True rumors especially tended to mutate toward accuracy; false rumors tended either to become more false or to remain false.

LIMITATIONS AND CONCLUSIONS

Two limitations of these three studies should be considered. First, these results may be caused by some form of recall bias wherein true rumors are recalled more easily than are false ones. When true rumors become fact, perhaps the ramifications of these facts (e.g., job layoffs, boss left, company was sold) tend to serve as cues to remind people of the original rumor. However, false rumors may be equally memorable if found to be bizarre in content. Second, we note again that rumors that remained unverified were procedurally excluded from the sample. Therefore, it is necessary to qualify the applicability of these results to organizational rumors that have been proven true or false.

Taken all together, however, the literature and our empirical results suggest two conclusions. First, organizational rumors tend to be accurate. The reputation of workplace rumor as inaccurate apparently is itself inaccurate! The reason for this disparity is puzzling. If the overwhelming majority of rumors that are recalled were true, why would the overall impression of rumor tend to be not credible? We have noticed this pattern repeatedly: When asked about rumor overall, people classify it as false or low-quality information. When asked to recall specific rumors, people tend to report true or high-quality information. To explain this disparity, we offer two speculations. First, social desirability bias may be operating; participants may assume that relying on rumors is a less than acceptable behavior. It may conflict with their self-image as intelligent persons. Second, the same cognitive processes that result in stereotyping of persons may result in stereotyping of rumors. For example, rumors may be vulnerable to illusory correlation: Because rumors are probably a minority of the information that is processed (e.g., news and information), false specimens of that minority may become relatively salient and then falsely correlated (cf. Chapman & Chapman, 1969). In an attempt to establish meaningful categories, people tend to therefore associate *rumor* with *false*.

Second, the literature and results suggest that for those rumors that prove to be true or false, the true tend to get "truer" and the false either stay the same or become more false. Rumor verity trends seem to bifurcate. We dub this intriguing possibility the *Matthew accuracy effect*. The Matthew effect in science refers to the finding that well-known scientists are accorded a disproportionately large share of credit and access to new scientific ideas and information whereas lesser known scientists are allotted fewer accolades and less access. Robert K. Merton (1968) coined this term after the same general principle expressed in a biblical text from the Book of Matthew: "For everyone who has will be given more, and he will have an abundance. Whoever does not have, even what he has will be taken from him" (Matt. 25:29, New International Version). The idea is expressed in such adages as "nothing succeeds like success" and "the rich get richer and the poor get poorer." Variants of this idea have been noted in many domains; in network science, nodes with many connections tend to obtain more, whereas those with few connections tend to lose what they have (Newman, 2003).

In the next chapter we will explore the mechanisms by which accurate–inaccurate rumor content is generated and changed.

Appendix 6.1
Student Survey 1: Request for Participation in a
Short Survey on Rumor Accuracy

Rumors are one of the ways that people obtain information in organizations, and rumors may impact us in a variety of ways. Of course, we all know that rumors may or may not be true, but we must sometimes make decisions on the basis of a rumor. That's fine if the rumor turns out to be true, but could cause problems if it's a false rumor. For us to be better "consumers" of rumors, it would be helpful to know how likely they are to be true. Your participation in this study will help us answer this question and thereby help us create guidelines for when (if ever) it is appropriate to trust a rumor.

Kindly respond to the attached brief survey on an instance in which a rumor occurred in the workplace. The survey takes only 10 minutes to complete and your cooperation will be greatly appreciated. Your participation is completely VOLUNTARY, and your returning this survey will be taken to mean that you have consented to participate in this research study. You may, of course, stop at any time without consequence or prejudice. Your responses will be ANONYMOUS (please do not put your name or student number on the survey) and the data will be kept confidential (only aggregates will be reported). At the end of the quarter, I will report the results to our class.

THANK YOU VERY MUCH.

A rumor is an unverified bit of information about something of importance to a group. Think of an instance when a rumor occurred in a workplace setting. You may have simply heard or read the rumor or you may have also passed it along to coworkers. **CHOOSE A RUMOR THAT HAS SINCE BEEN PROVEN TRUE OR FALSE BEYOND A REASONABLE SHADE OF DOUBT;** we are not interested in rumors that are still uncertain.

1. State the RUMOR here:

2. Please describe the SITUATION OUT OF WHICH THE RUMOR AROSE:

3. How ACCURATE (true) did the rumor prove to be? (circle one number): 1 100% False, 9 100% True.

4. From the time the rumor started until when the rumor was proven true or false, to what extent did the rumor tend to become MORE ACCURATE? 1 Became More Distorted, 9 Became More Accurate.

Now remember the situation **JUST PRIOR TO WHEN THE RUMOR WAS PROVEN TRUE OR FALSE. Answer all of the remaining questions for the point in time JUST PRIOR TO WHEN THE RUMOR WAS PROVEN TRUE OR FALSE.**

5. Overall, how ANXIOUS (worried/concerned) did the CONTENT OF THE RUMOR ITSELF make people feel who heard and/or passed the rumor? 1 Not at all Anxious, 9 Highly Anxious.

6. Overall, how ANXIOUS did the SITUATION OUT OF WHICH THE RUMOR AROSE make people feel who heard and/or passed the rumor? 1 Not at all Anxious, 9 Highly Anxious.

7. Overall, how ANXIOUS (worried/concerned) were people who heard and/or passed the rumor? 1 Not at all Anxious, 9 Highly Anxious.

8. Overall, how UNCERTAIN (filled with doubts and uncertainties about the SITUATION OUT OF WHICH THE RUMOR AROSE) were people who heard and/or passed the rumor? 1 Certain, 9 Uncertain.

9. Overall, to what extent did people KNOW WHAT TO DO in order to minimize negative consequences associated with the rumor or maximize positive consequences associated with the rumor? (Do not answer if no consequences whatsoever or neutral consequences only were associated with the rumor.) 1 Did Not at all Know What to Do, 9 Knew Exactly What to Do.

10. Overall, how CONFIDENT were people who heard and/or passed the rumor that this rumor was true? 1 Not at all Confident, 9 Highly Confident.

11. If the rumor had proven true, how POSITIVE (favorable) would the probable consequences have been for most of the people who heard and/or passed the rumor? 1 Very Negative, 9 Very Positive.

12. Overall, how IMPORTANT (significant, consequential) was the RUMOR to people who heard and/or passed the rumor? 1 Not at all Important, 9 Very Important.

13. Overall, how IMPORTANT (significant, consequential) was the SITUATION OUT OF WHICH THE RUMOR AROSE to people who heard and/or passed the rumor? 1 Not at all Important, 9 Very Important.

14. When a rumor is passed from one person to another, it may involve a great deal of interaction (discussion and clarification), or it may involve very little interaction. Overall, how INTERACTIVE was a typical discussion of the rumor? 1 Not at all Interactive, 9 Very Interactive.

15. A rumor may recirculate through a group (most people in the group hear the rumor from more than one person), or it may not recirculate (most people hear it once and never pass it on). To what extent did the rumor RECIRCULATE through the group? 1 Did not Recirculate, 9 Actively Recirculated.

16. A rumor may pass through an established communication network (e.g., an office grapevine) or through a group of people who never communicated before. Overall, how ESTABLISHED were the communication channels of the group of people who heard and/or passed the rumor? 1 Novel, 9 Established.

17. The grapevine is an established informal communication network. To what extent was this rumor passed through a grapevine? 0% Passed Through Grapevine, 100% Passed Through Grapevine.

Finally, a few details about yourself:

18. You are: Male / Female (please circle one).

19. Your age is: ____ (in years).

Mechanisms Facilitating Rumor Accuracy and Inaccuracy 7

In 2005 the most devastating storm in U.S. history—
Hurricane Katrina—hit New Orleans. According to
rumors and news reports, the Big Easy became a
hotbed of anarchy: Children and adults were raped in
the Convention Center, violent gangs shot at rescuers
and police helicopters, cars were hijacked at gunpoint,
and hundreds of dead bodies floated in the shark-
infested waters that submerged the city. These stories
turned out to be almost entirely false. Although some
looting occurred along with isolated shooting incidents,
the tales of widespread chaos were gross exaggerations
and fabrications; they were largely inaccurate.
—*Dwyer and Drew, 2005; Gillin, 2005*

n the previous chapter we saw evidence suggesting that
organizational rumors tend toward accuracy, and catastrophic rumors—as those about Katrina illustrate—tend
toward inaccuracy. Why might this be? In more specific
terms, what are the mechanisms by which accurate (or
inaccurate) rumor content is generated or changed? In this
chapter we summarize evidence from studies investigating
rumor accuracy and present our own recent empirical
investigations when pertinent. As in the previous chapter,
accuracy signifies verity, and *distortion* pertains to lack of
precision during rumor transmission. Because distortion
may obviously affect accuracy, we examine literature pertaining to rumor distortion also. For clarity, we parse

accuracy mechanisms into five sets: cognitive, motivational, situational, network, and group mechanisms; we summarize these mechanisms in Table 7.1. In reality, these processes may be inseparably blended, such as when cognitive schemas are informed by cultural concepts. Special attention is given to the neglected work of H. Taylor Buckner (1965) whose theory of rumor accuracy focused on network and motivational mechanisms. We also describe our own recent research that investigated Buckner's ideas.

Cognitive Mechanisms

Cognitive mechanisms affecting accuracy refer to processes associated with information processing. These include the narrowing of attention, memory limits, and perceptual biases.

ATTENTIONAL NARROWING

Systematic rumor distortion—resulting in inaccuracy—results from the narrowing of attention on the part of a person listening to rumors told serially and with no discussion. Research on the teller–listener–extremity effect in impression formation is relevant here: Subjects serially transmitted—without discussion—a message about an actor's culpable behavior (a football player's drunk-driving incident). The teller heard central statements (e.g., the football player was driving drunk) and statements about mitigating information (e.g., he didn't know that someone had spiked the punch). Those with first-hand information (tellers) rated the actor less extremely than did those who recounted the actor's story (listeners). Why would listeners tend to rate the actor more harshly? Tellers' accounts "tend to be more disjointed, temporally disorganized, and incomplete" (R. S. Baron, David, Brunsman, & Inman, 1997, p. 827). Baron et al. argued that disjointed teller accounts are harder for the listener to process and thus require increased attentional resources, which leads to ignoring mitigating information, which in turn leads to more extreme judgments. Baron et al. gathered support for this sequence by demonstrating that the effect becomes more extreme in subjects that hear white background noise while listening to the message (white background noise diminishes attentional capacity).

Attentional narrowing effects seem especially pronounced in initial tellings of the rumor—again in the context of serial transmission (ST) with no discussion. Consistent with G. W. Allport and Postman's

TABLE 7.1

Mechanisms Involved in Rumor Accuracy

Mechanism	Summary	Example
Cognitive: attentional narrowing	In the context of ST with no discussion, attentional narrowing leads to distortion in favor of salient information.	Tellers' accounts of a football player's drunk driving incident tended "to be more disjointed, temporally disorganized, and incomplete" and taxed listeners' attentional resources; listeners therefore focused on central features of these accounts (Baron et al., 1997, p. 827).
Cognitive: memory limits	In the context of ST with no discussion, memory limits lead to distortion that favors easily encoded or salient information.	Leveling of details in a series of ST demonstrations was not random; those details that were more difficult to encode or retrieve were dropped (G. W. Allport & Postman, 1947b).
Cognitive: perceptual biases	Perceptual biases lead to selective perception and interpretation so as to cohere with existing cognitive structures such as stereotypes and schemas.	False rumor content that a community worker (in charge of community social activities) was communist seems to have been made plausible by a rapid increase in news media reporting on the threat of communism (Festinger et al., 1948).
Motivational: accuracy	Accuracy motivation tends to produce more accurate rumors.	Ego-involved subjects—subjects for whom the topic was important—leveled details less than neutral subjects did in a ST laboratory study (Higham, 1951).
Motivational: relationship-enhancement	The desire to enhance or maintain relationship with others promotes rumor content that creates positive affect and positive impressions, or is stereotype-consistent.	Change in rumors surrounding a man found dead in the backseat of an automobile; the actual cause of death was resisted by those who first found the body and were thus "in the know"; the original rumor was, however, inaccurate (R. H. Turner & Killian, 1972).
Motivational: self-enhancement	Self-enhancement leads to rumor content that reinforces existing beliefs, attitudes, wishes, biases, suspicions, and desires or derogates outgroups to boost self-esteem.	MBA students were more willing to transmit rumors that reflected well on their own school and negatively on a rival school (Kamins et al., 1997).
Situational feature: high collective excitement	High collective excitement leads to "suggestibility" and diminished critical ability.	Because of high anxiety, suggestibility after catastrophic landslides was heightened, people set aside their critical set, rumors were not scrutinized, and people did not desire to verify them (Sinha, 1952).

continued

TABLE 7.1 (Continued)

Mechanisms Involved in Rumor Accuracy

Mechanism	Summary	Example
Situational feature: capacity to check	With an accuracy motivation, the capacity to check leads to increased accuracy.	Military rumors in Caplow's (1947) study were accurate partly because military personnel could ask superiors about the veracity of rumors (superiors could then confirm that the rumor was false).
Situational feature: time	For groups capable of ferreting out the facts, time increases accuracy; otherwise time leads to inaccuracy.	False rumors in the 1996 Field Interviews (see chap. 6., this volume) were quickly discarded.
Group: conformity	Conformity pressures lead to rumors consistent with the consensus.	Once consensus among prison inmates was achieved about who were "snitches," data were reorganized and conformity was demanded (Åckerström, 1988).
Group: culture	Rumors tend to be consistent with cultural axioms.	Rumors that earthquakes resulted from planet alignments and Himalayan deity indignation recurred over time (Prasad, 1950).
Group: epistemic norms	Higher group standards of evidence lead to accuracy.	Groups characterized as "skeptical" by public relations personnel tended to produce more accurate rumors than did those characterized as "gullible" (DiFonzo & Bordia, 2002a).
Network: interaction	Interaction increases precision accuracy.	Messages transmitted under conditions in which participants could ask questions retained precision accuracy whereas conditions prohibiting interaction exhibited distortion (Leavitt & Mueller, 1951).
Network: transmission configuration	ST and cluster configurations tend to promote distortion; multiple interaction promotes accuracy for critical set group orientations and inaccuracy for uncritical set orientations.	Group skepticism moderated the relationship between MI and accuracy in a sample of workplace rumors in Student Rumor Survey 2 (this chapter).
Network: channel age	Channel age is associated with accuracy.	Caplow (1947) attributed high accuracy rates in part to the ability of increasingly established channels of communication to label the quality of information sources.

Note. ST = serial transmission.

(1947b) ST leveling curves, R. S. Baron et al. (1997, Study 1) replicated the teller–listener–extremity effect for first- to second-generation transmissions, but not for second- to third-generation transmissions. The authors proposed that lower number of events (because of omissions) in the second to third generation permitted attention to mitigating information.

R. S. Baron et al. (1997) also speculated that attentional narrowing effects may be exacerbated by anxiety. Consistent with this idea, Ellis and Zanna (1990) showed that arousal narrows attention to salient stimuli and thus increases the impact of salient information on causal attribution. Because anxiety is closely linked with arousal, anxiety may therefore cause people to focus on salient parts of a situation (e.g., behavioral action rather than situational factors) in the rumor construction process. G. W. Allport and Postman (1947b) found similar effects: ST without discussion in front of an audience rather than without an audience resulted in greater leveling of rumor content. Although Allport and Postman accounted for this finding as the result of greater motivation to be accurate (participants passed on only that information about which they were absolutely confident), anxiety and attentional narrowing are also quite plausible.

Thus, attentional narrowing—in the context of ST with no discussion—seems to result in inaccuracies characterized by emphasis on salient or central information. Often this information may be about behavioral actions rather than situational constraints; such effects are likely to be exacerbated by anxiety or arousal.

MEMORY LIMITS

Memory limits led ST—with no discussion—participants to level the number of details recalled from an initial set of 20 to a final set of 5 (G. W. Allport & Postman, 1947b). Leveling of these details was not random; those details that were more difficult to encode or retrieve were dropped. For example, proper names and titles were almost always deleted (see also Bartlett, 1932). However, "odd, perseverative wording" (e.g., "There is a boy stealing and a man remonstrating with him"; Allport & Postman, 1947b, p. 89) tended to hang on. Items pertaining to movement (e.g., "There is a window with three flowerpots, one falling out," p. 95) and size (e.g., "big warehouse," p. 96) also tended to remain presumably because they are more vivid and thus more easily encoded. Allport and Postman also noticed that ST subjects, who were instructed to be as accurate as possible, tended to level to an easily remembered phrase. Thus, the limits and biases of memory itself—in the context of ST with no discussion—result in inaccuracies characterized by salient or easily remembered information.

PERCEPTUAL BIASES

Activating listeners' cognitive structures, such as stereotypes and schemas, may result in selective perception and interpretation of succeeding stimuli so as to fit the activated structure (Sedikides & Anderson, 1992); distortion of rumors in the direction of established structures (also known as *assimilation*) may result (G. W. Allport & Postman, 1947b). Trope and Liberman (1996) have noted this confirmation bias in social hypothesis testing; once a hypothesis is generated, there is a tendency to restrict attention and information processing. The hypothesis lends a frame to the evidence and people tend to look for evidence consistent with their hypothesis. For example, false rumor content that a community worker (in charge of community social activities) was communist seems to have been made plausible by a rapid increase in news media reporting on the threat of communism (Festinger et al., 1948). The communism rumor was elaborated over a 2-week period and other information was reinterpreted to agree with this rumor (it should be noted that no rebuttal efforts were made during this period). A similar phenomenon in collective behavior has been labeled *symbolization* (R. H. Turner & Killian, 1972). Symbolization is one way that crowds selectively define a situation by focusing tensions and actions in a simplified way on one object, as with a scapegoat. For example, the statement "White professors A and B are behind the [civil rights] sit-ins" tends to select and highlight evidence that points toward how these professors are the ones truly responsible for the sit-in. In like fashion, "evidence" supporting (false) rumors of Paul McCartney's death was found on a Beatles album cover: Paul wore no shoes, and in Britain, the deceased are typically interred without shoes (Rosnow, 1991).

The effect of perceptual biases in race rumor formation and perpetuation is well known (Bird, 1979; R. H. Knapp, 1944; P. A. Turner, 1993). The same stereotypes documented by G. W. Allport and Postman in 1947 are influential today. They posited that stereotypes that are characteristic of some rumors are a means of easily condensing—or, to use a more modern cognitive term, *chunking*—a number of ideas. One of us (DiFonzo) periodically asks students to anonymously list rumors they have heard about other races; such rumors invariably conform to stereotypes. Race rumors often seem to mutate to reflect the racial stereotypes of the rumor public (Maines, 1999). Rumors circulating in the African American community—such as that a boy had been mutilated in a shopping mall lavatory—specified the perpetrators as White; the same rumors circulating in the White community specified them as Black (M. Rosenthal, 1971). Stereotypes not only influence how evidence is interpreted but also lead to a premature cessation of evidence gathering (Trope & Liberman, 1996). Of course, reliance on stereotypes when interpreting individuals or instances is likely to result in inaccuracy. Anxiety seems to strengthen reliance on cognitive structures. In the context of interpersonal communication, Gudykunst (1995) proposed that high anxiety leads to reliance on stereotypes when one makes judgments regarding a stranger. Anxiety was associated with agreement of the rumor with group biases in our survey of rumor episodes recalled by top public relations personnel (DiFonzo & Bordia, 2002a). Anxiety thus seems to increase dependence on activated cognitive structures, especially stereotypes.

These perceptual biases sometimes lead to false confirmation when testing hypotheses, but there is evidence that people are cognizant of the diagnosticity of the evidence (Trope & Liberman, 1996). For example, Caplow (1947) observed that statements delimiting the probability of the rumor's truth (e.g., "this is probably not true . . .") were attached to the rumor. We note that perceptual biases have occurred in both ST laboratory (G. W. Allport & Postman, 1947b; Lyons & Kashima, 2001) and field situations in which not much information is known (Festinger et al., 1948) or formal sources of information are not trusted (P. A. Turner, 1993). The individual tendency to originate or distort a rumor toward activated schemas may be augmented or inhibited by situational and group processes (discussed later).

Motivational Mechanisms

Motivational mechanisms affecting accuracy refer to the goal of the interpersonal interaction that involves rumor. That is, what is the rumor-spreader trying to accomplish? Following the outline developed in chapter 3 (this volume), these processes include accuracy, relationship enhancement, and self-enhancement.

ACCURACY

People are often motivated to achieve an accurate picture of a situation; recall the fact-finding motivation introduced in chapter 3 (this volume). One implicit rule of conversation is that information transmitted be trustworthy (Grice, 1975; Higgins, 1981). When anxiety is not high, for example, and if participants are attempting to define a situation "realistically," then accuracy is a "primary consideration" (Shibutani, 1966, pp. 72–76). In these situations, the group checks reliability of information and tests hypotheses. When the group is given the proper resources to ferret out the facts, such efforts have been successful: "When accuracy is important to those participating in the experiment, there tends to be little distortion of *any* kind" [italics in original] (Shibutani, 1966, p. 92).

Accuracy motivation—as well as consequent hypothesis testing and salience of diagnostic information—increases with the importance of the topic. People are motivated toward accuracy when the costs of false confirmation are greater. People are also more aware of how diagnostic the information is when the costs are higher; they are careful to form conclusions based on valid evidence. This careful attention to accuracy even occurs in ST studies: Higham (1951) found that ego-involved subjects (subjects for whom the topic was important) leveled details less than did neutral subjects.

Accuracy motivation also increases when people are held personally responsible for what they say. Grapevine participants care about their reputation among sustained relationships; they may not care about it among strangers (Shibutani, 1966). The implication is that among grapevines consisting of sustained relationships, people are more motivated to be accurate. G. W. Allport and Postman (1947b) noted that ST in front of an audience rather than without an audience resulted in greater leveling of rumor content and they attributed this result to accuracy motivation: Subjects passed along only those items about which they were certain. Johan Arndt (1967) similarly noted that message distortions in word-of-mouth communications hinge on the ability to evaluate the message and the "rewards associated with precise transmission" (p. 65). Arndt speculated that in product rumors, "the knowledge that the receiver of word of mouth can buy the product and thus check the veracity of the message would appear to discourage extreme exaggerations. After all, the communicator has his reputation as a reliable source at stake" (p. 66).

RELATIONSHIP ENHANCEMENT

As noted in chapter 3 (this volume), people are often motivated to build and maintain relationships. Often this motivation manifests itself in an inclination to say something that is likely to make the hearer feel good, and a disinclination to share a rumor that will diminish the hearer's mood. This is the minimize-unpleasant-messages effect (Tesser & Rosen, 1975) already discussed. Business school students resisted passing negative rumors (compared with positive rumors) because such rumors might generate negative affect in the recipient (Kamins, Folkes, & Perner, 1997). Selective transmission of rumors in this fashion fosters inaccurate content by promoting the survival of only socially acceptable rumors that enhance relationships with one's ingroup (here relationship-enhancement motivation works in tandem with self-enhancement motivation, which is described later). However, as we discussed in the Rochester Institute of Technology (RIT)–University of Rochester (UofR) study presented in chapter 3 (this volume), when people seek to maintain close or long-term relationships, relationship enhancement may also lead to accuracy motivation; people try to be accurate so as to maintain their reputation. In that case, relationship-enhancement and accuracy goals coincide.

Relationship enhancement similarly manifests itself in a desire to foster a favorable impression of oneself in others. Scientists often become invested in their theories (Kuhn, 1996); so it is with rumors and their transmitters. The desire to manage and enhance a favorable impression acquired by being "in the know" may affect content; those in the know may resist rumor revision that would discredit their proposed version of the situation. R. H. Turner and Killian (1972) observed such resistance in rumors surrounding a man found dead in the backseat of an automobile; the actual cause of death—alcohol poisoning—was resisted by those who first found the body and were thus in the know. Spreaders of the baby-sitter murder rumors (Peterson & Gist, 1951) also modified rumors so as to enhance their own prestige. In a similar way, exaggerations (e.g., "The whole family had perished") and dramatizations (e.g., "a house had come *rolling down*" [italics in original]) occurred in rumors surrounding a massive landslide (Sinha, 1952). Why? Sinha proposed that in the lab, the transmitter is accuracy-motivated, but in the field, one transmits partly for effect; that is, the story is shared partly for diversion. Rumor content, especially in situations that resist definition, may thus resist change toward accuracy to enhance or maintain the impression one has formed in others (Arndt, 1967).

Another aspect of the relationship-enhancement motivation is more cognitive in nature: Despite implicit communication rules to transmit accurate and truthful messages, accurate transmissions may conflict with the goal of sharing a coherent message, that is, one that is understandable, plausible, and acceptable to the hearer (Ruscher, 2001). Stereotype-inconsistent material, for example, may therefore be dropped in the interests of "a tidy story" (p. 68). Peterson and Gist (1951) proposed such a motivational interpretation of how snowballing occurred in a rumor concerning murder of a baby-sitter: Transmitters selectively emphasized or de-emphasized aspects of the rumor, drawing from their beliefs about what was probable so as to make the rumor seem more plausible. Shibutani (1966) has similarly proposed that even accuracy-motivated rumor content tends to be consistent with "presuppositions of the public" (p. 86). Relationship-enhancement—

by coherence—motivation may be most apparent in situations in which the group is unable to ascertain the facts; rumor publics in the baby-sitter murder and landslide rumors did not have reliable evidence available.

SELF-ENHANCEMENT

Self-enhancement, also discussed in chapter 3 (this volume), is the desire to defend against threats to one's sense of self and maintain one's self-esteem. One way that self-enhancement motivation operates is to ensure the circulation of rumors that are complimentary to one's existing beliefs and attitudes. G. W. Allport and Postman (1947b) noted that rumor "firms pre-existing attitudes rather than forming new ones" (p. 182). F. H. Allport and Lepkin (1945) found that World War II rumors of waste and special privilege were more likely to be believed—and presumably continue to be transmitted—by people who opposed the Roosevelt administration (see chap. 4, this volume). In other words, rumor content may change to advance the process of rationalizing and justifying existing beliefs. This is a relatively cool (cognitive) process.

Another warmer (emotional) way that self-enhancement motivation operates is to promote the circulation of rumors that are complementary to existing unfulfilled wishes, biases, suspicions, and desires, especially in situations in which no consensus develops (Shibutani, 1966). Rumor distortions have been viewed by a vein of researchers as projections of repressed impulses introduced at each transmission node. This research is best typified by Jung's (1910/1916) analysis of a girls' school rumor about a student–teacher affair; the rumor represented a wish-fantasy. Through the mechanism of projection, rumors vent underlying emotional tension (i.e., they relieve, justify, or explain anxiety; Wilkie, 1986). For example, Lowenberg (1943) noted that psychotic patients display a fear of poisoning and that in times of national crisis, rumors of mass poisoning are common in "normals." He concluded that—as with the psychotics—rumors of mass poisoning are a projection of shock and fear. Why poisoning? Lowenberg pointed to psychoanalytic theories that shock and fear became associated with the oral zone during childhood weaning. In today's terms, we might say that the child formulates an illusory correlation between any illness or discomfort he or she experienced during this period and the act of ingesting new types of food. Adult anxiety in a crisis then rouses this early association and even normal adults become primed to believe rumors of mass poisoning. In more broad terms, another psychoanalyst, Ambrosini (1983), posited that rumors project intrapsychic anxieties on extrapsychic objects. Likewise, rumors have been explained as a justification for anxiety through the mechanism of cognitive dissonance (Festinger, 1957; Prasad, 1950; R. H. Turner & Killian, 1972). Dissonance is the psychological tension arising from contradictory attitudes or actions; for example "I feel anxious but there is nothing to feel anxious about." At a more conscious level, rumor distortion depends partly on what a person desires or expects to be true (Turner & Killian, 1972). For example, friends tended to transmit favorable rather than unfavorable rumors regarding their friend who had been abruptly withdrawn from class; nonfriends showed the reverse pattern (Schachter & Burdick, 1955).

Self-enhancement motivation also operates by fostering rumor content that derogates outgroups and thereby enhances the prestige of the ingroup. A rumor sketching a negative characterization of *them* makes us feel better about *we*—and, by extension, *me*. The Kamins et al. (1997) study discussed earlier in this chapter and in chapter 3 (this volume) supports this idea: MBA students were more willing to transmit rumors that reflected negatively on a rival school (fall in ranking) than they were willing to transmit rumors that the rival school's rankings rose. The RIT–UofR study presented in chapter 3 (this volume) marginally replicated this finding: With rumor recipient as ingroup and target of rumor as outgroup, negative rumors were marginally more likely to be transmitted than were positive rumors[1] (see Figure 3.4). In a similar way, rumors of violent acts and atrocities typically portray perpetrators as outgroup members. For example, P. A. Turner (1993) documented rumors circulating among both African and Caucasian groups that the other group was cannibalistic. Self-enhancement motivation explains why people typically encounter a large number of wedge-driving rumors—rumors that are hateful or hostile toward outgroups—but rarely hear rumors that are negative or critical of the ingroup. On the whole then, the evidence indicates that people prefer to transmit negative rumors about the outgroup.

Situational Features

Situational features refer to the conditions and circumstances of the rumor episode that bear upon accuracy. These features include collective excitement, ability to check rumor veracity, and time.

---

[1] $t(45) = 1.56$, $p_{1\text{-tailed}} = .06$.

HIGH COLLECTIVE EXCITEMENT

We have discussed how individual trait and state anxiety may exacerbate cognitive processes that usually inhibit accuracy. Collective excitement—situations in which many or all individuals in a situation are anxious—may intensify such effects by increasing *suggestibility* (distortion of perception) and diminishing critical ability. Crowd milling, for example, may catalyze restless individuals into an excited mob that immediately acts on an inaccurate rumor (R. H. Turner & Killian, 1972). Sinha (1952) observed that suggestibility after catastrophic landslides was heightened because of high anxiety: People set aside their critical set, did not scrutinize rumors, and did not desire to verify. Shibutani (1966) proposed two general sorts of rumor deliberation patterns that hinge on anxiety: *deliberative* ("If unsatisfied demand for news is moderate, collective excitement is mild, and rumor construction occurs through critical deliberation"; p. 70) and *extemporaneous* (in situations of intense collective excitement, rumor construction becomes behavioral contagion). Mausner and Gezon (1967) provided an example of extemporaneous rumor construction: A grade school temporarily closed because of unfounded fears of an outbreak of vaginal gonorrhea among girls (only 3 out of 173 girls had it, but many exhibited some symptoms); this rumor exemplified contagion in that it was marked by high collective excitement and suggestibility.

High collective excitement may also enhance the development of less stringent norms of verification. In critical situations when formal lines of communication are closed, informal networks that are temporary and unstable form. New norms for evaluating information and deciding behavior may emerge: "This is what everybody is saying!" (R. H. Turner & Killian, 1972, p. 32). Less stringent norm development is enhanced in close groups rather than in situations that promote communication, as in a crowd in which people may become sensitized to others in the group. However, people may already be sensitized because of existing group ties. In such "organized" groups, emergence of group norms in a fear situation (smoke billowing into a room) was quicker and more intense than in "unorganized" groups; organized groups showed more fear and reacted more quickly (Turner & Killian, 1972, pp. 38–41).

CAPACITY TO CHECK

Given an accuracy motivation, people strive to check the validity of information; rumor accuracy increases when they can do so (Shibutani, 1966). Military rumors in Caplow's (1947) study were accurate partly because military personnel could ask superiors about the veracity of rumors (superiors could then confirm that the rumor was false). In deliberative situations, people strive to check the veracity of information. For example, people called a rumor control center during a graduate student worker strike to check on the veracity of rumors; the center became a new source of external information and many inaccurate rumors were presumably squelched in this way (Weinberg & Eich, 1978). Even during catastrophes, people check the quality of the source of the rumor; for example, Port Jervis, New Jersey, residents had heard rumors that the dam would burst but left only when these rumors were spread by the fire department—an authoritative source (R. H. Turner, 1964).

Veracity checking is not possible or may be greatly encumbered in a number of situations. ST without discussion obviously exemplifies one of these situations. False eyewitness perceptions that are unduly trusted constitute another. Rosenberg (1967) described a news account that was inaccurate from the outset and remained inaccurate because newspapers that picked up the story failed to check its accuracy. Newspapers similarly failed or were unable to check rumors of mass anarchy following Hurricane Katrina (Dwyer & Drew, 2005). Situations with novel channels of communication constitute yet another situation in which ability to check veracity is difficult or impossible. Exaggerations and fabrications arose after a devastating earthquake had destroyed normal channels of communication; these reports could not be checked for a long time (Prasad, 1935). In a similar manner, military units undergoing radical personnel changes saw a flurry of initial inaccurate rumors until more normal lines of communication could be reestablished (Caplow, 1947).

The perceived urgent need to act before information can be checked constitutes a fourth situation in which checking is constrained (Prasad, 1935; Shibutani, 1966). People in situations in which delays may have adverse consequences may perpetuate inaccurate rumors because the consequences of taking time to check rumor veracity may be extremely negative should the rumor prove true. One must act quickly, for example, to alert one's friends that a computer virus, identified only by the presence of a teddy bear icon, has infected one's computer and spread to all addresses on one's address list ("JDBGMGR.EXE", 2002; see also Weenig, Groenenboom, & Wilke, 2001). If the rumor is true, damage to a friend's computer may be averted. (Concerned associates of ours actually spread this false rumor out of a perception that they had to act quickly.) The headlights hoax described in chapter 2 (this volume) spread quickly for the same reason: Almost all of the graduate students and faculty we interviewed immediately spread the rumor to friends and loved ones in part because they felt they had to act quickly to prevent violent death. Keep in mind that in these last two examples, the hoaxes spread among very skeptical people: academic psychologists!

A fifth situation in which checking is constrained is one in which no firm information is available (Buckner, 1965). The baby-sitter murder rumors persisted because police shrouded their investigation in secrecy (Peterson & Gist, 1951). Even when firm information is available, the information source must be trusted for rumors to become accurate (R. H. Turner & Killian, 1972). Rumors surrounding the death of John F. Kennedy, for example, almost certainly persist among those who distrust government authorities and the Warren Report. However, the false rumor that Procter & Gamble Corporation contributes to the Church of Satan has been periodically and successfully squelched by the publication of "truth kits" containing statements from trusted religious leaders, such as Billy Graham, stating the rumor to be a falsehood (Green, 1984; Koenig, 1985).

One's ability to check may also be constrained by rumor participants' proximity to valid sources of information. Accuracy of 12 planted rumors was related inversely to distance from original source; employees hearing it firsthand held more accurate rumors than did those hearing it second- or thirdhand (Walton, 1961). G. W. Allport and Postman (1947) similarly observed that some secondhand reports are accurate because someone in the rumor chain had access to firsthand knowledge, was motivated toward accuracy, or had opportunity to verify.

Closely related to a group's ability to check the validity of information sources is the group's ability to internally check consistency of information by comparing rumors. Rumors may be compared with one another to successfully deduce accuracy under the assumption that more authentic portions of the rumor will appear more often. For example, a dozen Korean War veterans recently recalled how they killed approximately 300 South Korean civilians in 1950 at the village of No Gun Ri (Choe, Hanley, & Mendoza, 1999). The accounts differed only in details; by retaining common elements of these accounts, news reporters were able to create an accurate reconstruction of this event. Such comparison is possible if a rumor is actively recirculating within a group (Buckner, 1965; DiFonzo & Bordia, 2002a).

TIME

The findings related to situational feature of time are mixed; with time, true rumors sometimes surface. For example, rumor survival was related to the accuracy of Caplow's (1947) military rumors. Yet Hershey found no relation between persistence and accuracy (as cited in Hellweg, 1987, p. 217). Buckner (1965) proposed that for groups that possess the ability and motivation to achieve accuracy, time tells all. Inaccurate rumors in such groups may initially proliferate during an invention stage (R. H. Turner, 1964) but, as we saw in the 1996 Field Study, false rumors are quickly discarded. However, for those groups that possess neither the inclination nor the ability to achieve accuracy, time results in further inaccuracy.

Group Mechanisms

Group mechanisms refer to aspects of the social entity through which the rumor spreads; especially those processes associated with group identity, norms, and influence. Those processes most pertinent to rumor accuracy include conformity processes, culture, and group epistemic norms.

CONFORMITY

Once consensus is formed, conformity is demanded (Festinger et al., 1948; Firth, 1956; R. H. Turner & Killian, 1972). In an attempt to ascertain which prison inmates snitch, hypotheses are tested and sources checked as in the rumor construction process; once a hypothesis is accepted, however, data are reorganized and conformity is demanded (Åckerström, 1988). In a similar way, in crowd formation, if some group members assent to one definition of a situation over others, it becomes difficult to advance other proposals (e.g., if someone in the crowd yells, "Police brutality!"; Turner & Killian, 1972). To the extent that such formulations are incorrect, inaccuracy is perpetuated.

CULTURE

Shibutani (1966) noted that, even though people retain critical ability in both deliberative and extemporaneous rumoring, the emergent rumors tend to be plausible to the rumor public—thus they tend to agree with cultural axioms. Rumor content is thus partly shaped by group biases. Information is invented, distorted, or ignored to fit the main theme of the rumor. Prasad (1950) categorized rumors surrounding earthquakes from 1934 and from 1,000 years prior, and from countries other than India. It is surprising that he found common content and themes. He posited that such commonality could not come from individual projection of "complexes" (p. 129), emotional stress, or archetypes.

Rather, he argued they arise from a common "attitude" (p. 129)—drawn heavily from cultural heritage—arising from the earthquake situation. Rumor construction is like a picture-completion task, with attitude driving the picture. In earthquake situations in which the causes of earthquakes were unknown, speculations based on "the traditional and cultural heritage peculiar to the group" (p. 7) were adopted. These common cultural attitudes explain rumor content; for example, the earthquake resulted from planet alignments and Himalayan deity indignation. Cultural effects are not limited to uneducated persons. Even scientists and intellectuals entertained these rumors.

Rumor content is thus, at least in part, anchored to group beliefs because social representations (collective understandings of general topics) are anchored to group beliefs (Lorenzi-Cioldi & Clémence, 2001). Organizational culture informs individual schemas and thus affects the individual's sense-making process (S. G. Harris, 1994), and therefore the content of rumor construction. Shibutani (1966) posited that skeptics are not immune to cultural anchoring: In deliberative rumor construction activities, the content may change so as to convince skeptics. For example, an authority may be cited, and the rumor may accord with "interests, sensitivities, and beliefs" (p. 85) of the group. Cultural anchoring of rumors is well documented. Knopf (1975) posited that rumor content is the crystallization of culturally sanctioned racial hostility. Kapferer (1989) stated that rumor content is the expression of collectively shared but repressed fears and beliefs. G. W. Allport and Postman (1947b) noted that "all rumors are liable to . . . cultural assimilation" (p. 157). They propose that as rumors circulate, they lose their individual features and come more to resemble broadly cultural ideas and familiar linguistic phrases (i.e., they become *conventionalized*). They also note that rumors are elaborated to conform to cultural frameworks. For example, in Bartlett's (1932) ST work, Hindu subjects were prone to adorn a tale with a moral in accord with Hindu fable.

GROUP EPISTEMIC NORMS

Closely related to culture, group norms of what evidence is counted as acceptable have been theorized to be associated with accuracy. Buckner (1965) posited that groups that possessed "meager standards of evidence" (p. 57) were less likely to achieve accurate rumor hypotheses. However, those groups characterized by skepticism tend to arrive at more accurate conclusions. We found correlational evidence supportive of Buckner's thesis (DiFonzo & Bordia, 2002a); groups characterized by PR personnel as skeptical tended to produce more accurate rumors than did those characterized as gullible.

Network Mechanisms

Communication networks are organizational structures of relations between entities: usually individuals, but also organizations and groups (Monge & Contractor, 2000). Attributes of the relations between these entities, rather than attributes of the entities themselves, are thus the focus of network analysis. Emergent communication networks are informal and naturally occurring (e.g., the grapevine), as opposed to formal networks, which usually correspond to organizational structure charts. Information diffusion—including rumor transmission—occurs on, within, or through these communication networks. In this section we consider how three aspects of information diffusion on communication networks—the extent to which discussion occurs in transmission, the pattern of information transmission, and the age of the information channel—each affect accuracy.

INTERACTION

Interaction refers to discussion that occurs between sender and receiver during transmission (Buckner, 1965). Interaction may involve redundant communication (repeating the message), clarification, comparison, and interpretation. It has also been labeled "free feedback" (Leavitt & Mueller, 1951) and "reciprocity" (D. L. Miller, 1985); we sometimes referred to it earlier as *discussion*. Interaction is generally associated with more precise transmission (Buckner, 1965, McAdam, 1962; R. H. Turner & Killian, 1972). Messages—consisting of descriptions of geometric patterns—transmitted under conditions of free feedback retained accuracy whereas serially transmitted messages exhibited distortion (Leavitt & Mueller, 1951). However, ST—without interaction—invariably leads to distortion (G. W. Allport & Postman, 1947b; D. L. Miller, 1985; Peterson & Gist, 1951). When people are allowed to verbally interact, even ST distortion is reduced (McAdam, 1962).

TRANSMISSION CONFIGURATION

Rumor transmission configurations can differ substantially. An ST network consists of members transmitting information from one to another along a single chain. *Cluster* (C) transmission patterns refer to transmission in which information is told to a cluster of people, some of whom don't pass it along, and some of whom pass it along to other clusters (K. Davis, 1972). Those who pass it along are called *liaisons*. *Multiple interaction* (MI) refers to transmission in which "many people hear the rumor from more than one source" (Buckner, 1965, p. 62). MI awaits a precise conceptualization but it clearly includes interaction and recirculation of the rumor. We have operationally defined MI as conceptually similar to rumor "activity" (DiFonzo & Bordia, 2002a). When rumor activity is high, many people hear versions of the rumor from multiple sources (MI), they interact (discuss) with one another, and the versions often recirculate (e.g., X tells Y, Y tells Z, then Z tells X). Most grapevine studies within organizations have found a C rather than ST or MI pattern of transmission (K. Davis, 1972; Hellweg, 1987). (In the following discussion, remember that C stands for cluster pattern of transmission, ST for serial transmission pattern, and MI for multiple interaction pattern.)

Transmission configuration has at least two implications for accuracy. First, ST and C patterns may grant liaisons more influence over rumor accuracy than do MI patterns. Keith L. Davis found that approximately 20% of the average network were liaisons (1972, p. 264). Some persons in the network—usually liaisons—contribute more to rumor construction and therefore affect content more than do others (R. H. Turner & Killian, 1972). Thus, in ST and C transmission, content toward or away from accuracy may especially depend on characteristics of the liaison subset. MI may diminish the influence of this subset.

Second, ST and C patterns of transmission are likely to show some distortion because of cognitive mechanisms (discussed previously) at each node of transmission. As noted, such distortion is mitigated through interaction, especially if the topic is outcome relevant to participants. MI patterns of transmission have the capacity to correct or accentuate such distortions. Buckner (1965) proposed that group orientation plays a moderating role in the relation between MI and rumor accuracy. *Group orientation* encompasses several situational, motivational, and network factors that result in either a critical or uncritical set. *Critical set* orientation refers to an unspecified combination of factors such as ability to check, high standards of evidence, and established channels; *uncritical set* orientation refers to the lack of these attributes. For groups with a critical set, MI should be associated with accuracy; more interaction and recirculation in these fortunate groups should result in more valid hypotheses. This idea is consistent with Nisbett and Ross's (1980, p. 267) suggestion that group interaction has the capacity to greatly mitigate common inferential biases. For groups with an uncritical set, MI should be negatively associated with accuracy; more interaction and recirculation in these groups will result in inaccurate and bias-laden hypotheses.

Reanalysis of data from a recent study of PR officers (DiFonzo & Bordia, 2002a; see Appendix 2.1) is partially consistent with the idea that MI and accuracy are associated in groups with a critical set orienta-

EXHIBIT 7.1

1996 Field Interview Group Orientation Attribute Measures

1. *Knowledgeability.* Most of the group was knowledgeable about the subject matter of the rumor (e.g., many witnessed the alleged event or nonevent; many were informed by the plant manager as to whether or not the company is laying workers off).
2. *Situation familiarity.* Most of the group is familiar with the situation in which a rumor such as this typically arises (e.g., journalists know that a few days before a national election, rumors that a candidate leads an immoral life often spring up and therefore journalists tend to be quite skeptical of these rumors).
3. *Channel age.* Most of the group heard the rumor within a stable interaction system and thus know the reliability of the teller from past experience (e.g., if Bill Smith tells a rumor and Bill Smith has been accurate or inaccurate in the past).
4. *Defense motivation.* Believing or disbelieving the rumor fills an emotional need for most people in the group; that is, they *want* to believe or disbelieve (e.g., rumors that the company will be handing out large bonuses this year).
5. *Situation urgency.* Most of the group was in an urgent situation and was unable to take the time necessary to investigate a rumor (e.g., "The dam has broken!").
6. *Channel novelty.* Most of the group was in a situation in which stable rumor channels were disrupted and hence the reliability of the rumor transmitter could not be evaluated (e.g., crisis situations in which many people were milling about, all interested and involved in the situation and seeking information).
7. *Information nonavailability.* Most of the group was in a situation in which absolutely nothing was known (e.g., such as when the police would not comment on whether or not an incident occurred).
8. *Gullibility.* Most of the group had very meager standards of evidence (e.g., they tended to accept what people said without questioning it).

Note. All attributes are adapted from Buckner (1965). Attributes 1 to 3 are conducive to critical set; attributes 4 to 8, to uncritical set.

tion. These professionals recalled harmful or potentially harmful rumor incidents and rated them on a variety of indices including MI and accuracy. MI in this sample was associated with rumor accuracy. In Buckner's framework, such a relationship ought to apply only to critical-set-oriented groups. To test this idea, we reanalyzed the data to assess critical set orientation. Buckner proposed that group skepticism and established communication channels are elements of a critical set orientation (see Exhibit 7.1: Group skepticism would be indicated by low group "gullibility" and how established channels of communication are by channel age and novelty). The group, as a whole, was neither skeptical nor gullible, but did possess established channels of communication.[2] Results of an experiment performed by Komarnicki and Walker

---

[2] We conducted one-sample *t* tests against the neutral (midpoint) scale value for group skepticism and how established group channels were: skepticism $t(60) = 1.10$, $p = .28$, established channels $t(59) = 3.31$, $p = .002$.

(1980) are also consistent with these ideas. As in G. W. Allport and Postman's (1947b) studies, participants were asked to pass along information they heard to the next person in line. Those communicating in line structures yielded the usual ST-type distortions. However, participants communicating in more complex structures in which they could change locations in line and immigrate to other lines yielded precision accuracy. More complex network structures mitigated ST-type distortions.

Buckner (1965) further proposed two group-level variables affecting MI: group structure and outcome-relevant involvement. First, MI is affected by group structure, which is how close or diffuse the group is. In diffuse groups, contact tends to be through chains and therefore multiple interactions are not likely. An individual in a diffuse network might hear a rumor only once. In close groups, members enjoy close and continuous contact; therefore MI is more likely. Close groups may be temporary (e.g., crowds) or long-standing (e.g., small towns, college fraternities, cliques, mental wards). In close groups the individual is likely to hear the same rumor many times. Empirical evidence supports this statement. People closely involved in friendship networks were more likely to have heard a rumor that a community worker was a communist (Festinger et al., 1948). Military rumors tended to diffuse within established groups rather than between them (Caplow, 1947). Second, Buckner proposed that MI is related to group involvement with the topic; groups that are highly interested in a rumor are more likely to exhibit MI.

Buckner's two-factor theory of MI may be summarized as follows. First, close groups with high involvement in the rumor should produce much interaction and recirculation—hence the high levels of MI. Caplow's (1947) study of military rumors, Schachter and Burdick's (1955) field experiment at a girls' school, Peterson and Gist's (1951) study of babysitter murder rumors, and R. H. Turner and Killian's (1972) studies of crowd behavior exemplify this situation. Second, diffuse groups with high rumor involvement should produce serial chains of communication and a few patches of recirculation resulting in moderate levels of MI. We speculate that some Internet rumors exemplify this category. Third, close groups with low rumor involvement will result in a few small serial chains and patches of recirculation, again producing only moderate MI. Finally, diffuse groups with low rumor involvement would produce very short serial chains and low MI. Sedivic's (1987) planted rumor did not disseminate widely in part because of low interest (involvement) and physical barriers to dissemination (departments were located far from one another and were thus diffuse). Additional support for this two-factor idea comes from Back et al. (1950) who conducted a participant observation study in which seven rumors were planted in an organization over 4 months. Two rumors about lost data (morale committee questionnaires) spread quickly to morale committee members, to whom it was important; the remaining rumors were relevant to the organization but varied in their spread.

CHANNEL AGE

Shibutani (1966) noted two types of communication channels: institutional (formal) versus auxiliary (normal everyday informal contacts). In deliberative (low anxiety) rumor construction situations, people use auxiliary channels. In extemporaneous (high anxiety) rumor construction situations, people use auxiliary channels and any other sources of information they can obtain. Channels are likely to differ with respect to age. Institutional and auxiliary channels are likely to be established or stable; other channels are likely to be novel or unstable.

Established, rather than novel, channels may lead to accuracy because information sources could be easily tagged for validity (Buckner, 1965). For example, Caplow (1947) attributed high accuracy rates in part to the ability of increasingly solid (established) channels of communication to label the quality of information sources (e.g., "This came from Joe so don't trust it; he never gives us good information"). Caplow noted that unreliable informants were excluded from the network, which thus increased rumor accuracy.

Recent Empirical Evidence

In this section we specify hypotheses based on the previous discussion— especially Buckner's (1965) framework—and report research testing these. In these investigations, we focused on factors related to group orientation. We hypothesized that rumors in groups possessing a critical set orientation ought to be more accurate; rumors in groups possessing an uncritical set ought to be less accurate. Because Buckner did not specify how critical set variables might interact, no hypothesis was made regarding the possible combinations of critical set variables (e.g., groups able to check but not possessing established channels). We also hypothesized that group orientation variables would moderate the MI–accuracy relationship.

1996 FIELD INTERVIEWS

We used data from the 1996 Field Interviews (described in chap. 6, this volume) to explore the first set of hypotheses and collected quantitative data regarding rumor accuracy and orientation. These data were subjected to qualitative analyses only (because of a small n) and served as a springboard for further discussion during the interviews. We determined accuracy by asking participants to estimate the percentage of the rumor (or rumor variants) that was true (accuracy rates were presented in Table 6.3). Group orientation attributes were explored with a series of questions that described each orientation attribute and asked respondents how characteristic the attribute was in the rumor incident they were describing. All attributes were adapted from Buckner (1965) and are presented in Exhibit 7.1. All items were followed by the open-ended query "What indicated this to you?" in an attempt to evaluate responses in terms of observable events.

Qualitative results were consistent with the hypothesis that a critical set orientation is associated with rumor accuracy. One case exemplified a less-than-critical-set orientation: Members in this organization, whose president was rumored to be working secretly for a government intelligence agency, were rated as not knowledgeable about the subject matter of the rumor, unfamiliar with this type of rumor situation, and not part of an established interaction network. In addition, most people in the group felt an emotional need to either believe or disbelieve the rumor, and were in a situation in which absolutely nothing was known (and thus checking could not occur). Rumors persisted for extended periods and remained substantially distorted compared with the remaining episodes (40% of the rumors were false).

The remaining cases exemplified the efficacy of groups with critical set orientations in discerning veracity. For example, false rumors among concerned workers that a parent company intended to sell a subsidiary eventually became more accurate as they circulated and recirculated among the subsidiary's workers. In this case, organizational members had been presented with this type of rumor situation in the past (this rumor concerned the latest in a series of company reorganizations), and, like the journalists in Buckner's (1965) example, they were acquainted with situations in which this type of rumor might arise.

Another case also illustrated the power of the group to use the rumor mill to collectively procure the facts. Prior to the announcement of a major reorganization that resulted in the closing of an entire operations center and the relocation of hundreds of employees, workers were obsessed with gathering information and rumors percolated incessantly throughout the organization. The rumors also became increasingly accurate, making the eventual formal announcement redundant. Leaks presumably spouted in the face of the irresistible force of employees' "need to know" to plan accordingly. One manager visiting the operations center remembered "getting a lot of questions asked of me." Even though she was unable to give out any information, she marveled at the productive use of rumors in collective reasoning:

> One person would see something, for example, that they're not going to fill this vacant position out here but we've got more people here—this doesn't make sense—why are they doing this?—and put this together with another piece of it—kind of talking out loud to one another—and they'd start saying "Geez, that makes sense!"

Another manager described it as the fitting together of "little pieces of a puzzle." In Buckner's terminology, this group was composed of stable communication channels in which each member's reliability was known; MI probably enhanced this group's ability to produce accurate rumors.

STUDENT RUMOR SURVEY 2

Data from Student Rumor Survey 2, which is described in chapter 6 (this volume), was also used to explore these hypotheses. Group orientation variables were group skepticism and how established communication channels were.[3] We performed hierarchical moderated regression analysis to test the moderating role of skepticism and (separately) established channels on both accuracy and the MI–accuracy relationship. Results—displayed in Table 7.2—indicated that skepticism predicted accuracy in both the main effects and moderated models. More skeptical groups tended to produce more accurate rumors overall. Yet in addition, as hypothesized, skepticism moderated the MI–accuracy relationship, as illustrated in Figure 7.1 by the slopes of regression lines linking MI to accuracy under high, average, and low levels of skepticism.[4] In high-skepticism groups, accuracy increases with MI; more interaction and recirculation brought about greater accuracy. In low-skepticism groups, accuracy did not improve with increased MI. Established channels also predicted accuracy in both main and moderated effects models. Contrary to hypothesis, however, established channels did not moderate the relationship between MI and accuracy.

---

[3] We reverse-scored group skepticism by asking participants an 8-point version of question 22 in Appendix 2.1. How established communication channels were was assessed with question 16 in Appendix 6.1. MI was obtained by averaging responses to items 14 (interaction) and 15 (recirculation) in Appendix 6.1.

[4] These slopes were computed with Table 7.2 moderated model regression coefficients under different values of the moderator variable skepticism (Aiken & West, 1991). The values used to reflect high and low skepticism were one *SD* above and one *SD* below sample means, respectively.

TABLE 7.2

Results of Hierarchical Moderated Regression Analysis Predicting Accuracy

Variable	Main effects model	Moderated model
Moderating variable: skepticism		
MI	.21^ (.12)	.17 (.12)
Skepticism	.30** (.10)	.29** (.10)
MI × Skepticism		.12* (.06)
ΔR^2		.02*
Model R^2	.04**	.06***
Adjusted R^2	.04	.05
Moderating variable: established channels		
MI	.12 (.12)	.12 (.12)
Established channels	.21* (.10)	.21* (.10)
MI × Established channels		.05 (.06)
ΔR^2		.004
Model R^2	.03*	.03*
Adjusted R^2	.02	.02

Note. MI = multiple interaction (see text). ^$p < .10$. * $p<.05$. **$p < .01$. ***$p < .001$.

Overall, these exploratory results suggest mixed support for the moderating role of group orientation variables such as skepticism. Additional research in this area should more clearly conceptualize and operationalize group orientation variables as well as the MI variable.

Implications for Organizational Rumors

We speculate that some of the previously mentioned mechanisms affecting accuracy are regularly involved in organizational contexts. First, for those rumor situations in which information is simply passed along (e.g., "I heard that the boss's wife had a baby today"), attentional narrowing and memory limitations may distort transmission. However, such distortion is likely to be counteracted by simple interaction because of redundancies and feedback. In sense-making situations (e.g., "I heard that our division is being downsized; what did you hear?"), organizational members are likely to be motivated toward accuracy, knowledgeable about issues surrounding the rumor topic (e.g., profitability of the division), and able to check (e.g., by using leaks from well-positioned sources). These features predispose accuracy. To the extent that com-

FIGURE 7.1

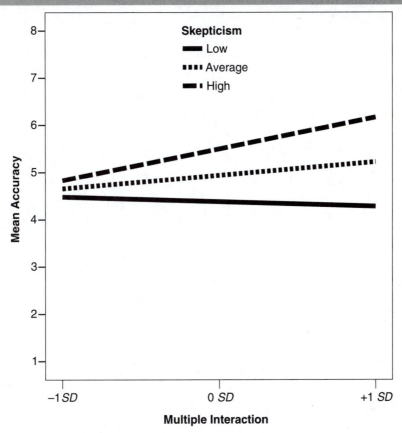

Computed slopes of regression line (predictor: multiple interaction; outcome: accuracy) at sample low, average, and high skepticism.

munication networks are established rather than novel, and when group norms favor skepticism, accuracy is also favored. Furthermore, high outcome-relevant rumors (e.g., about layoffs) are likely to be subjected to multiple interaction, especially in close networks; MI in these situations will enhance accuracy.

Thus far in this volume we have updated, explored, and expanded a number of enduring themes in rumor research: rumor concepts, effects, transmission, belief, sense making, and accuracy. We have addressed these themes from research done in a variety of contexts. In the next two chapters, we focus on two recurring themes that occur especially within organizational settings. The first of these is trust; the second, managing rumors.

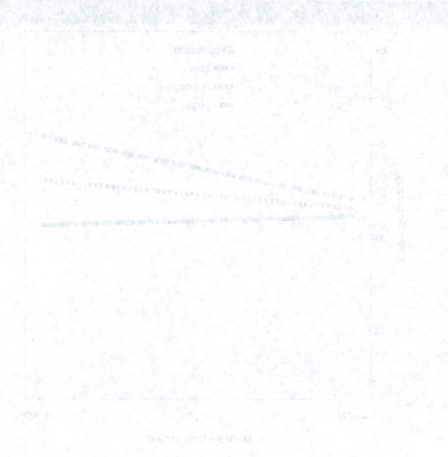

Trust and Organizational Rumor Transmission

8

For 9 hours on a hot Sunday afternoon in Sydney, Australia, police in riot gear battled 200 Aboriginal youths (Chulov, Warne-Smith, & Colman, 2004). Bricks, bottles, and firecrackers rained down on the police, 40 of whom were injured during the melee. The spark that ignited this tinderbox was a rumor that police cars had chased 17-year-old Thomas Hickey on his bicycle, causing him to fall and fatally impale himself on a steel-spiked fence. Police insisted they had been cruising the area looking for a bag-snatcher, found the impaled youth, and attempted to resuscitate him. Although a hot summer day and alcohol had contributed to this rumor-sparked riot, distrust played a foundational role.

A friend whose company was facing the prospect of severe downsizing mentioned to one of us (DiFonzo) that rumors were rampant. "What has management said about it?" I asked. He replied, "I wouldn't trust anything *they* say." We have often noticed that rumor seems to thrive where there is a dearth of trust. Yet this variable is rarely mentioned in rumor transmission literature (see chap. 3, this volume). We wondered, How is trust related to rumor transmission? In

An earlier version of this chapter can be found in DiFonzo, Bordia, and Winterkorn, 2003. We thank Rob Winterkorn for his invaluable assistance in collecting data analyzed in this chapter.

this chapter we approach this question by continuing to report the results of a longitudinal investigation of the division of a company undergoing a drastic downsizing. In chapter 2 (this volume) we introduced this study and reported the correlates of hearing rumors; in this chapter we address a different question: "How does trust in the organization affect rumor transmission?"

This question has not hitherto been quantitatively explored. We think it is important for organizational rumor transmission research, of course, but it is also important for another topic of research in applied psychology: namely, the role of trust in organizational phenomena. Interest in this latter topic has increased in recent years (Dirks & Ferrin, 2002; McEvily, Perrone, & Zaheer, 2003; Robinson, 1996; Rousseau & Tijoriwala, 1999). In particular, Dirks and Ferrin (2001) recently proposed two ways—a main effects model and a moderating effects model—by which trust affects organizational phenomena. We use these models to frame our understanding of how trust affects transmission. We begin with a discussion of how we think trust directly affects transmission, then proceed to how trust moderates the by now well-known relationships between uncertainty, anxiety, and rumor. We then present our study investigating these effects. Our findings suggest that trust—or more specifically distrust—is not peripheral to rumor transmission; indeed, it seems to play a central role.

Direct Effects of Trust on Rumor Transmission

Trust is the willingness to be vulnerable because a person thinks someone has his or her best interests at heart (Rousseau, Sitkin, Burt, & Camerer, 1998). Researchers have proposed slight variations of this definition; trust has often been operationalized as both a specific and generalized expectation of the benign nature of others' actions (Creed & Miles, 1996; Kramer, 1999). Distrust, naturally, is the obverse of this: It is the expectation of the malignant nature of others' actions. Distrust has been linked to rumor activity. After qualitative analysis of numerous rumor episodes, Shibutani (1966) concluded that when formal information is not trusted, people compensate with informal speculation, or rumor. For example, rumors in the former Soviet Union were spawned by distrust of formal news sources (Bauer & Gleicher, 1953). Despite these findings, we know of no follow-up studies quantitatively investigating trust's role in rumor transmission, especially within the organization.

Dirks and Ferrin (2001) proposed a main effects model in which trust acts directly on organizational variables and a moderator model in which trust moderates relationships between organizational variables. In the main effects model, trust acts simply to produce positive attitudes and cooperative behavior. Individuals' expectations of the benign nature of management lead to more positive appraisals of ambiguous events and to behaviors congruent with these appraisals. In a similar way, high trust in management should reduce rumor activity: "Management told us work assignments are slow lately because of a new central office accounting system. I trust them; they wouldn't lie to us." However, low trust undermines formal communications and increases the need for collective (informal) sense making. "Management *would* lie to us—they are heartless and mean-spirited. I don't believe their explanation; they intend to use this slowdown as a pretext for layoffs." Therefore, low trust should lead to more rumor activity. These ideas mesh well with Jean-Noel Kapferer's (1987/1990) emphasis on rumor as unofficial or unsanctioned information, and with that part of our definition (see chap. 1, this volume) focusing on rumor as a means of managing risk. In sum, people rely more heavily on and participate more frequently in the informal sense-making apparatus (the rumor mill) if they don't trust or if they feel threatened by the formal sense-making network (the boss or management).

Rousseau and Tijoriwala (1999) found evidence consistent with this straightforward role of trust in management during organizational change. Management explained a complex restructuring to registered nurses in a U.S. hospital as being necessary to improve quality of patient services. Trust predicted acceptance of these explanations. Nurses with low levels of trust tended to discount these official accounts for change or accounts focused on economic factors and to accept alternate explanations based on self-serving managerial motives. These researchers concluded, "High trust is likely to be associated with acceptance of information provided by management and a reduction of information-gathering efforts" (p. 524). Such alternate explanations are tantamount to rumors; the information-gathering efforts that surround them are tantamount to sense-making rumor activity. In short, distrust led to rumor activity.

In a similar way, recent organizational rumor research has incidentally noted that trust inhibited rumor activity (DiFonzo & Bordia, 1998). In interviews with corporate management, we observed an association between attitudes of distrust and rumor activity, whereas attitudes of trust seemed to reduce rumor activity. For example, corporate employees concerned about a potential major reorganization exhibited high levels of rumor activity and a lack of trust in management. Communications officials in one instance were considered almost malevolent by employees; this company experienced rampant rumor activity. However, another communications officer claimed that trust had been conscientiously built up over the years; this company experienced relatively short bouts of rumor and seemed to place faith in formal communiqués. We therefore propose that trust is negatively associated with the frequency of rumor transmission.

Moderating Effects of Trust

In the moderator model (Dirks & Ferrin, 2001), trust enhances or inhibits relationships between other variables. Dirks and Ferrin offered this example of the moderating effect of trust: High trust permits the relationship between conscientiousness (a dispositional trait) and organizational citizenship behavior (OCB). Conscientious personality should covary with OCB. Low trust, however, would inhibit the strength of such a relationship; even people who are dispositionally inclined to OCB will not exhibit such behavior in situations of low trust because to do so would violate social exchange norms. Under low trust then, conscientious personality would be unrelated to OCB. However, under conditions of high trust, conscientious behavior should be a good predictor of OCB; that is, the two variables would be related. In this example, trust plays the role of a moderator variable, a catalyst, an amplifier, a necessary but not sufficient condition.

It is important at the outset to note that a variable may have both direct and moderating effects. If we continue with the Dirks and Ferrin (2001) example, we see that trust may directly affect OCB (trust in management leads to being a good organizational citizen) and it may moderate the relationship between conscientiousness and OCB. We return to this point later in the discussion.

Dirks and Ferrin (2001) proposed that one mechanism by which trust moderates relationships is by affecting "one's interpretation of another's past action or events relating to the past action: Under high levels of trust, one is more likely to respond favorably to a partner's action than under low levels of trust" (p. 459). Trust thus helps people to interpret ambiguous actions by other people as friendly rather than hostile in intent. However, low trust engenders a hostile, rather than friendly, interpretation of events; even unambiguous and non-anxiety-producing events may become infused with hostile intent.

In the context of rumor, trust may moderate the relationship between rumor transmission and its antecedents. Uncertainty and anxiety have been linked with rumor transmission (see chap. 3, this volume). Trust should moderate these relations in a similar way; this is depicted in Figure 8.1. First, when trust is high, uncertainty and anxiety predict rumor transmission. When people trust management, they engage in rumor discussions only when they feel anxious or uncertain. Yet when trust is low, uncertainty and anxiety may not predict rumor transmission because distrust of management—"management is evil (or unjust or incompetent)"—leads to rumor transmission even when uncertainty and anxiety are minimal. When trust is low, management's actions are perceived to be hostile, even a small amount of anxiety and uncertainty becomes magnified and leads to rumors. Distrust of management may also lead to wedge rumors (rumors that are uttered mostly out of self-enhancement reasons). Again, uncertainty and anxiety result from

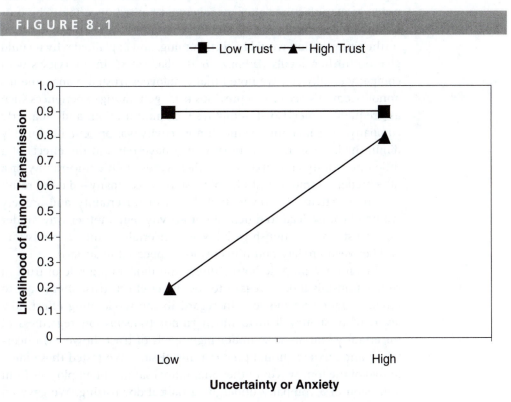

FIGURE 8.1

Hypothesized moderating role of trust on uncertainty–transmission and anxiety–transmission relationships.

interpretations of other's actions, and these interpretations hinge on trust.

Recent organizational rumor research findings are consistent with the idea of trust as a moderator; trust may have also played a moderating role in organizational rumor episodes we analyzed (DiFonzo & Bordia, 1998). In this research, distrust of the corporation may have engendered perceptions that were conducive to the generation of rumors regardless of levels of uncertainty or anxiety. That is, even small levels of uncertainty and anxiety may have found fertile ground in attitudes of distrust; thus a little uncertainty or a little anxiety—among attitudes of distrust in the company—may have been increased through negative interpretations and thus resulted in rampant rumor activity. High levels of uncertainty and anxiety, of course, would also lead to much rumor activity. In low-trust conditions then, the relationships between uncertainty and rumor, and between anxiety and rumor, would be weak, because people would be rumor active all the time.

Now consider a rumor episode we studied that seemed to exhibit high-trust conditions: Layoff rumors quickly abated at a large consumer products manufacturer after management limited uncertainty by outlining the general extent of layoffs, committed to a time line when further information would be forthcoming, and explained why it could give no further details (DiFonzo & Bordia, 1998). In interviews with company employees, we noted that employees trusted management's announcements because of previous trust-generating experiences such as frequent supervisor-to-employee communication and quarterly company-wide meetings. Some rumor activity was present, but quickly diminished. Trust in the company may have reduced the effects of a little uncertainty and anxiety. In other words, a little uncertainty or a little anxiety—among attitudes of trust in the company—did not result in rumor activity. However, high levels of uncertainty and anxiety would of course lead to much rumor activity. Put another way, under high trust, the relationships between uncertainty and transmission, and between anxiety and transmission, appeared to surface.

In sum, we propose both a direct and moderating role of trust in rumor transmission. In regard to the direct effect, trust should act to inhibit rumor transmission. In regard to the moderating effect, low levels of trust may lead to much rumor transmission regardless of uncertainty and anxiety; under high levels of trust, however, uncertainty and anxiety should predict transmission. We tested these ideas in two of the four waves of the longitudinal sample of employees from a division of a company undergoing radical downsizing. We gave an overview this study in chapter 2 (this volume); here we describe it in greater detail.

Sample, Procedure, and Instrument

Study participants consisted of 75 employees in a division of a subsidiary company of a large corporation.[1] Two employees distributed and collected each of the four waves (T1, T2, T3, T4) of the questionnaire. Each wave was administered approximately 1 month apart. Identifying information was removed from each survey. Work slowdowns and restructuring (merging of some departments in this and other divisions) were occurring prior to the first and second wave of surveys. Layoff announcements occurred between the second and third wave. Approximately 50% of employees were laid off between the third and fourth wave.

Uncertainty, anxiety, and trust were measured with a 7-point scale (see Exhibit 2.2). The number of different rumors heard during the past month was recorded. Of these, the number of different rumors passed was also recorded. By dividing the number of rumors passed along by the number of rumors heard, we assessed the proportion of heard rumors transmitted; this variable is the *likelihood of transmission* (LOT). LOT operationalizes rumor transmission as the propensity to pass along a rumor that one hears. LOT builds on previous measures of rumor transmission that listed rumors that participants had heard as well as whether or not they were passed along (Rosnow, Yost, & Esposito, 1986; see also K. Davis, 1972; Esposito, 1986/1987; Rosnow, Esposito, & Gibney, 1988; Schachter & Burdick, 1955). To maximize the reliability and validity of LOT, we had participants record a summary of the rumors that they had heard. As with previous measures of transmission (e.g., DiFonzo & Bordia, 2000), LOT was correlated with anxiety and uncertainty (see Table 8.1), which evidences the reliability and validity of this measure. Furthermore, the components of LOT—number of rumors heard and passed—both peaked at T2, which agreed with informal impressions conveyed by organizational informants.

---

[1] All 75 employees in this division received the questionnaire during wave 1 (T1); 61 (81%) returned it completed. Seventy-two employees received the questionnaire during T2; 48 (67%) returned it. Accurate response rates for T3 ($n = 40$) and T4 ($n = 29$) could not be calculated; however, estimates on the basis of layoff numbers at T3 and T4 indicated that at least 50% of surviving employees responded. Sample age group $F(3,163) = .22$, $p = .88$, tenure $F(3,163) = .17$, $p = .92$, and gender proportions $\chi^2(3) = 2.76$, $p = .43$, did not differ by wave.

TABLE 8.1

Zero-Order Correlations and Alpha Coefficients

	1	2	3	4	5	6	7	8
1. T1 LOT								
2. T1 uncertainty	.36**	.77						
3. T1 anxiety	.39**	.69**	.87					
4. T1 trust	−.47**	−.41**	−.32*	.86				
5. T2 LOT	.60**	.22	.23	−.49**				
6. T2 uncertainty	.32*	.52**	.46**	−.33*	.28	.84		
7. T2 anxiety	.40**	.61**	.68**	−.22	.27	.65**	.96	
8. T2 trust	−.55**	−.44**	−.30*	.83**	−.61**	−.41**	−.37**	.87

Note. $N = 60$ for T1–T1 correlations; $N = 46, 47$, or 48 for all other correlations. LOT = likelihood of transmission (proportion of heard rumors transmitted). Uncertainty and anxiety were transformed prior to correlation calculations. Alpha coefficients are in the diagonal. No alpha coefficients for T1 or T2 LOT could be computed because these were single-item measures. $*p < .05. **p < .01.$

Operationalizing rumor transmission in this way is appropriate given a number of different rumors in circulation over a period of time—a condition typical of organizational rumor episodes. In addition, LOT is independent of the number of rumors that a particular individual hears. The advantage of this independence becomes apparent when one considers that the alternative operationalization—number of rumors passed—depends in large part on the number of rumors that one hears; LOT accounts for this confound by being a within-subjects variable. By extension, LOT also accounts for factors known to affect the number of rumors heard, such as whether or not one is a liaison (K. Davis, 1972) and whether or not one is part of a close network (Buckner, 1965). Therefore, LOT affords the advantage that the results that obtain in this investigation cannot be caused by factors associated with the number of rumors heard.

Results

Raw variable means by wave are portrayed in Figure 8.2. T1 was a time of mounting tension. Work slowdowns and some departmental mergers had occurred; uncertainty and anxiety were at high levels. Employees were clearly hearing layoff rumors with specific and consistent numbers (25–60 employees), dates (first quarter), and departmental targets, as well as speculation about whether the division would be sold or outsourced. There seemed to be some confusion as to work

FIGURE 8.2

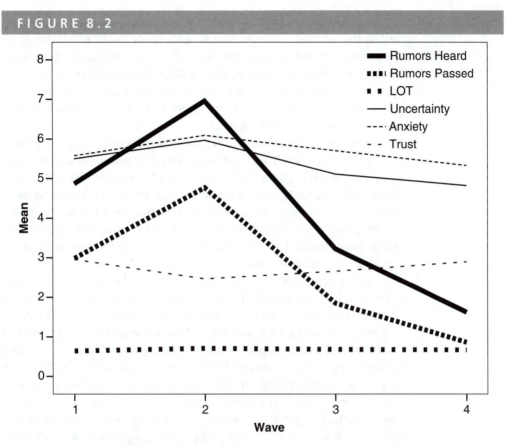

Mean number of rumors heard, number of rumors passed, likelihood of transmission uncertainty, anxiety, and trust by wave.

tasks also: Participants indicated in open-ended responses that work assignments were "not detailed," "indefinite," and "nonspecific." The picture presented is that of employees perceiving a dearth of work, speculating as to the meaning of this for the organization and for their jobs, and a reticent management. Comments evidenced a sense that employees knew the division was in trouble but "hoped against hope" that management would lead them with "a clear, well-thought-out, plan." (We note at this point that one's level of trust in management would greatly influence how these conditions were interpreted.)

T2 represents a climax; suspense peaked. T2 occurred prior to layoff announcements. Rumor activity, uncertainty, and anxiety peaked, and trust faltered. Employees' comments indicated the same queries as in T1, but also indicated increasing distrust—"The company made twice

as much money as they expected," the parent company is not committed to the division, management should "show us the commitment to
its programs," management should have "answered this question asked
directly to them; instead they deferred," and management is "keeping
everyone in the dark until the very end"—and increased anxiety—"Is
my job secure or not?" Many employees were dismayed that they had
not been told "the truth sooner."

T3 and T4 (after the layoffs) represent anger and moving-on. Uncertainty and anxiety fell, and rumor activity plunged (although the LOT
remained stable). Some residual rumors of future layoffs and sale of
the division occurred. Although on average trust rose, comments indicated that many employees were bitter: Management is not "honest,"
"Management tells its employees only what they want to in order to
keep them productive," "Employees are really being jerked around,"
"Who cares?" and "No sources can be trusted."

In the remainder of this section we describe results of tests for
effects on LOT. We specifically addressed the following questions: What
are the main effects of uncertainty, anxiety, and trust on LOT? What
are the moderating effects of trust? We performed eight hierarchical
moderated linear regression analyses.[2] We used only T1 and T2 data
in these regressions because of lower sample sizes at T3 and T4. Four
regressions tested the main effects of uncertainty and the main and
moderating effects of trust on an uncertainty–LOT relationship; results
are presented in Table 8.2. Another four regressions tested the main
effects of anxiety and the main and moderating effects of trust on an
anxiety–LOT relationship; results are presented in Table 8.3. Of each
of the four sets of analyses, two were cross-sectional and two were
longitudinal.

MAIN EFFECTS OF UNCERTAINTY
AND ANXIETY

Main effects for uncertainty (Table 8.2) and anxiety (Table 8.3)
obtained. When uncertainty was the sole predictor of LOT in each

---

[2] Missing data patterns were first analyzed longitudinally and no systematic patterns
of attrition were discovered. For example, participating in both T1 and T2 (versus only
T1) questionnaire administrations was not correlated with T1 uncertainty, anxiety, LOT,
or trust. All possible wave combinations (T1 vs. T2, T1 vs. T3, T2 vs. T3, etc.) were used.
After means and SDs were computed for each variable by wave, the dataset was screened
for correlation and regression analyses with Tabachnick and Fidell (1996/2001). Outliers
(those values whose z-scores were beyond ±3 SD from the mean) were changed to the
next most extreme score (1, uncertainty; 3, anxiety; 6, no. rumors heard, and 5, no.
rumors passed values). Multicolinearity was investigated with Mahalanobis distances;
one data point at T1 was deleted. Zero-order correlations were then calculated (Table
8.1 presents the T1 and T2 intercorrelations); all correlations did not go beyond ±.85,

cross-sectional analysis, it predicted LOT; hence there was a main effect for uncertainty. This result replicates previous research showing a relationship between uncertainty and transmission (Rosnow, 1991). The effect disappeared, however, after trust was added, indicating that distrust accounted for a large part of the LOT variance resulting from uncertainty. Put simply, in a matchup between distrust and uncertainty, the distrust variable wins hands down.

Anxiety displayed a similar pattern of results; when anxiety was the sole predictor of LOT, in each cross-sectional analysis, it predicted LOT. Hence there was a main effect for anxiety, and this result also replicates previous research showing the anxiety–LOT relationship (Rosnow, 1991). The effect disappeared or was greatly diminished, however, after trust was added, indicating that distrust accounted for a large part of the LOT variance resulting from anxiety. In a matchup between trust and anxiety, the distrust variable again wins convincingly.

These results point toward a more central, perhaps a more proximal, role for trust than heretofore theorized. With trust, we can account for a much higher proportion of LOT variance than without it. These results also extend previous rumor transmission research to a new operationalization of transmission: LOT.

MAIN EFFECTS OF TRUST

Results suggest strong support for the main negative effects of trust on both current and longitudinal rumor transmission, as predicted. As shown in Tables 8.2 and 8.3, in the cross-sectional analysis for T1, trust was a significant negative predictor of LOT in the main effects models that included either uncertainty or anxiety. It remained a significant negative predictor in the moderated effects models. In other words, trust dampened same-time LOT over and above the effects of uncertainty, anxiety, or trust-moderation. This pattern also obtained in the T2 cross-sectional analysis. Note that this same pattern also obtained for both longitudinal analyses.[3] Trust dampened future LOT over and above the effects of same-time or future-time uncertainty, anxiety, or trust-moderation. In sum, trust dampened both same-time and future LOT

---

indicating no bivariate collinearity. Bivariate scatterplots appeared to be elliptical, indicating linearity and homoscedasticity.

[3] T1 trust was a significant negative predictor of T2 LOT in the main effects models that included either T1 anxiety or uncertainty, and it remained a significant negative predictor in the moderated effects models. T1 trust was even a significant negative predictor of T2 LOT in the main effects models that included either T2 anxiety or T2 uncertainty, and it remained a significant negative predictor in the moderated effects models.

TABLE 8.2

Hierarchical Moderated Regression Analysis Predicting LOT at T1 and T2 Using Uncertainty

	T1 Cross-sectional analysis: moderating variable: T1 trust Outcome variable: T1 LOT (N = 60)		
Variable	**Main effects models**		**Moderated model**
T1 uncertainty	.09*** (.032)	.05 (.033)	.05 (.033)
T1 trust		−.13*** (.043)	−.13*** (.043)
T1 uncertainty × T1 trust			.02 (.022)
ΔR^2		.12***	.009
Model R^2	.13***	.25****	.26****
Adjusted R^2	.11	.22	.22

	T2 Cross-sectional analysis: moderating variable: T2 trust Outcome variable: T2 LOT (N = 47)		
Variable	**Main effects models**		**Moderated model**
T2 uncertainty	.06^ (.032)	.02 (.028)	.02 (.028)
T2 trust		−.18**** (.039)	−.16**** (.043)
T2 uncertainty × T2 trust			.03 (.021)
ΔR^2		.30****	.03
Model R^2	.08^	.38****	.41****
Adjusted R^2	.06	.35	.37

	Longitudinal analysis A: moderating variable: T1 trust Outcome variable: T2 LOT (N = 46)		
Variable	**Main effects models**		**Moderated model**
T2 uncertainty	.06^ (.033)	.04 (.031)	.03 (.030)
T1 trust		−.14*** (.042)	−.12** (.043)
T2 uncertainty × T1 trust			.04^ (.025)
ΔR^2		.19***	.04^
Model R^2	.07^	.26****	.31****
Adjusted R^2	.05	.23	.26

	Longitudinal analysis B: moderating variable: T1 trust Outcome variable: T2 LOT (N = 46)		
Variable	**Main effects models**		**Moderated model**
T1 uncertainty	05 (.035)	.002 (.035)	.003 (.036)
T1 trust		−.15*** (.046)	−.15*** (.047)
T1 uncertainty × T1 trust			.003 (.020)
ΔR^2		.19***	.000
Model R^2	.05	.24***	.24**
Adjusted R^2	.03	.20	.19

Note. Data reported are beta coefficients with standard errors in parentheses. LOT = likelihood of transmission (proportion of heard rumors transmitted). T1 = Time 1. T2 = Time 2. ^$p < .10$. **$p < .01$. ***$p < .005$. ****$p < .001$.

TABLE 8.3

Hierarchical Moderated Regression Analysis Predicting LOT at T1 and T2 Using Anxiety

T1 Cross-sectional analysis: moderating variable: T1 trust
Outcome variable: T1 LOT (N = 60)

Variable	Main effects models		Moderated model
T1 anxiety	.13***	.09* (.038)	.09* (.037)
T1 trust		−.13*** (.041)	−.11** (.040)
T1 anxiety × T1 trust			.07* (.029)
ΔR^2		.13***	.06*
Model R^2	.15***	.28****	.34****
Adjusted R^2	.13	.26	.31

T2 Cross–sectional analysis: moderating variable: T2 trust
Outcome variable: T2 LOT (N = 47)

Variable	Main effects models		Moderated model
T2 anxiety	.09^ (.048)	.04 (.041)	.05 (.041)
T2 trust		−.18**** (.038)	−.16**** (.039)
T2 anxiety × T2 trust			.06 (.040)
ΔR^2		.31****	.034
Model R^2	.07^	.39****	.42****
Adjusted R^2	.05	.36	.38

Longitudinal analysis A: moderating variable: T1 trust
Outcome variable: T2 LOT (N = 46)

Variable	Main effects models		Moderated model
T2 anxiety	.09^ (.049)	.07 (.044)	.09* (.044)
T1 trust		−.14**** (.040)	−.14**** (.040)
T2 anxiety × T1 trust			.08^ (.042)
ΔR^2		.21****	.05^
Model R^2	.07^	.28****	.33****
Adjusted R^2	.04	.25	.28

Longitudinal analysis B: moderating variable: T1 trust
Outcome variable: T2 LOT (N = 46)

Variable	Main effects models		Moderated model
T1 anxiety	.06 (.042)	.03 (.039)	.06 (.038)
T1 trust		−.14**** (.042)	−.11** (.042)
T1 anxiety × T1 trust			.08* (.037)
ΔR^2		.20****	.08*
Model R^2	.05	.25***	.33****
Adjusted R^2	.03	.22	.29

Note. Data reported are beta coefficients with standard errors in parentheses. LOT = likelihood of transmission (proportion of heard rumors transmitted).
^*p* < .10. **p* < .05. ***p* < .01. ****p* < .005. *****p* < .001.

even when uncertainty and anxiety were accounted for; these main effects were strong and consistent.

MODERATING EFFECTS OF TRUST

Results in Table 8.3 give strong support for the moderating effects of trust on both current and longitudinal anxiety–LOT relationships, as predicted.[4] In the cross-sectional analysis for T1, the addition of the interaction term between anxiety and trust accounted for an additional 6.1% of the variance in LOT. The beta coefficient for this interaction term was both positive and significant, indicating that high levels of trust lead to a strong anxiety–LOT relationship, whereas low levels of trust lead to a weak anxiety–LOT relationship. Figure 8.3 illustrates this relationship by showing the slopes of regression lines linking anxiety to LOT under high, average, and low levels of trust.[5] As trust throughout the sample was low, it should be noted that these values are not absolute; indeed, high trust fell at approximately the scale midpoint. Examination of Figure 8.3 illustrates that at low levels of trust, LOT was uniformly high; low-trust participants passed along most of the rumors they heard regardless of levels of anxiety. At high levels of trust, however, anxiety covaried with LOT. This same relationship was evidenced in T2 cross-sectional analysis, but was not significant.[6]

In the longitudinal analysis evaluating the moderating effect of T1 trust on the T1 anxiety–T2 LOT relationship, the addition of the interaction term accounted for an additional 8.3% of the variance, and was also significant; this interaction is illustrated in Figure 8.4. The same pattern as in the cross-sectional plot is evident here. The remaining longitudinal analysis evaluated the moderating effect of T1 trust on the T2 anxiety–T2 LOT relationship; the same pattern was again evident but only marginally significant at conventional alpha levels.[7] Even at conventional significance levels, however, we observed that T1 trust

---

[4] Hypothesized interaction effects for T1 and T2 were also tested in the hierarchical linear regressions. In this procedure, the predictor and moderator variables are centered before the interaction term is computed (Aiken & West, 1991). *Centering* refers to subtracting the mean of the variable from each value. Interaction effects—indicating moderation—are then tested in regressions after all main (centered variable) effects have been entered.

[5] These slopes were computed with Table 8.3 moderated model regression coefficients under different values of the moderator variable trust (Aiken & West, 1991). The values used to reflect high and low trust were one *SD* above and one *SD* below sample means, respectively.

[6] $p = .12$.

[7] $p = .07$.

FIGURE 8.3

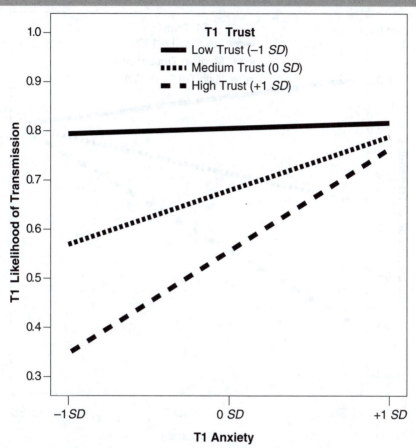

Computed slopes of regression line (predictor: T1 anxiety; outcome: T1 likelihood of transmission [LOT]) at sample low, average, and high T1 trust in the company.

moderated the relationships between T1 anxiety and both T1 LOT and T2 LOT.

Results (presented in Table 8.2) assessing the moderating effect of trust on both current and longitudinal uncertainty–LOT relationships evidenced similar patterns, but were weaker. Cross-sectional interaction terms were not significant; longitudinal interaction terms were also not significant at conventional levels.[8]

---

[8] $p = .11$ and $p = .14$.

FIGURE 8.4

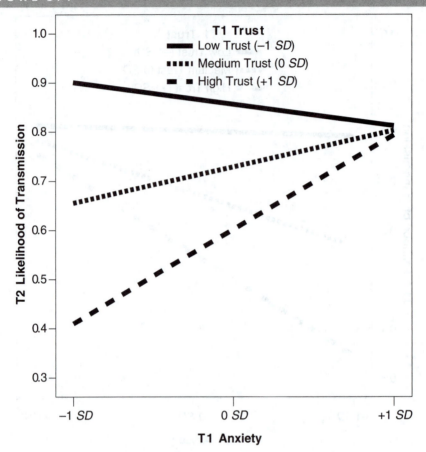

Computed slopes of regression line (predictor: T1 anxiety; outcome: T2 likelihood of transmission [LOT]) at sample low, average, and high T1 trust in the company.

In sum, trust moderated anxiety–LOT relationships: During T1 it moderated the relationships between anxiety and T1 LOT; during T2 it marginally moderated the relationship between anxiety and T2 LOT. T1 trust even longitudinally moderated the relationship between T1 anxiety and T2 LOT, and marginally moderated the relationship between T2 anxiety and T2 LOT. Similar but nonsignificant patterns obtained for uncertainty.

Trust as a Key Variable in Rumor Transmission

Results suggest that trust is perhaps a more important—and more foundational—variable in rumor transmission than is uncertainty or anxiety. Strong support was found for the main and moderating roles of trust in both cross-sectional and longitudinal anxiety–LOT relationships. Trust negatively predicted same-time and future-time rumor transmission. Trust during one time period also moderated the relationships between anxiety from the same time period and both current and future rumor transmission. Although in the predicted direction, results were nonsignificant for the moderating role of trust in uncertainty–LOT relationships.

Results not only extend the corpus of literature—rapidly increasing in size—on the various roles that trust may play in organizations (Kramer, 1999); they also are consistent with the framework proposed by Dirks and Ferrin (2001) to explain when trust would manifest itself as a main or moderating effect. These researchers proposed that trust would manifest itself as a main effect in situations of "weak" strength— that is, in situations that do not "provide clear or powerful cues that lead individuals to interpret the events in a similar way" (p. 462). In situations in which situational strength was in the "mid-range," they proposed that trust would recede to a moderating role. Situational strength in some situations may be in between weak and mid-range and may thus manifest itself as both a main and a moderating variable. Our results offer support for this conceptualization in two ways. First, uncertainty-transmission effects (although practically important) have been found to be weak to moderate ($r = .19$; Rosnow, 1991); we should therefore expect trust to manifest itself as a main effect only, which indeed occurred in every analysis we performed. Second, recalling that anxiety-transmission relationships are strong ($r = .48$; Rosnow, 1991), we should therefore expect trust to manifest itself as a moderator or as both a main effect and moderator variable. The latter indeed occurred: Trust always manifested itself as a main effect and sometimes as a moderating variable.

These results provide further insight into the high levels of rumor activity typical of situations in which formal sources of information are not trusted. Distrust may provide fertile soil for rumors that cannot easily be squelched by dispelling uncertainty and reducing anxiety. Such an instance occurred in the case of the external organizational rumor plaguing the soft drink Tropical Fantasy in 1991. Remember that false rumors circulated among the African American community that the soda was owned by the Ku Klux Klan and contained substances that would sterilize Black men. The rumor caused sales to drop by 70%. Commenting on the popularity of similar rumors in the African American community, Lorraine Hale, an African American psychologist, stated,

> Having come from a slavery background, where we were so brutalized for so long, the sense of fear we have as a people is very real. There's a mass paranoia that the objective here is to kill us out, as easily and quickly as possible. We don't articulate it, but we act on it. This leads to watchfulness and caution and suspicion, enough to question the contents in a soft drink. (as quoted in Lerbinger, 1997, p. 159; see also P. A. Turner, 1993)

In our terminology, distrust in a slightly uncertain situation led to high levels of rumor transmission. The rumor may have resisted media and government agency attempts to dispel uncertainty until then-mayor of New York City David Dinkins, himself an African American, publicly drank the soft drink (Freedman, 1991). In our terminology, trust in the formal source of information was restored for this situation. The point is, again, that trust was key.

Results also support the view of trust as a stable variable. Evidence points toward stability of trust attitudes over time. Previous longitudinal research by Robinson (1996) found a significant moderate correlation ($r = .34$) between trust in employer measured at initial employment and then after 30 months. We note that our 1-month T1 trust to T2 trust intercorrelation was the highest of all study variable pairs ($r = .83$; see Table 8.1).

Trust may also be a self-perpetuating attitude aided by the social mechanism of rumor. Robinson's (1996) research showed that trust at time of hire exerted both main and moderation effects 18 and 30 months later. In particular, initial trust predicted and moderated later interpretations of breach of psychological contract. Consistent with this research, our results also evidenced longitudinal effects of trust for impending layoffs that were often seen as unfair. Indeed, low-trust individuals engaged in more rumor transmission. Higher rates of transmission of negative rumors among low-trust individuals may help entrench interpretations that ensure subsequent deteriorations in trust (cf. similar effects of gossip in Burt & Knez, 1996). As our study was mainly concerned with rumors about negative outcomes, future research should test this idea among organizations experiencing rumors about positive outcomes. Such positive rumors presumably would help to enhance trust over time. We also note that future research should strive to identify other modes of measurement besides self-report.

Practical implications of these results include the importance of addressing attitudes of trust in formal sources of information (see also DiFonzo & Bordia, 2000). Dispelling uncertainty and reducing anxiety may not dampen rumor activity without attention to levels of inter-group trust. Rumors of plant closings and downsizings, for example, may not be diminished by announcements to the contrary, unless the source of the rebuttal is judged to be honest and trustworthy (Bordia, DiFonzo, & Schulz, 2000). These implications seem particularly relevant to situations involving organizational change, the focus of this study. Explanations by management may effectively become impotent when given to employees who do not trust management. Interpretations—based on employee perceptions of the company as caring, honest, and trustworthy—may determine the extent to which official explanations are accepted and acted on.

Conclusion

In summary, the results of our study suggest that trust is a key variable in rumor transmission and is likely to play a central role in organizational rumor activity in at least two ways. First, distrust in the organization is likely to fuel rumor activity. For example, if an employee perceives the company to be uncaring and dishonest, he or she is unlikely to rely on their explanations to account for recent changes in personnel that affect the quality of his or her job. Second, trust is likely to alter the relationships between uncertainty, anxiety, and rumor. When trust in the company is low, employees may be especially prone to engage in rumor discussions regardless of their levels of uncertainty or anxiety; when trust is high, such rumor discussions are necessary only under conditions of high uncertainty or anxiety. For example, if I, as an employee, perceive the company as uncaring and dishonest, even small amounts of uncertainty and anxiety are enough to make me concerned. I am then likely to participate in rumor discussions because I think that my coworkers in the rumor mill—but not the management—have my best interests at heart. Even rumors appearing during times of quiescence and stability would receive lots of my attention because they might protect me from dreaded consequences that the company did not care about. However, when I trust the company, there is no need to pay much attention to rumors because the company explanation can be relied on; I need turn to rumors only when the company is unable to quell my uncertainty or anxiety. Future research should seek to replicate these patterns in other arenas—both field and experimental—

and should seek to further clarify the nature of the relationship between trust and transmission. Future transmission research—in whatever venue—should routinely measure trust in formal communication sources.

In the next chapter, we continue in an organizational vein and discuss empirical evidence pertaining to the management of rumor.

Rumor Management

9

In the late 1990s, we were hired by the Procter & Gamble Corporation (P&G)—a major manufacturer of household products—as expert witnesses in a court case involving perhaps the most famous external corporate rumor of the 20th century (Fine, 1992; Green, 1984; Marty, 1982; Mikkelson, 2003; Pinsdorf, 1987; we introduced this rumor in chap. 1, this volume). Having first targeted the McDonald's Corporation in the late 1970s, the famous—and false—Satanism rumor has bedeviled P&G since 1981 (Koenig, 1985, p. 42). The rumor, which is entirely false, states that the president of P&G appeared on *The Phil Donahue Show* to say that he was "coming out of the closet" with regard to his Satanism. The rumor, in all its forms and facets, is categorically false, yet at times its spread was wide enough to result in approximately 15,000 phone calls per month to P&G. P&G's response to this rumor has been multipronged. Enlisting the help of high-ranking religious leaders, they compiled a "truth kit" to debunk it, which they sent to individuals who contacted them and to churches in areas where the rumor was breaking out. At times they marshaled a nationwide press campaign denouncing the rumor. Finally, they sued—often successfully—competitors who had spread the rumor. These efforts have dampened rumor activity.

W e have shown in this volume how rumors can be a problem. The false rumor that McDonald's uses worm meat in its burgers led to a drop in sales of up to 30% in some areas (Tybout, Calder, & Sternthal, 1981). As noted earlier, the false rumor that Procter & Gamble is associated with Satanism led to 15,000 calls a month on the consumer help-line (Austin & Brumfield, 1991). Rumors of layoffs were associated with increased change-related stress among employees of a metropolitan hospital undergoing restructuring (Bordia, Jones, Gallois, Callan, & DiFonzo, in press). Rumors that a police chase led to the accidental death of an Aboriginal boy led to rioting and attacks on police in Sydney, Australia (Chulov, Warne-Smith, & Colman, 2004). In situations like these, effective management and control of rumors is vital to the management of the crisis situation. How can rumors be effectively managed? In this chapter we review the literature on rumor management, including our own empirical work, and present guidelines for preventing and neutralizing rumors. We begin with a general review of the literature on rumor-quelling strategies. Next, we explore in more detail the role of rumor rebuttals (or denials) in reducing belief in rumors. Finally, we provide some general guidelines on rumor management.

Rumor-Quelling Strategies

In understanding the role of rumor-quelling strategies in curbing rumors, it is useful to consider each strategy in the context of the life cycle of rumors. Recall that the life cycle of rumors can be divided into three stages: Generation, evaluation (or belief), and transmission (DiFonzo, Bordia, & Rosnow, 1994). Rumor is generated in times of uncertainty and anxiety regarding topics of high importance. Next, the rumor is evaluated for plausibility or belief; this process occurs at the individual and group levels. A rumor that meets the standards of plausibility gets widely circulated in the transmission stage. The rumor-quelling strategies can be aimed at each stage. Some strategies can reduce generation (and thereby prevent rumors or reduce the inclination to participate in a rumor discussion); others reduce belief in the rumor; and still others target transmission.

Table 9.1 provides a summary of rumor-quelling strategies drawn from a review of psychological and business literature. From each paper listed, we gleaned recommendations aimed at curbing rumors. The specific recommendations were then condensed into general categories of quelling strategies. The articles summarized in Table 9.1 include

TABLE 9.1

Inventory of Rumor-Quelling Strategy Literature

Reference	RQS investigated or proposed	RQS class (ultimate aim)
F. H. Allport & Lepkin, 1945	"Rumor clinic": publication of rumor and strong rebuttal with evidence.	Reduce belief
Austin & Brumfield, 1991	1. Rebut with facts from neutral stakeholders to enquirers.	Reduce belief
	2. File lawsuits for libel; use private detectives.	Reduce transmission
	3. Remove trademark or change trademark (to reduce activation of negative cues).	Reduce belief
	4. Rebut to consumers in affected regions (not enquirers).	Reduce belief
K. Davis, 1972, 1975	Prevent them by	
	1. providing information regarding important events.	Reduce uncertainty
	2. providing emotional and economic security.	Reduce anxiety
	3. fostering a cooperative environment.	Reduce belief
	Refute them by	
	4. vanquishing the rumor with truth.	Reduce uncertainty
	5. not repeating the rumor.	Reduce transmission
	6. rebutting early.	Reduce transmission
	7. rebutting by appropriate spokesperson.	Reduce belief
	8. rebutting face-to-face.	Reduce belief
	9. listening for gaps in information.	Reduce uncertainty
	10. listening for feelings.	Reduce anxiety
Esposito & Rosnow, 1983	Internal rumors:	
	1. Keep employees informed.	Reduce uncertainty
	2. Heed rumor (assess and address underlying concerns).	Reduce anxiety
	3. Act promptly; don't repeat.	Reduce transmission
	4. Enlighten personnel.	Reduce belief
	External rumors:	
	5. Rebut.	Reduce belief

continued

TABLE 9.1 *(Continued)*

Inventory of Rumor-Quelling Strategy Literature

Reference	RQS investigated or proposed	RQS class (ultimate aim)
Festinger et al., 1948	1. Give detailed information.	Dispel uncertainty
	2. Integrate old leaders into new activities.	Reduce transmission
	3. Leader rebuts rumor in a public forum.	Reduce uncertainty, anxiety, and belief
	4. Remove rumor instigator.	Reduce transmission
Goswamy & Kumar, 1990	1. Give "prohibitory orders" banning assembly curfew.	Reduce transmission
	2. Arrest or detain opposition leader.	Reduce transmission
	3. Increase counterpropaganda.	Reduce belief
Gross, 1990	Denial by rumored party.	Reduce belief
Hershey, 1956	1. Keep normal communication channels open.	Reduce uncertainty
	2. Don't use public address system to rebut rumor.	Reduce transmission
	3. Present facts about the topic rather than disprove rumor.	Reduce uncertainty
	4. Prevent idleness and monotony.	Reduce transmission
	5. Campaign against rumors; ridicule rumor mongering.	Reduce transmission
	6. Develop faith in the source of management's communications.	Reduce belief
	7. Educate supervisors in rumor dynamics.	Reduce uncertainty, belief, and transmission
	8. Distract people's attention from rumor area.	Reduce anxiety and transmission
	9. Ask the question "What anxiety or attitude does this rumor reflect?" Then relieve tension by correcting the situation that caused it.	Reduce anxiety
Iyer & Debevec, 1991	1. Rebuttal	Reduce belief
	2. No rebuttal	Reduce belief
Jaeger, Anthony, & Rosnow, 1980	Rebuttal	Reduce belief
Kapferer, 1989	1. Rebuttal	Reduce belief
	2. Police investigations	Reduce transmission
Kapferer, 1990	Press release	Reduce uncertainty and belief

Kimmel & Keefer, 1991	1. Reduce uncertainties about the disease.	Reduce uncertainty
R. H. Knapp, 1944	1. Give complete and accurate information (prudent censorship).	Reduce uncertainty
	2. Create and sustain faith in leaders.	Reduce anxiety
	3. Tell news quickly and completely.	Reduce uncertainty and anxiety
	4. Make information accessible (e.g., educational meetings).	Reduce uncertainty
	5. Prevent idleness, monotony, and personal disorganization.	Reduce transmission
	6. Campaign deliberately against rumor mongering.	Reduce transmission
Koenig, 1985	1. Open business rumor control centers (24 hours).	Reduce uncertainty
	2. Have a skeptical outlook.	Reduce belief
Koller, 1992	1. Rebuttal	Reduce belief
	2. Positive advertising	Positive advertisement
	3. No response	Reduce belief
Litwin, 1979	Use key communicators to spread accurate information.	Reduce uncertainty
McMillan, 1991	1. Remove doors (improve access to managers).	Reduce uncertainty
	2. Confirm rumors.	Reduce uncertainty
	3. Hold regular monthly town meetings.	Reduce uncertainty
	4. Install a toll-free phone line for inquiries.	Reduce uncertainty
Ponting, 1973	Rumor control center	Reduce uncertainty
R. H. Turner, 1994	1. Intervene quickly.	Reduce transmission
	2. Collect rumors, assemble independent panel of local experts to investigate them, and issue a point-by-point rebuttal rather than a general denial.	Reduce belief
	3. Widely disseminate this rebuttal through formal channels.	Reduce transmission
Weinberg & Eich, 1978	Rebut rumor with a neutral source (a credible "rumor control center").	Reduce belief

Note. RQS = rumor-quelling strategy.

strategies aimed at all three stages in the rumor life cycle. The most common recommendation for reducing generation of rumors is to reduce uncertainty. This goal can be achieved by providing accurate and timely information and having open channels of communication. However, only a few authors suggest reducing anxiety, which perhaps reflects the difficulty in achieving this goal; K. Davis (1975) and Hershey (1956) recommended reducing anxiety by providing emotional and economic security to employees, and R. H. Knapp (1944) suggested inculcating trust in leaders.

The most frequent recommendation aimed at reducing belief in the rumor was the use of rebuttal, including suggestions to strengthen rebuttals by garnering the support of neutral spokespersons. For example, R. H. Turner (1994) found that Chinese earthquake rumor abatement strategies include assembling a local panel of experts to evaluate the rumors and issue a point-by-point rebuttal rather than a general denial; these methods have been reported to be nearly universally successful. Belief could also be reduced by increasing skepticism (Koenig, 1985), fostering a cooperative, trusting environment (K. Davis, 1975), and even using counterpropaganda (Goswamy & Kumar, 1990). Finally, several rumor-quelling strategies were aimed at reducing transmission. These included strategies that dissuade people from spreading the rumor, including punitive steps such as police investigations (Kapferer, 1989) and lawsuits (Austin & Brumfield, 1991). Of course, reducing generation and belief should also indirectly reduce transmission of rumors.

We wondered how commonly these strategies were used and how effective they were in quelling rumors. These questions were part of our investigation of 74 highly experienced public relations (PR) professionals introduced in chapter 2 (this volume; DiFonzo & Bordia, 2000). Recall that the respondents had on average over 26 years of experience in PR or corporate communication roles and came from several sectors, including automotive, aerospace, banking and finance, health care, retail, and transportation. In this part of the study, we presented the PR professionals with a list of 17 strategies to prevent or neutralize (i.e., counteract) rumors. These strategies (see Figure 9.1 and Appendix 2.1) represented an exhaustive list gleaned from existing literature on rumor management and from the results of our own interviews with managers and PR officers. For each strategy, participants were asked if they had used the strategy to prevent or neutralize rumors; each participant then rated the effectiveness of the strategy. Results showed that these strategies were commonly used and 15 of the 17 strategies had been used by over a third of the participants. Rumor prevention strategies, such as stating the values and procedures that will guide organizational changes, were the most commonly used. Strategies that

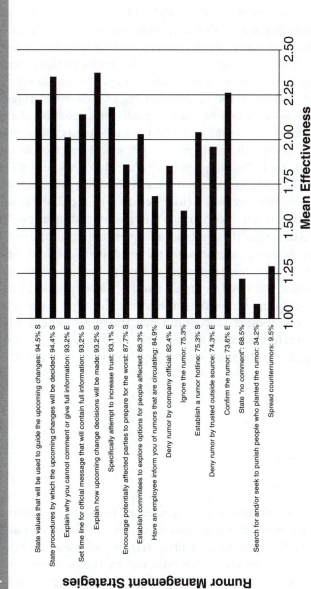

FIGURE 9.1

Rumor strategies and mean effectiveness ratings. Strategies are in decreasing order by percentage of respondents who had ever used it to prevent or neutralize rumors. Mean effectiveness rating is on a scale on which 1, 2, and 3 indicate low, medium, and high average effectiveness, respectively. *S* indicates a structuring-uncertainty strategy and *E* indicates one that enhances official communication (see text). From "How Top PR Professionals Handle Hearsay: Corporate Rumors, Their Effects, and Strategies to Manage Them," by N. DiFonzo and P. Bordia, *Public Relations Review, 26,* p. 182. Copyright 2000 by Elsevier. Reprinted with permission.

involved counteroffensive measures, such as searching for or seeking to punish people who planted the rumor and spread counterrumors, were the least likely to be used.

To group the strategies into common underlying dimensions, we conducted a principal components analysis on the effectiveness ratings. The analysis revealed two underlying dimensions: structuring uncertainty and enhancing formal communications. Structuring uncertainty means to limit it in some way. Uncertainty is a major cause of rumors and structuring it is not surprisingly a way to prevent or control rumors (Davis, 1972; Hirschhorn, 1983). These strategies included stating values and procedures that will be used to guide the upcoming changes and providing time lines by which official announcements will be made. These strategies restrict the range of uncertainty ("I don't know what will happen, but I will find out next week" or "I don't know if I will be affected by the restructuring, but I know that they will take work unit performance into account before deciding to break them up"). Strategies that structured uncertainty were rated overall as more effective than were strategies that enhanced formal communications.

The *enhancing formal communication* strategies involved denying the rumor by internal or external sources, or confirming the rumor. Confirming the rumor was rated as highly effective, albeit sparingly used; this strategy may be applicable only in rare instances, but is very effective in neutralizing rumors. Once confirmed, the rumor generally loses its unique informational value and is likely to subside. We now turn to the strategy of rebutting rumor and the effectiveness of rebuttals in rumor quelling.

Rumor Rebuttals

One of the most common strategies used in response to a harmful rumor is to deny the rumored allegation (Kimmel, 2004b). This denial may take many forms, such as a press release, full-page newspaper advertisements, statements by CEOs on company Web sites, testimonials and endorsements by neutral third parties, and so on. Although commonly used, rebuttal is a controversial strategy. Business writer Owen Edwards (1989) asserted, "About the only way not to counter a rumor is to deny it, since any denial tends to give rumor added clout. The more vehement the denial, the more credible the story becomes" (p. 228). However, Professor of Sociology Frederick Koenig strongly recommended it: "If a company is the target of a rumor, it should deny it immediately as forcefully and publicly as possible, showing the evidence that proves it is unfounded" (quoted in Goleman, 1991).

As we showed in chapter 4, rumor rebuttals reduce belief in rumor. Academic literature suggests, however, that some variables may moderate this effect. Iyer and Debevec (1991) exposed participants to allegations of harmful effects of environmental tobacco smoke (ETS). The allegations were attributed to one of three sources: a neutral source (a TV station), a negative stakeholder (R. J. Reynolds), and a positive stakeholder (American Cancer Association). Next, the allegation was rebutted by a neutral source (*The Boston Globe* newspaper) or by a low credibility source (R. J. Reynolds) in an inflammatory tone or in a conciliatory tone. Iyer and Debevec also had a condition involving no rebuttal. The dependent measure was attitude toward ETS. The results showed that the conciliatory denial was effective (more positive attitudes toward ETS) when the allegations arose from a positive stakeholder. A neutral source rebuttal was similarly more effective when the source of the allegation was neutral. Yet when the source of the allegation was a negative stakeholder (R. J. Reynolds), not rebutting the allegation led to the most favorable attitude. This result is not surprising, as a rebuttal from R. J. Reynolds after an allegation from the same source (i.e., R. J. Reynolds) would be a strange occurrence. Thus, on balance, Iyer and Debevec (1991) found support for the effectiveness of rebuttals, but the results suggest that denial source characteristics (neutral vs. low credibility source) may render a denial more or less effective.

In our own research, we have approached rumor rebuttals as persuasive messages; their aim is to persuade the audience to disbelieve the rumor. The social–psychological literature on persuasion and attitude change has addressed characteristics of the source and content of the message that determine the persuasiveness of the message (Petty & Wegener, 1998). For example, a message delivered by a source of high credibility is more persuasive than is a message delivered by a low-credibility source. In a similar way, a message with high-quality arguments is more likely to persuade the audience than is one with low-quality arguments. With the aid of this framework, we now discuss two sets of moderating variables that we investigated: denial source characteristics and denial message characteristics.

DENIAL SOURCE CHARACTERISTICS

Rebuttal effectiveness is enhanced when the source of the rebuttal matches the scope of the rumor. For example, in an organizational context, if the rumor is about a departmental policy or process, the department head is the appropriate source to rebut the rumor. A line employee would be too low in the official structure, not likely to be in a decision-making role, and therefore not be a persuasive source. However, the CEO of the organization would be too far removed from departmental matters and therefore not expected to comment on a department-level rumor. In fact, the involvement of the CEO may even raise suspicion among staff that matters may be grave. As one PR officer observed,

> If the building is on fire, the chairman should go and take over because it's very serious. If a manager on the sixth floor has a fire, you don't send the chairman, because what ends up happening is that it's just a little fire, and if he runs in there, he will get this fire smell all over his clothes, and it takes a long time for the smell to go away. (DiFonzo et al., 1994, pp. 59–60)

We tested these ideas in the context of a rumor about student entry requirements in a psychology department in a university in Australia (Bordia, DiFonzo, & Travers, 1998). Places in the undergraduate program were in high demand and students were often anxious about getting admitted. Rumors about entry requirements were widespread. The study was conducted in a laboratory setting. Participants were exposed to a rumor that the grade point average required for entry into second-year undergraduate courses would be going up next year. The participants were first-year students and therefore the rumor was realistic and important. The rumor was denied by one of four sources: a fellow student, a lecturer in the department, the head of the department (HOD), or the CEO of the university (known as the vice chancellor or VC). We expected that the HOD would be the most effective in reducing belief and anxiety associated with the rumor because the HOD would be the one to make the decisions about entry requirements and therefore the most knowledgeable about departmental matters. Therefore, we also hypothesized that the HOD would be rated as the most appropriate source to deny this rumor. The student and lecturer sources are not in decision-making roles and therefore lack the credibility required to refute the rumor. The VC would be too high in the university administration hierarchy and therefore not likely to be relevant as a source on a department-level matter. Finally, we hypothesized that the denial would be successful in reducing belief and anxiety associated with the rumor; belief and anxiety were measured before and after presentation of the denial statement. As expected, overall, denial did reduce belief and anxiety associated with the rumor. Furthermore, the HOD condition had the greatest reduction in belief and anxiety, as shown in Figure 9.2. In addition, Figure 9.2 shows that the HOD was rated as the most appropriate source.

Although our prediction about source appropriateness was supported, we wondered what underlies a judgment about appropriate-

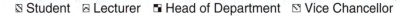

FIGURE 9.2

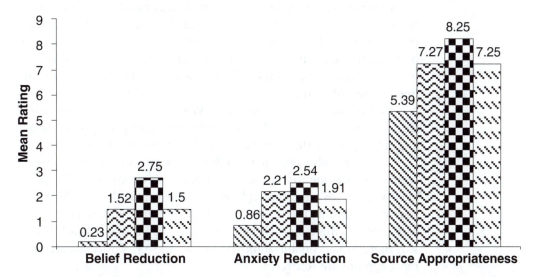

Mean belief reduction, anxiety reduction, and source appropriateness ratings for rumor denials issued by sources that varied in appropriateness. Rumor that the grade point average required for entry into second-year undergraduate courses will be going up next year. Data from Bordia et al., 1998.

ness. And, as we saw in chapter 8 (this volume), rumors often circulate in tense and conflict-ridden settings, such as organizational restructuring. In such situations, employees can be suspicious of management intentions and not believe rumor rebuttals. Thus, perceptions of source honesty should be particularly important for effective rebuttal. Indeed, research on source characteristics in persuasion notes that perceptions of source honesty play a very important role in assessments of message accuracy (Priester & Petty, 1995). We conducted another study to test these ideas (Bordia, DiFonzo, & Schulz, 2000). In this study we predicted that sources high on perceived honesty and appropriateness would be effective in reducing belief and anxiety associated with the rumor. The study was conducted on an Australian university campus at which a rumor was spreading among the undergraduate students that the undergraduate library was being closed down. We rebutted this rumor by one of the following three sources in a between-groups design: a library staff member on the loans desk, the librarian, or the VC.

The results on denial effectiveness replicated Bordia et al. (1998): Both belief and anxiety were significantly lower after the denial.

Moreover, as predicted, the denials were the most effective in reducing belief in the rumor when the sources were perceived to be high on honesty and appropriateness (see Figure 9.3; note that honesty was not a manipulated variable; it was simply measured). In other words, honesty and appropriateness had an additive effect in reducing belief in the rumor. With regard to anxiety reduction, only source honesty had a main effect; that is, anxiety was reduced most when the source was perceived to be honest. These results dovetail nicely with our findings regarding the moderating role of trust on rumor transmission reported in chapter 8 (this volume). When the information source is trusted (i.e., honest), a rebuttal is effective in dispelling uncertainty and anxiety; when the source is not trusted, the rebuttal is less effective.

The results also provided insights into what may underlie assessments of source appropriateness. Appropriateness was positively correlated with knowledgeability ("How knowledgeable do you think this source is regarding the rumor?") and status in the management structure. Because this rumor alleged the closure of a university facility and was therefore an organization-level topic, the VC was considered the most appropriate source.

FIGURE 9.3

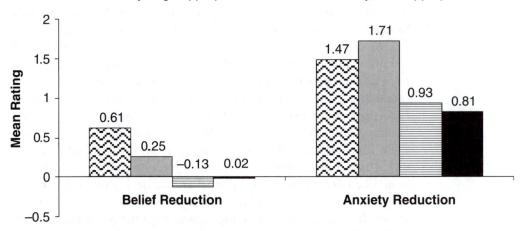

Mean belief reduction and anxiety reduction for rumor denials issued by sources high or low in appropriateness and honesty. Rumor that undergraduate library will close down. Data from Bordia et al., 2000.

DENIAL MESSAGE CHARACTERISTICS

Another set of studies provided insights into message characteristics required for belief and anxiety reduction. First, denials that assist recipients in attaining a sense of control over potential threats can relieve anxiety (Bordia, DiFonzo, Haines, & Chaseling, 2005). In these studies we tested the effectiveness of rebuttals in reducing belief and anxiety associated with the Good Times virus rumor. This rumor, which spread over the Internet in late 1990s, alleged that a virus was being circulated by e-mail and merely reading a text message would infect the computer. The rumor caused concern among e-mail users and warnings of the alleged virus were forwarded to friends and coworkers, creating increased Internet traffic and concerned inquiries to technical support staff. Accurate information debunking the rumor was also available on the Internet.

In our studies, we presented the hoax e-mail to participants and measured belief and anxiety associated with this rumor. Next, we presented another e-mail that rebutted the rumor and again measured belief and anxiety. In the first study we found that the denial was successful in reducing belief and anxiety associated with the rumor. Moreover, this denial was more effective than a control condition in which participants were exposed to a message that was unrelated to the virus rumor. In the second study, we compared the denial with a control message that was on the topic of computer viruses but did not explicitly deny the rumor. Instead, the message provided information on how to safeguard against computer viruses. It is interesting to note that although the denial was significantly better than this control message in reducing belief in the rumor, the difference in anxiety reduction was small and not statistically significant. The control message, by providing information and coping strategies, alleviated some anxiety. In the third study, we incorporated these anxiety-alleviating elements into the denial ("Being informed about viruses is the best defense for future protection of your computer files. A computer virus is a snippet of computer code that must infect a host program to spread. The best way to detect these pathogenic computer codes is to install an antivirus program checker"). This denial, which aided participants in regaining a sense of control, was effective in reducing belief and anxiety; these results are shown in Figure 9.4.

Second, another line of research has suggested that the inclusion of rebuttal context may moderate denial effectiveness. These studies examined the effects of a rebuttal in the presence or absence of a prior accusation. Koller (1993) found that the rebuttal source is evaluated more negatively when there is no prior accusation. In the absence of a

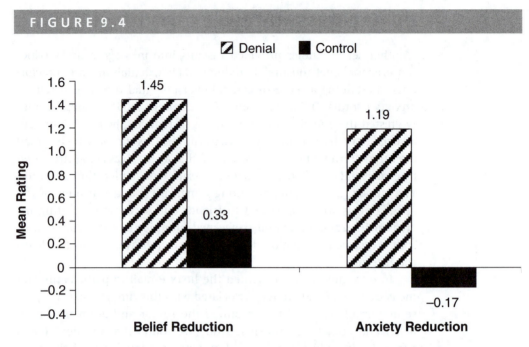

FIGURE 9.4

Mean belief reduction and anxiety reduction for denial of the Good Times rumor. Data from Bordia, DiFonzo, Haines, and Chaseling, 2005, Study 3.

prior accusation, the audience finds the rebuttal puzzling and suspicious and evaluates the rebutter negatively. In an early study demonstrating this effect (Yandell, 1979), three experimental conditions were created. First, an actor was accused of damaging a typewriter, and the actor subsequently denied having done so. The second condition involved a denial in the absence of an accusation. In condition three, the actor confessed to damaging the typewriter. The actor was more likely to be seen as being guilty in the second (denial-only) condition compared with the first (accusation + denial). In fact, ratings of guilt in the second condition were as high as when the actor confessed to damaging the typewriter. Yandell concluded in attributional terms that the accusation provided a situational explanation for the denial. However, a denial in the absence of an accusation was attributed to guilty conscience and led to an impression of guilt. A similar effect was noted by Wegner, Wenzlaff, Kerker, and Beattie (1981) in their study on the innuendo effect of newspaper headlines. They found that whereas the denial only ("Bob Talbert not linked with Mafia"; $M = 3.73$) led to less negative impressions than did the assertion ("Bob Talbert linked with Mafia"; $M = 4.25$), the negative impressions were not as low as in the control condition ("Bob Talbert celebrates birthday"; $M = 3.00$). In fact, the denial condition was not significantly different from the assertion or the control condition.

How might we understand these results? Holtgraves and Grayer (1994) applied attribution theory and Grice's (1975) maxims of conversation to the study of denials in a courtroom setting. Grice's maxim of quantity states that a speaker should be as informative as the situation demands. Holtgraves and Grayer postulated that a denial, in the absence of an accusation, leads to the violation of the quantity maxim. When faced with an overinformative denial, the audience is motivated to explain this violation, which results in an attribution of guilt and low ratings of the person on characteristics such as trustworthiness. Their findings supported the predictions. Thus, rebuttal context affected rebuttal effectiveness.

This line of research has primarily been conducted in the context of allegations aimed at individuals. We applied this research to the context of rumors of product contamination and rebuttals by corporations (Bordia, DiFonzo, Irmer, Gallois, & Bourne, 2005). We investigated whether the inclusion of rebuttal context moderated the effectiveness of denial. First, we wanted to compare a message that states the rumor and then rebuts it (rumor + denial) with a message that rebuts without repeating the rumor (denial-only). Second, we also wanted to compare these rebuttals with a condition that follows the advice of some PR practitioners and responds only with "our policy is not to respond to rumors" (i.e., a no-comments approach). Third, we wanted to see how these three strategies (denial-only, rumor + denial, or no comments) fared in comparison to a rumor-only condition.

The study was conducted in a laboratory setting and participants were presented with a fictional newspaper story that reported a statement by a consumer products manufacturer, PBR. The story noted that PBR was plagued by a rumor that one of the ingredients in its products was harmful to consumers. Four conditions were created. The text in the four conditions is presented in Exhibit 9.1. In the rumor-only condition, the newspaper story reported the rumor about PBR. In the rumor + denial condition, the rumor was reported followed by a statement by PBR that repeated the rumor and then rebutted it. In the denial-only condition, no mention was made of the rumor. Instead PBR statement adopted a rebuttal stance and insisted that its products were safe for consumers. Finally, in the no-comments condition, the rumor was presented and the PBR statement said that PBR does not comment on rumors. We measured the following responses to the news story: the amount of uncertainty regarding the reasons for the press statement, suspicion of PBR, attribution of the statement to an

EXHIBIT 9.1

Text for Conditions of Rebuttal-Context Investigations

Rumor only	Rumor + denial	Denial only	No comments
PBR Product Safety Rumors *Nigel Wilson, Economics Correspondent* PBR is one of Australia's largest food product manufacturers. Rumors have been circulating recently about PBR's product safety. According to the rumors some of the ingredients in PBR's products are harmful to consumers. When we contacted PBR regarding the rumors, they said an official statement regarding the rumors would be released the next day.	**PBR says, "Rumors are false and malicious"** *Nigel Wilson, Economics Correspondent* PBR is one of Australia's largest food product manufacturers. Rumors have been circulating recently about PBR's product safety. According to the rumors some of the ingredients in PBR's products are harmful to consumers. At a press conference yesterday, a PBR company spokesman made the following statement: "PBR is a target of malicious and false rumors. These rumors claim that our products are contaminated and are therefore harmful to our consumers. Let me clearly state that PBR's products are *not* harmful to consumers. These rumors are baseless and spread by competitors wanting to damage our reputation and sales. We routinely conduct extensive testing of our products to ensure they meet the highest safety standards. To verify our claims we invited the National Health Authority to conduct independent tests. The National Health Authority found that our products are completely safe and not only meet but exceed national standards on food safety."	**PBR says, "Our products are safe"** *Nigel Wilson, Economics Correspondent* PBR is one of Australia's largest food product manufacturers. At a press conference yesterday, a PBR company spokesman made the following statement: "Let me clearly state that PBR's products are *not* harmful to consumers. We routinely conduct extensive testing of our products to ensure they meet the highest safety standards. To verify our claims we invited the National Health Authority to conduct independent tests. The National Health Authority found that our products are completely safe and not only meet but exceed national standards on food safety." PBR did not elaborate on the reason for making this announcement.	**PBR Product Safety Rumors** *Nigel Wilson, Economics Correspondent* PBR is one of Australia's largest food product manufacturers. Rumors have been circulating recently about PBR's product safety. According to the rumors some of the ingredients in PBR's products are harmful to consumers. At a press conference yesterday, a PBR company spokesman declined to comment. According to the spokesman, "PBR's policy is not to respond to rumors."

internal (something about PBR) versus an external (something about the environment) cause, perceptions of a cover-up by PBR, an overall evalutation of PBR, and finally intentions to purchase PBR products.

The results of the study provide unequivocal support for the denial strategy and no support for a no-comments strategy (see Figure 9.5; all differences in conditions discussed here are based on statistically significant differences). The no-comments condition was very similar to the rumor-only condition on most of the variables. In fact, it was even worse than the rumor-only condition on perceptions of cover-up. That is, on reading that the company was declining to comment on the rumor, participants felt that the company had something to hide.

Next, we compared the denial-only condition with the rumor + denial condition. As expected, level of uncertainty for the reasons for the press statement was the highest for the denial-only condition. Moreover, the press statement was attributed to more internal causes in the denial-only condition than in the rumor + denial condition. Also, perceptions of the cover-up were higher, and evaluation of the company lower, in the denial-only condition compared with the rumor

FIGURE 9.5

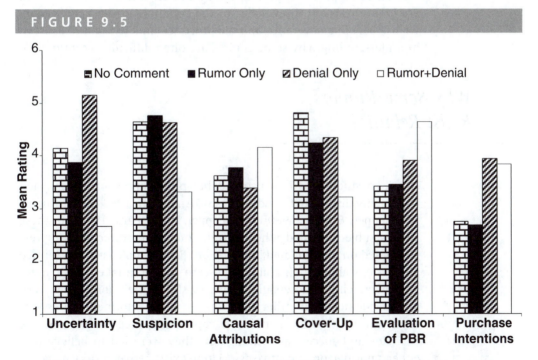

Mean ratings of uncertainty, suspicion, external attributions, cover-up intentions, company evaluation, and purchase intention. Rumor that PBR products are dangerous. All constructs measured on a 1 to 7 Likert-type scale. Data from Bordia, DiFonzo, Irmer, et al., 2005.

+ denial condition. Finally, there was no difference in the two denial conditions for purchase intentions.

Overall, these results suggest the following: (a) a no-comments strategy at best has the same effect as saying nothing, and at worst leads to greater perceptions of cover-up; (b) both denial-only and rumor + denial are significantly better than saying nothing (i.e., rumor-only or no comments) for evaluation of the company and purchase intentions; and (c) repeating the rumor in the denial provides a context for the denial statement and thereby reduces the uncertainty regarding the reasons for the denial. It also helps deflect the reasons for the denial to external causes and may lead to an overall positive assessment of the company.

Although these results provide some support for rebuttal strategies, we do not mean to imply that rumor management is easy or that rebuttals are a panacea for rumors. Indeed, rumors are notoriously difficult to control or manage. As discussed in chapter 3 (this volume), rumors serve a variety of needs and motivations and will therefore be resistant to disconfirming information. Indeed, social cognition literature on belief perseverance has found that impressions, once formed, are highly resistant to evidence to the contrary. In the next section, we use belief perseverance and the processes underlying it to assist us in understanding why some rumors are often difficult to refute.

Why Some Rumors Resist Rebuttal

A series of studies has demonstrated that initial impressions, even when thoroughly discredited, tend to persist (Anderson, 1983, 1985; Anderson, Lepper, & Ross, 1980; Ross, Lepper, & Hubbard, 1975). In these studies, subjects formed either a positive or negative directional impression based on manipulated information. For example, subjects formed impressions about their ability to discern real from fake suicide notes (they were either successful or unsuccessful in their ability to discern real suicide notes). In other experiments, subjects formed impressions about the relationship between a paper-and-pencil measure of risk behavior and success as a firefighter (they were led to believe that either a positive or a negative association exists between risky behavior and success). The manipulated information in these experiments was in the form of feedback from the experimenter (you are "correct" or "incorrect") or biased case histories about the risky behavior measure and successful firefighting. A manipulation check was then performed to measure the direction and strength of the impression.

Subjects were then *debriefed,* that is, informed in some way that the data on which they had based their initial impression was totally predetermined. In the earlier examples, debriefing consisted of the experimenter telling subjects that the feedback given was predetermined and unrelated to their actual responses, or that the firefighter case histories were fictitious. Subjects subsequently completed dependent measures of the strength and direction of the impression. Results uniformly showed that although weakened, initial impressions persisted (i.e., persevered) after debriefing. These results are similar to our findings on rumor denials. For example, with regard to the belief that "I am good [bad] at detecting true versus false suicide notes," people's strength of belief (a) is highest when they are given feedback consistent with the belief and (b) is reduced, but not eliminated, when the evidence is discredited. We similarly found that belief in a rumor (a) is highest when the rumor is given and (b) is reduced, but not eliminated, when the rumor is rebutted (in general). In other words, mud sticks— but not completely. Beliefs and rumors, when discredited, still tend to persist, but in a weakened state.

This belief perseverance phenomenon has been explained by three mechanisms: confirmation bias, causal inference making, and denial transparency. *Confirmation bias* is the tendency to conform incoming, contradictory data so that it does not challenge existing biases (Nisbett & Ross, 1980). Confirmation bias in this case discounts evidence contradictory to the first impression (subjects discount discrediting evidence so as to maintain their belief about their ability to discern suicide notes). Confirmation bias also acts here to selectively interpret concurrent information (reactions to false feedback) so as to bolster impressions (Ross et al., 1975). Once formed, impressions become relatively autonomous, that is, independent of the evidence on which they were founded. "The attributor doesn't 'renegotiate' his interpretations of the relevance or validity of impression-relevant information" (Ross et al., 1975, p. 890). Thus, at least on paper, it is easy to see how impressions become immune to logical challenges. In addition, as we noted in chapter 3 (this volume), rumors serve various psychological needs, and people are likely to engage in motivated reasoning to hold on to or legitimize cherished beliefs.

Causal inference making is the predilection to attribute unwarranted cause–effect relationships to merely contiguous events (Nisbett & Ross, 1980). Explaining an event increases its subjective likelihood (Ross, Lepper, Strack, & Steinmetz, 1977). In a similar way, as we showed in chapter 5 (this volume), rumors influence behavior because they provide ready-made causal explanations and lead people to deduce cause–effect relationships even in the absence of such an effect.

Finally, Wegner, Coulton, and Wenzlaff (1985) posited *denial transparency* as a more parsimonious account of persistence phenomena.

Denial transparency is a term that expresses the ineffectiveness of denial in negating propositions (denials are transparent in that people see through them; i.e., they are ineffective). The theory contends that persons classify all propositions as true initially, no matter how briefly. Propositions deemed false are then appended with a *not true* tag which is generally more difficult to remember than the affirmative proposition. For example, in the absence of other information, "Bob Talbert is not connected with the Mafia" will tend to be recalled as "Bob Talbert *is* connected with the Mafia." A denial does not erase a proposition; rather, it accompanies it.

For a denial to be effective, it should be reliably recalled with the target and the accusation. Given that recall of negations take more cognitive effort, Wegner et al. (1985) reasoned that if the denial ("I am not a cheat") is proposed in the affirmative ("I am honest"), it has higher likelihood of being recalled. In other words, victims of rumors should strive to be associated with positive impressions to replace the negative impressions created by the rumor. A similar idea was proposed by Tybout et al. (1981) who found that attitudes toward McDonald's restaurants in response to the rumor that the burgers contained worm meat were improved when worm meat was relabeled as a French delicacy or when participants were asked to think of certain details of the McDonald's restaurant they visited (e.g., whether it had indoor seating or not). In other words, rumor control should be a multipronged approach that may include an outright rebuttal and other reputation-enhancing strategies. Indeed, most effective rebuttals adopt this approach. Consider the example of Stroh Beer (Koenig, 1985). In 1983, the Stroh Brewery Company was plagued by rumors that the company had donated money to Jesse Jackson's presidential campaign. The company took out advertisements in the *Chicago Tribune* and in addition to stating that the rumors were "completely, totally false," the brewery company provided information on its donations to the Statue of Liberty renovation effort.

Recommendations for Managing Rumors

With these research insights in mind, we can answer our original question: How can rumors be effectively managed? Rumors can be prevented by reducing uncertainty and anxiety in the workplace. Managers need to anticipate events that may lead to uncertainty, anxiety, and a loss of a sense of control (and result in rumors) and strive to address these with a systematic communication strategy (Clampitt, DeKoch, & Cashman, 2000). Although managers may not be able to address all sources of uncertainty (all decisions may not have been made), strategies aimed at structuring uncertainty are likely to prevent rumors (Di-Fonzo & Bordia, 1998). As shown in chapter 8 (this volume), trust plays a vital role in how formal and informal communication is perceived. In an environment of distrust, even small amounts of uncertainty are threatening and may increase credulity. Yet in a climate of trust, dread rumors are unlikely to find a foothold. Therefore, trust-building measures (e.g., open and participative communication practices) are likely to reduce credulity and spread of negative rumors.

To curb rumors, one must act quickly. The longer a rumor circulates, the harder it is to control because of the following two features of rumor dynamics: First, as a rumor circulates, it tends to evolve into a more believable version and therefore becomes harder to contain. Second, the more times people hear the rumor, the more likely they are to believe it (the repetition effect noted in chap. 4, this volume). Therefore, people responsible for communication management need to be plugged into the informal networks and be aware of rumors as quickly as possible. In light of the fact that management can often be disconnected from line employees, by the time management hears of the rumor, it may have already circulated for a while. One manager reported using a "sonar man," a trusted subordinate who informed the manager of rumors circulating among employees.

When a rumor outbreak is being faced, the first decision to be made is whether to ignore a rumor or do something about it. As Figure 9.1 shows, over 75% of respondents to the survey of PR professionals indicated that they had ignored rumors. However, this strategy is relatively ineffective (Smeltzer, 1991). A rumor should be ignored only when it is considered harmless and expected to die on its own (DiFonzo et al., 1994). In particular, if asked for a response, managers should always comment on the rumor. As described earlier, a no-comments response conveys that one has something to hide and increases the uncertainty surrounding the issue. For example, Frith (2001) described how a no-comments policy, enacted by the AMP Corporation, fanned rumors of merger. If the rumor is true, it (or at least the elements of it that are true) must be confirmed. This strategy was rated as highly effective in our survey of PR professionals. Rumors, although exaggerated, often contain a grain of truth. Confirming the part that is true can reduce the uncertainty. In one case, a bank accidentally mailed a few credit cards to the wrong address. Rumors began spreading that large numbers of credit cards were mailed to the wrong address. The bank quickly informed the customers, confirming that some cards had been mailed incorrectly but also noting that the rumor exaggerated the problem (DiFonzo et al., 1994).

In many instances, a denial is required to reduce belief in the rumor, inoculate future recipients of the rumor, control the damage caused by the rumor, or just set the record straight (indeed, the absence of a denial may be taken as evidence of guilt). It is important to base the denial in facts. For one, it is the ethical thing to do. Acceptance of responsibility and ethical action improve the evaluation of the company. Also, organizations are rarely able to keep secrets for long. Leaks will occur, the facts will emerge, and management will lose credibility. In one company, a costly human error had occurred. The PR office was not informed and thus could not prepare a response for the press. A journalist discovered the incident and published a story, without proper response from the company. The PR officer described the incident as follows:

> Monday morning, a reporter called me and said that she understood that we had a real problem. I checked a little bit with the management and though they knew there was a problem, they did not mention it to anyone. The next day the reporter called me again. She really seemed to have some facts here. On the fourth day she told me that it was quite serious, she knew the numbers, the error would cost hundreds of millions, so I went back to the management and said, "What's going on?" They said, "Yes, we do have this problem." She ran the story that afternoon. (DiFonzo et al., 1994, p. 59)

The effectiveness of persuasive messages depends on the source credibility and message quality; so too with rumor denials. Sources that match the scope and seriousness of the rumor should be used. The source of the denial should also be perceived as honest and trustworthy. Indeed, neutral outside sources are likely to be very effective. For example, Alpac Bottling Company's efforts to counter allegations that syringes were found in soft drink cans got a boost when an independent bottling inspector announced, "I've inspected this type of plant machinery for years, and I know it just couldn't happen. It's a hoax" (Fearn-Banks, 2002, p. 233). The messages should be clearly worded, be easy to understand, and contain evidence (if available) discrediting the rumor. For example, denials from the designer Tommy Hilfiger that he made racist comments on the *Oprah Winfrey Show* included statements from Oprah Winfrey that not only did he not appear on her show, but she has never even met Tommy Hilfiger ("Tommy Rumor," 1999).

Finally, if it is likely that the denial will be received by people who have not heard the rumor, the denial should provide information on the reasons for and context that has led to the denial (i.e., acknowledge the existence of rumor). For example, the Stroh Brewery Company, when denying rumors of donations to a presidential campaign, clearly stated the rumor and denied it: "There are rumors in the Illinois and Indiana areas that the Stroh Brewery Company is making contributions to presidential candidates. These rumors are not true" (Koenig, 1985, p. 61). The half-page advertisement in the *Chicago Tribune* went on to provide information on the company's contribution to nonpolitical programs, the slanderous nature of the rumor, and the reward of $25,000 for information on the origins of this rumor.

In this chapter, we have reviewed research pertaining to rumor management and have explored the implications of this research for those attempting to prevent or manage rumors. In the next and final chapter, we summarize the concepts outlined thus far by addressing the questions raised at the outset and proposing a more comprehensive research agenda.

Summary, Model, and Research Agenda | 10

Perhaps the most bizarre rumor to surface in the aftermath of Hurricane Katrina, which devastated New Orleans in 2005: Dolphins, specially trained by the U.S. Navy to guard docked submarines by shooting poison dart guns at terrorist divers, had been swept out to sea during the hurricane. Because of this, according to the rumor, all divers and Gulf Coast bathers were at risk (Mikkelson, 2005). The rumor—judged "probably false" by the hoaxbuster Web site http://www.snopes.com— has enjoyed widespread circulation.

In this volume, we have addressed a series of questions— some old, some new—that surround rumor. We related these to current social and organizational psychological theory and we grounded much of our conclusions in empirical research. Where does this leave us? In this chapter we first summarize our conclusions on each question. We then propose an integrated model of rumor phenomena. Last, we set forth a detailed research agenda.

Summary

WHAT IS RUMOR?

In chapter 1 (this volume), we defined *rumor* as unverified and instrumentally relevant information statements in circulation that arise in contexts of ambiguity, danger, or potential threat, and that function to help people make sense and manage risk. This definition specifically addresses the content, contexts, and functions of rumor, and contrasts these with those of gossip and urban legends. Rumor content is unverified and instrumentally relevant information, whereas gossip is evaluative social talk and urban legends are interesting stories. Rumors arise in contexts of ambiguity, danger, or threat—either physical or psychological—and function to make sense of ambiguity or manage risk. In contrast, gossip arises in the context of social network formation and maintenance, and allows groups to become more cohesive and to define their membership, norms, and power structure. Urban legends arise in more socially cohesive contexts and serve to entertain and to convey group mores, norms, and cultural truths. We presented the Information Dimension Scale (IDS) to differentiate six dimensions of information. Four of the dimensions pertained to content: extent to which the information has evidentiary basis, is important, is about individuals, and is slanderous; two pertained to function: extent to which the information is entertaining and useful. We then measured the information dimensions of exemplars of rumor, news, gossip, and urban legends. Our exemplars exhibited different information dimension patterns in line with our conceptualization of each genre of hearsay. For example, our rumors were rated as low on evidentiary basis and high on importance and usefulness. The rating given to news mirrored these elements except for evidentiary basis, which was rated as high. Our gossip, however, was considered by participants as low in importance and usefulness, and high in slanderous content about individuals and entertainment value. And our urban legends were rated low on evidentiary basis, importance, and usefulness, but high on entertainment.

The use of the information dimensions to differentiate species of hearsay is a helpful advance in the study of rumor. It implies that, as with biological species and types of mental illness, classification depends on the presence of a number of characteristics and that nebulous forms exist. It is sometimes difficult to characterize information as either rumor or gossip; the information may indeed exhibit patterns characteristic of both. "The boss is having an affair with the CEO" may be like a rumor in some ways—it is rated low on evidentiary basis (there is no proof) and high on importance (because it affects work processes)—but like gossip in others—it is about individuals, slanderous, and entertaining. The IDS anticipates these nebulous forms and offers a way of characterizing information with continuous rather than discrete yardsticks. Instead of classifying information as either rumor or not rumor, we say that it exhibits an information dimension pattern that is strongly, moderately, or weakly characteristic of rumor.

WHAT ARE THE CATEGORIES OF RUMOR?

In chapter 2 (this volume), we posed basic descriptive questions. The rumor pie has been sliced several different ways, but most often according to the motivational tension characterizing the rumor: dread, wish fulfillment, or wedge-driving (R. H. Knapp, 1944). In organizational contexts, we offered our own categorization schemes on the basis of rumor's central functions of sense making and threat management. Our schemes classified rumor according to rumor public (internal or external to the organization), object of collective concern (e.g., job security, stock value), and content (e.g., turnover, costly errors). We also classified internal rumors about organizational change on the basis of four aspects of change that employees want to make sense of or manage the effects of: changes to job and working conditions, the nature of the organizational change, poor change management, and consequences of change for organizational performance. Categorization schemes such as these are important because they reveal what people are concerned about, they reveal underlying attitudes and beliefs, and they help to prepare practitioners concerned with rumor prevention and management.

HOW FREQUENT ARE RUMORS?

Although research on rumor frequency is scant, the best available evidence indicates that organizational rumors are rather frequent: harmful or potentially harmful rumors reached the ears of top-level corporate public relations (PR) officers almost once per week on average (DiFonzo & Bordia, 2000). The majority of these corporate rumors seemed to be internal and concerned with personnel changes and job security; external rumors were most often concerned with organizational reputation and stock prices. A recurrent theme throughout this research was that organizational rumors tend to occur in the context of change such as downsizing, mergers, new technology, and restructuring. Our analysis of internal change rumors at a large public hospital (Bordia, Jones, Gallois, Callan, & DiFonzo, in press) found that the largest portion—almost half—of internal rumors about change was concerned with changes to job and working conditions. In addition, the overwhelming majority of internal change rumors were driven by fear of dreaded consequences (i.e., they were dread rumors). We interpret these frequency patterns as further evidence of the sense-making and threat management functions of rumor: Employees, concerned about the ramifications of change, participate actively in the rumor mill to prepare actively or emotionally for potential negative events.

WHAT EFFECTS DO RUMORS HAVE?

Rumors clearly play a causal or contributory role in a variety of attitudinal and behavioral outcomes. A long line of rumor research has noted how rumors have contributed to panic, affected economic activity, exacerbated racial tensions, incited riots, and affected health behaviors, even when these rumors were not strongly believed. We reported how a false rumor about the deadly consequences of blinking headlights at nighttime motorists whose lights were off resulted in the nearly universal diminution of this prosocial practice of traffic culture, despite the fact that our sample was a highly educated, skeptical, and good-natured group of psychology faculty and graduate students. These findings accord with theory that people are especially sensitive to loss (Kahneman & Tversky, 1979) and attempt to prevent loss even when such negative events are extremely unlikely. In a similar way, rumors supposedly heard from "brother-in-law Harry" were rated as noncredible, but systematically affected individual stock-market trading behavior as much as did the same information presented as front-page *Wall Street Journal* news. These rumors drew "investors" away from a buy-low-sell-high trading strategy and therefore resulted in reduced profits compared with control participants (DiFonzo & Bordia, 1997). The notion that rumors have effects was also supported by results of our study of 74 highly experienced corporate PR officers; this sample rated rumor effects overall as moderately severe (DiFonzo & Bordia, 2000). Three general categories of effects were derived: external ramifications, internal attitudes, and internal behaviors. Of these, the effects of rumor on internal attitudes were rated as the most severe. This finding is supported by Bordia et al.'s (in press) hospital change study results suggesting that employees hearing negative rumors were more stressed than were those not hearing rumors.

We also reported the results of a more comprehensive investigation of the effects of rumor in a longitudinal study of an organization that underwent a radical downsizing. The number of negative rumors heard was associated with uncertainty and anxiety. The number of negative rumors heard was inversely associated with key employee attitudes: positive ratings of formal communication quality, trust in the company, job satisfaction, and organizational commitment. The number of negative rumors heard was also associated with intention to leave and—intermittently—lower productivity. Furthermore, the cumulative number of rumors heard was also associated with these outcomes and was generally a better predictor of these outcomes than was the number of recent rumors heard. This pattern of evidence suggests that hearing negative rumors is associated with a variety of negative outcomes. In addition, the evidence suggests that hearing negative rumors month after month materially contributes to a number of negative organizational attitudes, intentions, and behaviors.

WHY DO PEOPLE SPREAD RUMORS?

In chapter 3 (this volume) we reframed rumor transmission antecedents within a motivational framework. Rumor transmission is motivated by three broad psychological needs. The first need is to know and understand one's circumstances so as to be able to act or cope effectively. This need motivates fact-finding strategies. Uncertainty about a topic of high outcome-relevance leads to a feeling of lack of control and anxiety and motivates the search for information (i.e., fact-finding). Rumors provide explanation and prediction and fulfill this need. Second, the need to develop and sustain social relationships motivates relationship-enhancement strategies. In the context of rumors, people take into account the interaction context and may use rumors to bond with the conversational partner and achieve other relationship-enhancement goals. For example, people are more likely to transmit rumors they believe to be true so as to enhance their status in the social network as a reliable source of information (a relationship-enhancement goal). Third, the need to further material and psychological needs of the self motivates self-enhancement strategies. Motivated by self-gain, people transmit rumors as propaganda to undermine opponents, present the outgroup in a negative light, and justify existing (often prejudicial) beliefs and attitudes.

We also presented the results of an empirical study that explored the role of motivations in people's intention to transmit rumors. We manipulated the valence (negative or positive rumor), target (rumor about the ingroup or outgroup), and recipient of the rumor (an acquaintance from the ingroup or the outgroup) and asked participants about their intention to transmit the rumor and underlying motivations. We found that the fact-finding motivation was highest when the context was that of a negative rumor about the ingroup to be transmitted to another ingroup member. Mediation analysis revealed that the fact-finding motivation underlaid the intention to transmit a negative rumor about the ingroup to another ingroup member (as opposed to an outgroup member). That is, people may transmit a negative rumor about the ingroup to another ingroup member to ascertain the veracity of this rumor. However, the relationship-enhancement motivation was highest when the rumor was positive in valence, about the outgroup, and being transmitted to an outgroup member. Mediation analysis revealed that positive rumors about the outgroup were more likely to be transmitted to outgroup members (compared with negative rumors about the outgroup) and the relationship-enhancement motivation underlaid this effect. It would appear that by being the bearers of good news, people hoped to generate liking for themselves in a conversation partner. Finally, the self-enhancement motivation was highest when the rumor was positive and about the ingroup and the recipient was an outgroup member. However, transmission intention in this context was low, perhaps because this condition threatened relationship-enhancement goals. Thus, in our experimental context, the self-enhancement motivation took a backseat to relationship-enhancement motivation. The motivation-based approach highlights the variety of influences on rumor transmission, integrates previous research into a tripartite model of motivational antecedents to rumor transmission, and suggests that future research should incorporate the fact-finding, relationship-enhancing, and self-enhancing motivations in arriving at a more comprehensive understanding of rumor spread.

WHY DO PEOPLE BELIEVE RUMORS?

In chapter 4 (this volume), we addressed this question using Egon Brunswik's lens model of judgment in which distal attributes are inferred from proximal cues. That is, what cues do people use to infer the veracity of a rumor? We reviewed and (when possible) meta-analytically combined studies bearing on this question; we identified four such cues. People are more likely to believe a rumor if the rumor accords with the hearer's attitude (especially to the extent that the rumor accords with a specific attitude), comes from a credible source, is heard repeatedly, and is not rebutted. Rumors of government corruption and waste, for example, are more likely to be believed if the hearer specifically opposes the current government administration (e.g., the Roosevelt administration and not merely the government in general; F. H. Allport & Lepkin, 1945), hears it from a source deemed credible, hears it repeatedly, and does not hear a rebuttal of the rumor. We reported a study of stock-market brokers and traders in which we found that these and other cues were used to infer belief in stock-market rumors. Other cues in this domain included stakeholder status of the source (do they have anything to gain by spreading the rumor?), consistency with a larger pattern, consistency with emerging data, and agreement with expert consensus.

HOW DO RUMORS HELP PEOPLE MAKE SENSE OF UNCERTAINTY?

In chapter 5 (this volume), we explored the psychological mechanisms involved in the process of sense making at the individual and interpersonal levels. At the individual level, we explicated rumor sense making using frameworks within social cognition: explanation theory, causal attribution, illusory correlation, and antiregressive prediction. Rumors influence the individual explanation process by drawing the attention of an individual to an event or a particular aspect of an event, by offering an initial explanation for an event, by activating knowledge structures that influence the search for further information, and by motivating the sense maker—usually through anxiety-provoking rumor content—to continue searching for a satisfactory explanation. Cognitive knowledge structures are important at each stage of the explanation process, and knowledge structures about causes seem to be especially important in understanding how rumors affect individual sense making. We proposed that rumors help people make sense of the world by means of the ready-made and stable-cause explanations that are often embedded in them. By *ready-made* we mean that most explanations come from the social milieu—often embedded in rumors—and are probably not derived from an individual's own causal analysis. For example, people may observe that the office is being renovated and hear through the rumor mill a ready-made explanation for these renovations: The company will be restructuring. By *stable cause* we mean that the nature of the cause is more often lasting than temporary. For example, the restructuring is occurring because management has a stable dispositional trait: greed. We speculated—on the basis of a perusal of published rumors and experimental evidence—that most rumors contain such stable-cause attributions.

The significance of the idea that rumors are embedded with stable-cause attributions is that such attributions have been implicated in several well-known systematic judgment biases. We explored a couple of these with regard to rumor. First, rumors often result in erroneous judgments of correlation. They lead people to see relationships that in reality do not exist. Stock-market "investors" presented with rumors that were unassociated with stock price changes were strongly convinced that these rumors covaried with these price changes (DiFonzo & Bordia, 1997). Second, rumors often lead people to make antiregressive predictions (the recent trend will continue) and abandon more predictive base-rate information. Stock-market rumors have long been implicated in such antiregressive trading behaviors (e.g., Rose, 1951). For example, hearing a rumor that Goodyear profits are up led investors to predict that the stock price would increase rather than regress toward the mean of past prices. Our own experimental research found that stable-cause attributions are at the heart of antiregressive trading behavior brought on by rumors (DiFonzo & Bordia, 2002b). It is interesting that rumors in our studies did not have to be believed to have an effect; they merely had to make sense.

We also explored the dynamics of collective rumor sense making by examining the content, functions, and flow of statements made during Internet rumor discussions. We first addressed the question, "What types of statements constitute rumor discussions and what is their relative prevalence in a typical rumor episode?" We reviewed the Rumor Interaction Analysis System to content analyze rumor discussions on the Internet. We found that the largest portion of discussion content was about sense making: Participants attempted to ascertain whether or not the rumor was true. Participants also provided information, asked questions, authenticated credentials and information, shared relevant personal experience, expressed belief and disbelief, and attempted to persuade others; these activities support the collective goal of sense making. We next addressed the question, "What is the typical makeup of sets of statements contributed by rumor discussion participants?" That is, when people contribute to a rumor discussion, what is the relative composition of the types of statements they make at any one point in the discussion? We found 11 distinctive patterns of statement sets that discussants made at any one time; we dubbed these *communicative postures* and interpreted these within a collective sense-making framework. For example, the explanation-delivering posture was composed of a high number of prudent statements (e.g., "I don't know if this is true, but I heard that . . .") and providing information statements (statements that bring information to the discussion). Other postures included those that evaluated, verified, falsified, or accepted the explanation; shared or sought information; suggested courses of action; and sustained motivation to continue sense making. Thus, the posture that one takes at any one point in a rumor discussion fulfills an important collective sense-making function.

We finally wondered, "How do postures and statements typically change over the life of a rumor discussion?" Again, sense making is the key to understanding the progression of postures over the life of a rumor discussion. We observed that interaction episodes typically proceeded as follows: Explanation-delivering and directing postures were more common in the first quarter of rumor interaction, explanation evaluation peaked during the third quarter, and casual participation (a posture not associated with sense making) peaked at the end. A similar analysis of statement types over rumor lifetimes yielded a similar pattern. Thus, collective Internet rumor sense making seems to proceed in a multistage process of bringing the rumor to the attention of the group (Stage 1), sharing information (Stage 2), evaluating explanations (Stage 3), and then resolving the problem (Stage 4). The idea that rumor discussions are composed of various roles that may change over time is not new (Shibutani, 1966; R. H. Turner & Killian, 1972); however, our discussion advances, operationalizes, and tests these ideas.

Individuals and groups make sense using rumor, but this sense is at times quite bizarre. The inaccuracies in sense making beg the question, How accurate are rumors and how do they become more—or less—accurate? In chapters 6 and 7 (this volume) we addressed several questions related to rumor content change on the dimension of accuracy.

HOW DOES RUMOR CONTENT CHANGE?

Four patterns of content change have been identified: Content is leveled (the number of details is reduced), content is added (the rumor becomes more detailed or elaborate), content is sharpened (certain details are accentuated), and content is assimilated (content is shaped through leveling, sharpening, or adding to be in greater accord with cognitive schemas). Scholars generally agree that everyday rumors are sharpened and assimilated, but there has been some difference of opinion about whether rumors are generally leveled or added to. That is, do real-life rumors tend to become smaller or larger? We argued that it depends on transmission patterns stemming from situational ambiguity and rumor importance. Leveling—but not adding—has tended to occur in laboratory studies of rumor (in which participants are told to simply pass information along) and in planted-rumor field study situations (in which a rumor is planted and tends to simply be passed along rather than discussed intensely). Leveling occurs in some real-life rumor episodes marked by low ambiguity and when a group is primarily engaged in serially transmitting the information. In contrast, adding—but not leveling—has occurred mostly in field observation studies set in high-ambiguity and high-importance contexts such as catastrophes and murders. In other words, adding occurs in real-life ambiguous situations of importance in which a group is attempting to interactively discuss and collaborate on the rumor. Our argument highlights the sociological versus psychological divide over rumor. Since the time of G. W. Allport and Postman (1947b), psychologists have tended to view rumor activity as serially transmitted information from one participant to another, and the focus is on the individual's effect on rumor content at each transmission node. Sociologists have tended to see rumor as transmitted in more circular patterns for the collective purpose of explanation construction, and the focus is on how the group as a whole collaboratively affects content. Our view is that rumor primarily functions to help people make sense, but the dynamics of this sense making vary. Some rumor episodes (we speculate the minority) are characterized more by simple, perhaps even serial, transmission, whereas other rumor episodes are better characterized as interactive discussions. The former will tend to exhibit leveling; the latter, adding.

WHAT IS RUMOR ACCURACY?

In chapter 6 (this volume) we also presented a much needed conceptualization of the term *accuracy*. We proposed two types of rumor accuracy: *Verity* refers to correspondence with reality; *precision* refers to correspondence with some previous version of the rumor. Rumor accuracy varies on how true it is, and also on how precisely it has been transmitted. Rumor verity is analogous to instrument validity in test construction; rumor precision is analogous to instrument reliability. We proposed a categorization scheme based on rumor verity and distortion toward or away from verity. There are three types of true rumors: Stars are those that were precisely transmitted, converts became truer as they were transmitted, and grainies became slightly distorted as they were transmitted (although they are still mostly true). There are also three types of false rumors: counterfeits are those that were precisely transmitted, fallen stars started well but ended badly, and hopefuls started false but show signs of slight improvement (although they are still mostly false).

HOW IS RUMOR ACCURACY MEASURED?

Field observational studies of accuracy have tended to measure rumor verity. These investigations typically collected rumors or elements of a rumor in circulation in a field setting, ascertained which rumors or rumor elements were true, and calculated the percentage that were veritable. Lab and field experiments have tended to measure rumor precision. Lab experiments typically measured the distortions that occurred in participants who serially transmitted—either with or without discussion—a description of a stimulus such as a drawing; these methodologies resembled the telephone game or whisper down the lane. Field experiments usually planted a rumor within a setting, collected the rumor in circulation at some later time, and compared the terminal version with the original. It is important to note that rumor precision was taken as a proxy for rumor verity. That is, in the same way that test makers are interested in measurement reliability because it affects validity, rumor researchers who measured precision were ultimately interested in—and generalized their result to—rumor verity. Although there are two different types of accuracy, we don't think it will be helpful to promote the widespread use of these two terms; rather, it is enough to be aware of the distinction when one considers and designs rumor accuracy research. Therefore, when we and other rumor researchers refer to rumor accuracy, rumor verity is intended.

HOW ACCURATE ARE RUMORS OVERALL?

Is rumor's reputation as false information generally true? The answer seems to be that rumor accuracy varies widely, but some settings—notably organizational grapevines—generally produce accurate (i.e., true) rumors. We examined the handful of rumor accuracy field studies; accuracy varied substantially, but those rumors circulating in organizational grapevines tended to be highly accurate. We presented results of our interviews about rumor accuracy with managers and communications personnel in several organizations; their estimates of the accuracy of specific rumors were quite high, especially when the rumor had been in circulation for a time. We reported two additional studies in which we collected true and false workplace rumors from employed students in the United States and Australia, assessed their accuracy, and measured their accuracy trend (i.e., the extent to which they become more accurate or less accurate over time). When given the option of recalling a true or false rumor, most overwhelmingly recalled true rumors; indeed, most recalled converts (true rumors that became more accurate over time). When students were asked to recall both true and false rumors, true rumors were again overwhelmingly composed of converts; false rumors were either counterfeits or fallen stars. These studies suggest that organizational rumors that have since been proven true or false tend to be accurate: The reputation of workplace rumor as inaccurate is itself inaccurate! These studies also suggest what we have dubbed the Matthew accuracy effect: Of those organizational rumors that prove true or false, the true tend to get "truer" and the false either stay the same or become more false.

WHAT CAUSES ACCURACY AND INACCURACY?

In more specific terms, what are the mechanisms by which accurate (or inaccurate) rumor content is generated or changed? In chapter 7 (this volume), we reviewed literature pertinent to rumor content change with regard to accuracy and proposed five sets of mechanisms by which rumors become more accurate and less accurate; we proposed cognitive, motivational, situational, group, and network processes. Cognitive distortions result from limits to attention and memory, and from schema activation: The narrowing of listener attention in the context of serial transmission with no discussion results in inaccuracies characterized by emphasis on salient or central information. Memory limits—again in the context of serial transmission without discussion—result in inaccuracies characterized by easily remembered information.

Perceptual biases accrue from the interpretation of stimuli to be more in accordance with activated cognitive structures such as schemas and stereotypes.

Motivational mechanisms also affect rumor content: Accuracy motivation on the part of rumor participants—given the needed resources—is likely to result in more accurate rumors. Relationship-enhancement motivation results in the selective transmission of rumors that are likely to find a ready reception with the hearer; these rumors may or may not be more accurate. Self-enhancement motivation results in the transmission of rumors that boost the self-esteem of the teller, put his or her ingroup in a favorable light, or denigrate his or her outgroup; these rumors are often less accurate. Situational features affecting accuracy include high collective excitement, capacity to check rumor veracity, and time: High collective excitement leads to greater inaccuracy because people become more suggestible and less critical and adopt lower norms for the acceptance of information. The capacity to check rumor validity not surprisingly increases rumor accuracy. Constraints on this capacity occur in numerous ways: serial transmission without discussion, erroneous information from credible sources, novel channels of communication, the urgent need to act quickly to avoid threat, the lack of firm information on a matter, distance from valid sources of information, and the inability to compare rumors with other people. Time tends to result in either greater accuracy or greater inaccuracy.

Group processes include conformity, culture, and epistemic norms. Conformity processes—bringing individual behaviors and attitudes in line with group consensus—may lead to greater or lesser accuracy, depending on the veracity of group consensus. Rumors similarly tend to accord with the beliefs, values, and practices contained in group culture. Part of this culture is the epistemic norms—the group standards for evidence; to the extent that group standards are high, rumor accuracy is more likely. Network mechanisms include interaction, transmission configuration, and channel age (i.e., length of time established channels of communication have existed). Interaction—discussion that occurs during rumor transmission—tends to produce more accurate rumors. Three transmission configurations were identified: serial transmission with or without interaction, cluster transmission (one person tells persons in a group and some of these persons pass it on to other clusters), and multiple interaction (MI; rumor is actively discussed and recirculated). Serial and cluster transmission patterns are generally less active than are MI patterns. We theorized that serial and cluster transmission would lead to distortion at each transmission node because of the cognitive processes discussed earlier. MI patterns of transmission would tend to either mitigate or accentuate these and other errors.

Groups with what H. Taylor Buckner dubbed *critical set orientation* would yield more accurate rumors with greater MI; groups with an uncritical set orientation would yield less accurate rumors (Buckner, 1965). *Group orientation* here refers to the combination of variables affecting a group's capacity and inclination to ferret out the facts; these variables include such factors as ability to check, high standards of evidence, and the presence of established channels of communication. Finally, communication channel age was theorized to be related to accuracy; rumors passed along established channels tend to be more accurate because the tellers' credibility can be tagged. Novel channel credibility is naturally less able to be ascertained.

In chapter 7 (this volume), we also presented new research findings designed to explore and test some of the motivational, group, and network mechanisms discussed here. Interviews with communication personnel were consistent with the idea that a critical set orientation was associated with greater rumor accuracy. When so motivated and when the group is able to ferret out the facts of a situation, they do so. Results from a survey of employed students suggested that channel age and the group epistemic norm of skepticism each predicted rumor accuracy. Furthermore, MI moderated the relationship between skepticism and accuracy; that is, MI produced more accurate rumors in skeptical groups and less accurate rumors in gullible groups. MI did not moderate the relation between channel age and accuracy, however. These tentative results are mostly consistent with key tenets of Buckner's (1965) theory of rumor accuracy, although much work remains.

HOW DOES TRUST AFFECT RUMOR TRANSMISSION?

We have often observed that where distrust grows, rumors flow; in chapter 8 (this volume) we systematically investigated this idea. We presented a longitudinal study of an organization undergoing a radical downsizing. On the basis of a framework proposed by trust researchers (Dirks & Ferrin, 2001) we hypothesized that distrust—expectations of the malignant nature of management's intent—would engender more negative appraisals of ambiguous events—negative rumors—and behaviors congruent with these appraisals. And indeed we found what we expected: Distrust strongly predicted the likelihood of transmitting negative rumors heard and was a better predictor than both uncertainty and anxiety. When formal sources of information are not trusted, people resort to sense-making rumor discussions. Furthermore, when management is not trusted, their actions are appraised as potential threats, which increase the need to regain a sense of control and understanding; employees attempt to do this through participation in the rumor mill.

Results also suggested that trust moderated the relationship between anxiety and rumor transmission. When trust is high, rumor activity depends on anxiety; but when trust is low, rumor activity is uniformly high. These same patterns were found for uncertainty, although they were weaker. In other words, if a person distrusts management, he or she will tend to transmit rumors heard regardless of his or her level of uncertainty or anxiety. Management's actions are seen as antagonistic; even a small amount of anxiety and uncertainty becomes magnified. Also, spreading a negative rumor that denigrates management may be self-enhancing. These findings point toward trust as perhaps a more important variable in rumor transmission than uncertainty or anxiety. At the very least, it should be routinely measured in future investigations of rumor transmission.

HOW CAN HARMFUL RUMORS BE MANAGED?

In chapter 9 (this volume), we reviewed the literature on rumor-quelling strategies and summarized these in terms of whether they intervened in the rumor generation (e.g., reduce uncertainty), evaluation (e.g., reduce belief via rumor rebuttals), or transmission (e.g., threaten legal action) stage. The majority of the writing on prescriptions for rumor management recommends strategies aimed at reducing generation of and belief in rumors. We also reviewed results of a survey of highly experienced public relations (PR) professionals (with over 26 years of experience on average) on the prevalence and effectiveness of rumor-quelling strategies. The results showed that rumor prevention strategies (e.g., minimize uncertainty by stating values and procedures that will guide organizational change) were the most popular, whereas punitive strategies (e.g., identify and punish rumor-mongers) were the least popular. Also, a priori strategies that structured uncertainty were rated as more effective in managing rumors than was after-the-fact rumor control via formal communication methods (e.g., rebutting the rumor by internal or external sources). However, not all rumors can be prevented, and rumor rebuttal remains an important rumor management tool (Koenig, 1985).

HOW EFFECTIVE ARE REBUTTALS IN REDUCING BELIEF IN A RUMOR?

We considered rumor rebuttals as persuasive messages; their aim is to persuade people to disbelieve the rumor. We reviewed empirical research suggesting that, as with other persuasive messages, rumor rebuttals are more effective when delivered by sources that match the scope of the rumor, when sources are perceived to be honest, when the rebuttal message discredits the rumor and provides useful (and anxiety-alleviating) information on the topic of the rumor, and when the rebuttal message provides a context for the rebuttal (i.e., is framed in the context of a prior accusation or rumor). Our findings also suggest that a rebuttal is better than a no-comments strategy in combating a rumor. However, rebuttals are not a panacea and some rumors refuse to go away. This resistance of some rumors to rebuttals can be explained by the belief perseverance phenomenon: Although belief in rumors weakens when they are rebutted, some cherished beliefs endure and the negative impressions created by a rumor persist. Rebuttals that convincingly deny the rumor and associate the target with positive characteristics seem more likely to restore positive attitudes toward the rumor target.

Integrative Model

Figure 10.1 offers a pictorial representation of some of the main elements discussed in this volume. Let's describe each component of the model. Recall first our definition of rumor: unverified and instrumentally relevant information statements in circulation that arise in contexts of ambiguity, danger, or potential threat, and that function to help people make sense and manage risk. The context of rumor activity—symbolized by the background labeled *Environmental Characteristics*—is ambiguity and threat. Such situations may pose physical or psychological threat. In organizational settings, change is often the reason behind ambiguity and threat; restructurings, downsizing, new technology, staff changes, and other events like these raise questions among and carry potentially deleterious effects for employees.

In the midst of change, ambiguity, or threat, groups and individuals engage in sense making, which is represented by the large oval. Rumor is the making of sense—represented in our model as a piece of the puzzle that the group is attempting to assemble. The sense making happens at both the group and individual levels—hence the labels *Group Sense Making* and *Individual Sense Making*. At a group level, rumors are information statements in circulation among and through the rumor public; two arrows circling back on one another represent this. In addition, characteristics of the group play an important role in group sense making. These characteristics include group culture—including beliefs, values, and group epistemic norms—and network

FIGURE 10.1

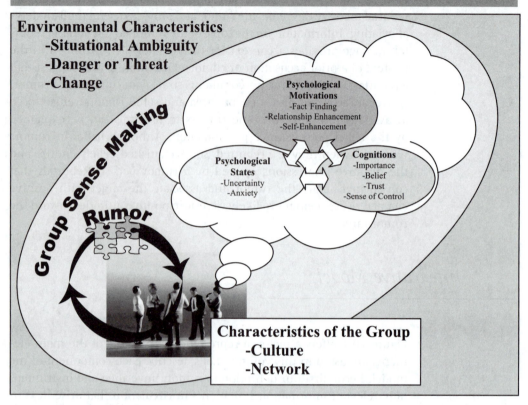

Environmental Characteristics
   -Situational Ambiguity
   -Danger or Threat
   -Change

Group Sense Making

Rumor

Psychological Motivations
-Fact Finding
-Relationship Enhancement
-Self-Enhancement

Psychological States
-Uncertainty
-Anxiety

Cognitions
-Importance
-Belief
-Trust
-Sense of Control

Characteristics of the Group
   -Culture
   -Network

Integrative model of rumor.

characteristics (see DiFonzo & Bordia, in press, for a discussion of network characteristics and rumor transmission).

At the individual level, sense-making processes are affected by motivations, psychological states, and cognitions. Motivations for rumor transmission include fact finding, relationship enhancement, and self-enhancement. Uncertainty and anxiety are aversive psychological states of mind. Cognitions include the level of trust the individual has in official information sources or in the targeted group, beliefs about the veracity and importance of the rumor, and the loss of a sense of control. Each element affects the others. For example, uncertainty often leads to fact-finding motivation. Distrust of the target group may engender self-enhancement motivations and lead to greater anxiety. Relationship-enhancement motivation may lead to heightened belief in a rumor sanctioned by the group.

Future Research Agenda

What's next for rumor research? In this section we set forth an agenda that highlights emerging trends, addresses gaps in knowledge, and outlines specific investigations.

CONCEPTUALIZATION AND CLASSIFICATION OF RUMOR, GOSSIP, AND URBAN LEGEND

In chapter 1 (this volume) we introduced the IDS to distinguish forms of rumor from gossip and urban legend and tested these ideas in a laboratory setting; we found that our small set of information exemplars fit predicted IDS patterns. What IDS patterns obtain for information communicated in nonlaboratory settings? This question may be addressed by collecting rumor, gossip, urban legends—and the many intermediate and nebulous forms that exist—from archived sources (e.g., snopes.com, urbanlegends.com, online discussions of rumor), by recording conversations in public places, or by using diary methods, and then rating them with the IDS. Special attention should be paid to the pattern of functional and contextual differences we have hypothesized. Such investigations would shed much needed light on the roles—unique, complimentary, or common—that each form of communication plays during ordinary social discourse.

Research in this vein would clarify the ongoing ambiguity associated with these forms. This research should also expand, refine, and validate the IDS. We have hypothesized that the primary motivations for participating in rumor discussions are to understand, to belong, and to self-enhance, whereas the primary foci of gossip and urban legends are to belong and to self-enhance. We have similarly noted that some rumors survive and some don't; what IDS differences exist between "fit" and "unfit" rumors? We think that the "fittest" rumors should be those that most help groups understand, belong, and self-enhance. Finally, we have raised the possibility that nonfalsifiable rumors are more likely to survive; any expansion of the IDS should include a falsifiability dimension.

RUMOR FORMS, FREQUENCIES, EFFECTS, AND EFFECT MECHANISMS

In chapter 2 (this volume) we overviewed research on the types of rumors that occur, their prevalence, and their effects. We tended to focus on organizational settings. What rumor forms, frequencies, and effects exist in other domains, such as religious communities, conflicted ethnic or racial enclaves, populations engaged in behaviors adversely affecting health, local communities considering environmental policy, elections for public office, terrorist cells, protest crowds, populations affected by natural disasters, Internet blogging networks, schoolchildren friendship groups, and consumers considering product purchases? Cataloging and counting rumors and rumor effects in such contexts would illuminate the contours of rumor sense making in these arenas. Perhaps of greatest practical concern are rumors that adversely affect health and health detection behaviors, escalate ethnic conflict, interfere with natural disaster responses, and are purposely planted as propaganda.

Of special interest are the cumulative effects of hearing rumors. The longitudinal study we presented indicated that hearing negative rumors month after month affected—among other variables—job satisfaction, trust, productivity, and withdrawal behaviors. This study should be replicated and the analysis should be extended to positive rumors: Positive rumors—heard repeatedly—should affect organizational attitudes and behaviors in an opposite manner. In this vein of research, special attention should be paid to the mediating mechanisms by which rumors affect outcomes. To wit, are rumor effects mediated through social learning, equity calculations, or schema activation? Finally, our understanding of rumor propaganda effects on the evaluation of both rumor target and rumor transmitter is currently limited (*rumor propaganda* refers to rumors intentionally planted to influence public opinion or behavior; DiFonzo & Bordia, in press). Rumors are often spread in the context of rival, competing, or conflicted groups; how does hearing negative rumors about Group A affect the evaluation of Group B? Even when such rumors are not believed, do they have their intended effect? Such knowledge would be timely and practically useful in light of the heightened polarization and conflict of our post-9/11 world.

MOTIVATIONS IN RUMOR SPREAD

In chapter 3 (this volume) we presented a tripartite framework of motivation in rumor spread: fact finding, relationship enhancement, and self-enhancement. Most work has been done, albeit indirectly, on the fact-finding motivation of rumor transmission. Several interesting questions remain, however. First, it has been repeatedly asserted that people transmit rumors to reduce anxiety or to indirectly cope with an unfavorable situation by understanding and interpreting it (this is a fact-finding motivation). Yet we are not aware of any research that tests this anxiety-reduction function, that is, how effective rumors are at reducing anxiety.

In contrast to fact finding, we know little about the relationship-enhancement goal in rumor transmission. For example, what are the effects of rumor transmission on others' evaluation of the transmitter? A person may hesitate to share a negative outgroup rumor with a member of the outgroup, for example, because he or she thinks it impolite to do so. A second example: Sharing a negative ingroup rumor with members of one's ingroup, especially in the context of a highly polarized ingroup–outgroup conflict, may cost a person a great deal of ingroup social capital. Investigating questions of this sort would lead to a fuller understanding of the relationship-enhancement motivation and would explore the social costs of sharing a rumor.

Much work also remains in exploring the self-enhancing motivation in rumor spread. First, the notion of self-enhancement is that people, desirous of boosting their self-image, build themselves up by putting others down in the form of negative outgroup tales. This idea needs further systematical testing, especially with the aim of teasing out relationship-enhancing motivations. Sharing a negative rumor with another school chum about a rival school is at once self- and relationship-enhancing; indeed, it may be that people share these sorts of rumors mostly for the social benefits they accrue and not to boost their self-esteem. These goals may perhaps be differentiated by experimental manipulations that temporarily raise or lower participants' self-esteem and expose them to self-enhancing and non-self-enhancing rumors; participants with lowered self-esteem should spread self-enhancing rumors more readily. Second, theorizing on self-esteem suggests that it is multidimensional (Baumeister, Campbell, Krueger, & Vohs, 2003). People with unstable or narcissistic forms of self-esteem—typically based on group membership—may be more prone to protect and enhance their self-image by spreading negative outgroup rumors, whereas those whose self-esteem is based on a realistic appraisal of accomplishments and relationships may not. For the threatened narcissist, negative outgroup rumors may serve as a form of aggressive self-esteem enhancement; this idea is ripe for testing. Third, as discussed in chapter 3 (this volume), the self-enhancement motive has often been capitalized on by those who have consciously planted rumors to be spread to drive a wedge between groups. Yet no attention has been paid to the motivations of those who orchestrate and spread such rumor propaganda. What is the extent and the effectiveness of rumor propaganda efforts, and how may their effects be prevented or neutralized? We have outlined these intriguing—and practically useful—questions elsewhere (DiFonzo & Bordia, in press).

Several interesting hypotheses surround how these three motivations operate overall. First, in what circumstances is each motivation generally operative? We speculate that relationship enhancement is the conversational norm from which one might deviate only when the possibility of tangible loss becomes salient (resulting in fact finding) or when one's sense of self is threatened (resulting in self-enhancement). Second, we posited that anxiety, uncertainty, and involvement lead to fact-finding motivation (a direct effect) which in turn leads to rumor transmission. In other words, fact-finding motivation mediates the effects of anxiety, uncertainty, and involvement on rumor transmission. This hypothesis has yet to be empirically tested. Third, we posited that relationship-enhancement motivation moderates the relationship between belief and rumor transmission. When people are motivated to enhance long-term relationships, they tend to pass along only those rumors that they believe; in the absence of this motivation, belief may not be closely related to transmission. This hypothesis also has yet to be empirically investigated.

In the broader view, much work remains to be accomplished in conceptualizing and investigating how each motivation is related to each antecedent. We speculate that differing types of negative events lead to differing motivations: Anxiety over possible loss of well-being leads to fact finding, anxiety about possible relationship deterioration leads to relationship enhancement, and anxiety over potential damage to self-image leads to self-enhancement motivation. Anxiety thus provides the goal of the motivation. We further speculate that uncertainty, involvement, and belief simply intensify motivation; for example, fear of losing one's job from downsizing motivates fact-finding motivation, and this motivation is especially strong when the management issues a no-comments statement (uncertainty is high), it is one's department—as opposed to another—that is likely to be downsized (outcome-relevant involvement is high), and downsizing seems plausible because management has downsized before in similar economic climates (belief is high).

Of course, some of the most interesting questions involve the effects—especially the cumulative effects over time—of each motivation on rumor selection, belief, and content change. To wit, we speculate that outgroup-negative rumors are most fit for survival over time in the context of a group that is primarily motivated by self- and relationship-enhancement, rather than fact-finding, motives. This hypothesis could be tested within a broader research paradigm that varied the motivation of experimental participants and then exposed them to various ingroup–outgroup positive–negative rumors and measured the likelihood of transmission to an ingroup–outgroup recipient. The research methodology would be especially fruitful if it also included the opportunity for participants to transmit rumors more than once and to several neighbors; for example, give Participants A, B, C, and D—all of the same ingroup—the opportunity to share either an outgroup-positive rumor or an outgroup-negative rumor with each other individually over several rounds of interaction. In conditions in which participants were first motivated to self- or relationship-enhance, these motivations should be accentuated by normative social influences (e.g., attitudinal conformity) and quickly result in the selection of (and higher levels of belief in) outgroup-negative—as compared with outgroup-positive—rumors. In conditions in which participants are motivated to fact find, this pattern of results should be weaker.

We leave this section on a methodological note. In the research we reported in chapter 3 (this volume), we saw that relative motivation was affected by varying rumor valence (positive–negative), rumor target (ingroup–outgroup), and rumor recipient (ingroup–outgroup). For example, the relationship-enhancement motivation was highest for the condition in which the rumor was positive and about the outgroup and the recipient was an outgroup member. This paradigm holds promise—these manipulations may be used, for example, to test the effect of motivation on rumor transmission and content—but we think these procedures need refinement and replication with other scenarios.

CUES TO CONFIDENCE IN RUMOR

Belief is an understudied and interesting aspect of rumor phenomena; several questions need to be addressed. First, a descriptive question: How much confidence do people place in commonly circulated rumors? In unpublished pilot work we asked college students to rate their belief in a set of external organizational rumors selected from snopes.com. We found very low levels of belief overall, but our sample of rumors—and participants—was woefully narrow. Of particular significance in future work would be confidence ratings of rumors related to specific attitudes of interest, such as attitudes about competing groups. For example, the false rumor that the AIDS virus was created in a western laboratory and tested on 100,000 Africans is believed by one third of a sample of African American churchgoers (another third are unsure about it; "Black Beliefs," 1995); the high level of belief in this rumor tells us much about the state of race relations in America today. Work is also needed to describe in more detail the shape of the relationship between belief and other outcomes; that is, we wonder how much belief is necessary for rumors to be transmitted or to affect other attitudes and behaviors. The nature of the relationship between belief and transmission may be linear or it may be catastrophic (a little belief affords large effects). In a similar way, even low-confidence negative rumors may affect behaviors, as when people decline to purchase a product rumored to contain carcinogens.

Second, why do people believe the rumors they do? In chapter 4 (this volume) we applied Brunswik's lens model of social judgment to frame this question and concluded that certain cues—agreement with attitude, source credibility, repetition, and absence of rebuttal—were operative. We first note the dearth of experimental evidence on the first three cues (agreement with attitude, source credibility, and repetition); much work could (easily) be done to experimentally validate the use of these cues in rumor confidence judgments and to derive the relative weight each cue is accorded. Second, in line with the previous chapter on motivations, the agreement with attitude cue might be fruitfully divided into cooler (the rumor agrees with a currently held attitude that is not closely tied to one's self-identity) versus warmer (the rumor agrees with an attitude that is closely tied to one's self-identity) cue subsets. The key marker between a warm versus cool cue is thus whether or not it bolsters a defensive reaction against a perceived threat; warm cue rumors are therefore self-enhancing. For example, strongly identified Democrats in 2004 may have been more likely to believe the false rumor that George W. Bush hypocritically misquoted the Bible because the rumor was self-enhancing, that is, it was a defamatory story attacking a perceived threat (the same could also be said of Republicans who felt threatened by Senator John Kerry). These cues should be experimentally tested; we speculate that self-enhancing cues are stronger than cues that indicate mere agreement with one's attitude. In broader terms, rumors that self-enhance are probably more likely to be believed than are rumors that don't, especially by people with low, unstable, or narcissistic self-esteem. In lens model terms, it seems likely that self-enhancement cues may be accorded greater weight in assessing one's confidence in a rumor.

RUMOR AS SENSE MAKING

In chapter 5 (this volume) we considered rumor sense making at the level of the individual and the group. At the individual level, we argued that many rumors convey a stable-cause explanation. Do they indeed? This hypothesis could be tested by procuring blind judges to evaluate a sample of rumors from a variety of domains and coding them for the presence or absence of a stable-cause explanation (x causes y and this cause is relatively stable over time). Less retrospective approaches could query participants about recent rumors:

> Think of a recent bit of information you heard about which
> you [or your group, acquaintances, friends, coworkers, or
> family] are unsure. Describe the information and the situation

surrounding it [these descriptions could be coded for stable-cause explanations]. Rate the extent to which this information explains or makes sense of a current situation or event. What current situation or event, if any, does this information explain? According to the information, what is the cause of the situation or event? Finally, rate the extent to which this cause will [or will not] last over time.

We also presented evidence suggesting that rumors lead people to perceive strong relationships between variables that are weak or nonexistent. This idea could be applied to increase knowledge of how racial stereotypes spread. It may be that rumors embedded with stable-cause explanations teach people to associate race with particular behaviors. This idea could be first explored by collecting race-related rumors: "Think of a recent bit of information you heard—about which you [or your group, acquaintances, friends, coworkers, or family] are unsure—that involved a member of another race." Participants could then describe the information and the situation surrounding it and these descriptions could be coded for stable-cause explanations. Research in this vein would be particularly interesting among child and school-age populations.

At the group level, research is needed to replicate the findings—reviewed in chapter 5 (this volume)—pertaining to the statement content, communicative postures, and dynamic flow in rumor interaction episodes over the Internet. These investigations should also explore the same phenomena in face-to-face interaction episodes through tape recording and transcription: Are the same patterns evident? Other interesting questions: What would the patterns of content, posture, and flow look like in a highly anxious group or one that perceived an imminent threat? The sense-making process might be more rapid and less deliberative in nature. In a similar vein, how would they look in a highly identified ingroup in the context of ethnic conflict with an outgroup? The sense-making process might include a conformity-demanding posture in which ingroup criticism was not permitted. Finally, how might these patterns change in the context of a more highly cohesive set of participants, say those in a very close-knit social unit? We speculate that the sense-making process may again proceed more quickly as compared with the Internet rumor discussions we analyzed.

RUMOR ACCURACY

In chapters 6 and 7 (this volume) we reviewed several questions related to rumor content change, accuracy base rates, and mechanisms related to how rumors become more and less accurate. We explored the literature on rumor content change and proposed that leveling (loss of details) occurs mostly in some real-life rumor episodes marked by low ambiguity and in which a group is primarily engaged in simply passing along the information, whereas adding (gain of details) occurs mostly in situations of high ambiguity and importance and the group is quite interactive and collaborative. This hypothesis should be tested experimentally to put to rest the persistent scientific legend that rumors always level. Research on this topic dovetails with an emphasis in social psychology on understanding social processes in the context of the act of communicating.

With regard to rumor accuracy base rates, we call for a revival of accuracy studies in naturalistic environments. With the proliferation of computer messaging archives, such studies ought to be far less labor-intensive than the bulk of those performed in the 1960s and 1970s. Rumors communicated via the Internet ought to be collected from a variety of domains and to sample a variety of situation types, such as high-involvement collaboration and low-involvement minimal-discussion serial transmission. (At the same time, efforts can be made to ascertain the relative frequency of these two situations.) After collection, the percentage of rumors or rumor elements that are true should then be ascertained. Of course, if such efforts can measure mechanisms affecting rumor accuracy discussed in chapter 7 (this volume), all the better; such data will of course be difficult to collect naturalistically and retrospectively. A series of diary-type web-based studies may be the most promising methodological avenue for collecting information of this type in field settings. Participants could be charged with the ongoing task of journaling rumors they hear and responding daily to items aimed at measuring cognitive, motivational, situational, group, and network data. If accuracy trends are also recorded, it may be possible to assess how widespread the Matthew accuracy effect is (accuracy trends bifurcate).

The set of accuracy mechanisms reviewed in chapter 7 (this volume) represents a rich source of theoretical propositions to be explored and tested. We propose several ideas here pertaining to each set. With regard to cognitive mechanisms, much could be gained by adopting the teller–listener–extremity effect paradigm—which uses serial transmission—but also allowing discussion (interaction) at each transmission node (Baron, David, Brunsman, & Inman, 1997, also proposed this). Because discussion allows for greater precision in transmission, accuracy should increase. In addition, we proposed that anxiety increases the reliance on extant cognitive structures (e.g., stereotypes) during transmission. This hypothesis could be tested by assessing each participant's level of implicit or explicit stereotyping, then manipulating participant anxiety before performing the tasks involved in the teller–listener–extremity effect paradigm. Lower anxiety and allowing participant discussion during transmission should each lead to less extreme judgments. These effects should be especially pronounced when the relevant cognitive structures (e.g., the stereotypical football player) are experimentally and subliminally primed (e.g., with a tachistoscope).

With regard to motivational mechanisms of accuracy, the methodology used by Lyons and Kashima (2001) could be extended by allowing discussion at each transmission node; fact-finding, as compared with relationship- and self-enhancement motivations, should increase accuracy. Second, very little work has been done on the conceptualization, measurement, and effect of the motivation to be "in the know" or to transmit rumors "for effect" (Sinha, 1952); we suspect that this motivation powerfully affects rumor accuracy. Third, the effects of self-enhancement motivation on accuracy (and rumor content change) is an area ripe for investigation; we have already outlined these ideas in the rumor motivations section earlier.

With regard to situational features, to our knowledge, no experimental work has followed up on R. H. Turner and Killian's (1972) idea that high collective excitement results in less stringent norms about what information is acceptable, especially in close—versus diffuse—groups. In addition, a group's corporate capacity to check rumor verity is an area in need of greater conceptual clarity and measurement. One goal of this work would be to reliably measure a group's capacity to check, and to relate this to overall rumor accuracy levels during any given rumor episode. One interesting question here: "How does the capacity to check fare against antiaccuracy motivations?" That is, how accurate are rumors in groups that have a high capacity to check rumor veracity but are strongly motivated to believe or disbelieve them? This question seems highly amenable to experimentation. We speculate that capacity to check trumps motivation when they are in conflict; rumors that are clearly false will not thrive, even among a group that strongly desires them to be true. We reason that in situations in which the rumor can be objectively checked, even relationship- and self-enhancing motivations come to act in service of accuracy because sending true information is a deeply engrained social rule. This research question has important practical implications; as previously discussed, many troubling rumor effects arise in situations of conflict in which people are strongly motivated to believe the worst about rival groups.

With regard to group mechanisms, the application of conformity literature to rumor phenomena seems a promising line of inquiry. In what circumstances does the transmission of an unverified bit of information cease to be sense-making activity and become a means of influence? When is external acceptance of a rumor demanded? In more specific terms, how does the well-known set of factors affecting conformity (e.g., unanimity, public balloting, group cohesion, low self-monitoring, group size) affect external acceptance of a rumor? Research of this sort would explore how, for example, "racialized narratives" (Maines, 1999) are not only common sets of beliefs circulating within communities, but also mandatory. A second group mechanism—culture—is witnessing resurgence in social psychology in general. Indeed, Lyons and Kashima (2001) found that culture informs rumor content change in serial transmissions of rumor. To what extent are rumors "culturally anchored" as proposed by Shibutani (1966)? The question first requires a sharper conceptualization—and measurement—of what we mean by *cultural anchoring*. The question might best be investigated in the context of well-developed cultural differences such as collectivism and individualism. For example, would the terminal story of the drunken football player in Baron et al.'s (1997) teller–listener–extremity effect study highlight more collectivistic than individualistic themes among Chinese as compared with American participants?

Finally, the investigation of network mechanisms is surely one of the most promising current avenues of accuracy research. In general, these research paths can be fruitfully guided by Buckner's (1965) conceptualizations of group orientation and MI; researchers can begin by sharpening these constructs, then systematically evaluating Buckner's (and our) hypotheses about how they act and interact to affect accuracy. Perhaps the greatest research fruit can be picked from this woefully underresearched question: "How do network transmission configurations—the network structure of information flow—affect rumor accuracy?" In chapter 7 (this volume) we posited first that different configurations differentially affect the influence of information liaisons; serial and cluster transmission grant more influence to liaisons than do MI configurations. This hypothesis could be evaluated by experimentally manipulating network transmission configuration and recording content changes at each node; liaisons should affect content less in the MI condition.

Second, Buckner posited that MI increased the speed of rumor content change relative to other configurations, but that group orientation moderated the direction of this change toward or away from accuracy. For example, groups that are accuracy motivated—as compared with relationship-enhancement motivated—should produce more accurate rumors and produce them more quickly in multiply interactive than in serial or cluster-transmission configurations. However, groups that are motivated by relationship enhancement—as compared with accuracy—should produce less accurate rumors and (also) produce them more quickly under MI than under serial or cluster transmission.

This idea has not been experimentally tested. The mechanisms that we propose are at work in these hypotheses can also be investigated: MI, as compared with serial and cluster transmission configurations, affords the opportunity for greater checking of information (both cross-checking across sources—as when Person C hears rumor variations from both Persons A and B—and checking of precision accuracy—as when Person C ensures that she heard the rumor correctly from Person A by discussing it with Person A). MI seems to afford greater opportunity for group forces, such as conformity, culture, and common perceptual biases heightened by collective excitement, to operate, especially in contexts in which the capacity to check is minimal.

We have been discussing how configurations of information flow—MI, serial transmission, and cluster transmission—affect rumor accuracy. We dubbed these configurations *network transmission configurations*. It is obvious, however, that these configurations occur in the context of actual social networks and these social networks can themselves be configured differently; we call networks *social space configurations*. Elsewhere we have reviewed these social space configurations and how they affect rumor transmission over time and across social space (DiFonzo & Bordia, in press). Three examples: In the usual representation of a *torus* configuration, each individual is relationally connected to his four closest "neighbors"—north, south, east, and west—in a two-dimensionally uniform distribution that resembles a grid. A *ribbon* configuration occurs when the person is connected to four neighbors aligned as in a line—two on that person's left and two on the right. A typical *family* configuration occurs when most of the people that one is connected with are also connected with each other (Latané & Bourgeois, 1996) and therefore form communities. These concepts have great relevance for accuracy research. Theorists and researchers can investigate how network transmission configurations are related to social space configurations, especially as they relate to accuracy. It seems likely that social space configurations may predispose and possibly constrain certain network transmission configurations. For example, we speculate that MI is more likely to occur in family than in ribbon configurations in view of the fact that family configurations predispose interaction within communities. Another interesting question for this research vein is, "How would social space configuration affect the spatial distribution of rumor accuracy over time?" We speculate that pockets of accurate and inaccurate rumors are more likely to occur in "clumpier" types of social space configurations such as the family (see DiFonzo & Bordia, in press, for a closely related presentation of hypotheses about the spatial distribution of rumors over time). This area is rich with potential and virtually untapped.

TRUST AND RUMOR TRANSMISSION

In chapter 8 (this volume) we explored the effects of trust on rumor transmission by reporting results of a longitudinal study of an organization undergoing a radical downsizing. One main finding was that distrust of management was a better predictor of rumor transmission than were anxiety and uncertainty. This finding—the first of its kind—should be replicated in other organizational settings. The current body of experimentally based knowledge about rumor merely mentions trust. In studies of rumor transmission, trust should become a central and regularly measured antecedent, along with anxiety, uncertainty, belief, loss of a sense of control, and importance. In addition to the sense-making (solving a puzzle) context, rumor should also regularly be considered in the context of intergroup conflict and threat; these of course involve perceptions of trust.

The broader extensions of this research are ripe for discovery and practically significant as well: Beyond management and staff, what roles does trust play in the spread of negative rumors related to any set of groups, especially those in conflict? The role of rumors in intergroup relations has only occasionally been systematically studied (e.g., Kakar, 2005; Knapp, 1944); in addition to indicating the underlying fears, beliefs, and attitudes of each party, future research could directly measure trust in the rival camp. We expect that distrust is strongly related to belief and transmission of negative rumors—even after anxiety and uncertainty are accounted for. (In addition, more general attitudes of basic mistrust, anomie, and powerlessness should correlate with belief in and transmission of all sorts of negative rumors.) Longitudinal research could investigate the direction of causality in a fashion similar to our analysis in chapter 2 (this volume): Does distrust lead to negative rumor transmission, or does transmitting negative rumors (through a process of schema activation or cognitive dissonance) lead to distrust? We suspect that both occur. We suspect that both anxiety and distrust feed off of one another, although we think that because attributions of malevolent intent inevitably lead to worry, the distrust → anxiety relation is the stronger of the two. Finally in this vein, trust should be experimentally manipulated in studies investigating rumor interventions. Raising trust should itself reduce negative rumor transmission. In addition, raising trust should aid rumor management efforts that try to reduce uncertainty and anxiety.

Broadening this research raises an issue in need of conceptual clarification. In our longitudinal study we measured trust in management. In this case, management was both the source of formal information and, in the context of the downsizing, the outgroup (anecdotal reports and observation of rumor content showed evidence of us-versus-them thinking). What of situations—quite common in conflict situations—in which the outgroup and the source of formal information are different entities? Trust of each entity (e.g., trust in the rival group and trust in the press) should be measured. What role does each play in the generation and survival of negative rumors? We speculate that distrust of the press may be the more serious of the two.

In chapters 2 and 8 (this volume) we introduced several new dependent variables related to rumor transmission: the number of different rumors heard, the number of different rumors passed, and the likelihood of transmission (the proportion of rumors heard that were passed). These measures need further testing and validation. We suggest that the diary method of data collection be used to more carefully record rumors heard and passed as well as a description of the transmission episodes. We also suggest that self-reports of these variables be compared with reports from friends and coworkers. Other measures, such as the number of different occasions on which a rumor was told and the number of different people to whom it was spread (Pezzo & Beckstead, 2006), should also be considered. Each construct is in need of conceptual sharpening: What does each signify? For reasons outlined in chapter 8 (this volume), we think that the likelihood of transmission quotient should become the standard rumor transmission outcome variable for actual rumors. Results from these studies would then be conceptually comparable to similar measures of behavioral intention in laboratory studies (e.g., "How likely, on a scale of 0% likely to 100% likely, are you to share this information with a coworker?").

RUMOR MANAGEMENT

The effective control of harmful rumors is of great practical relevance in a variety of domains, including public health, natural disaster and crisis management, civil and military administration, organizational communication, and PR. In chapter 9 (this volume) we reviewed research in this area. It is clear that a great deal more needs to be done. Although informed advice is readily available in the practitioner literature, very little systematic empirical research has been conducted on this topic.

More research is needed on ways to prevent rumors. Intergroup distrust (i.e., distrust between management and employees or between rival ethnic groups) plays an important role in the spread of rumors; when distrust is high, ambiguous events are interpreted as threatening. How can the likelihood of this happening be reduced? Greater contact between the rival groups (committees comprising management and employee representatives or citizen forums with diverse ethnic representation) may foster trust, reduce uncertainty about motives, and lower the likelihood that outgroup-derogating rumors would find traction. Management of anxiety and uncertainty during change is difficult. Strategies that structure the uncertainty should be useful in preventing rumors. We recommend that laboratory and field studies with experimental (involving communication strategies that structure uncertainty) and control conditions be conducted to assess the effectiveness of rumor prevention strategies.

More research is also needed on the effectiveness of rumor rebuttals. The role of the source of the rebuttal is important, but several questions arise: How does trust in the source affect rebuttal effectiveness? Higher trust will lead to greater rebuttal effectiveness, but is this a linear relationship or monotonic? Just how much trust is necessary? How do perceptions of the source of the rebuttal change after the rebuttal? Ingroup sources are perceived as credible and are likely to be more effective. However, what happens when an ingroup source rebuts a rumor that was derogating to the outgroup? Does the source garner respect for standing up for truth or lose authority and respect for selling out? How does the motivational context of the rebuttal source influence effectiveness? If the rebutter has something to gain, the rebuttal would be less effective. In a similar vein, how do the motivations of the target (or the rumor public) affect their acceptance of the rebuttal? We would expect that people motivated by fact-finding would be more persuaded by credible arguments, whereas those motivated by self-enhancement would be persuaded by strategies that assuage hurt esteem. Studies that manipulate motivations and then test the effectiveness of different rebuttals will help test these ideas. Finally, what are the long-term effects of rebuttals? Is there a sleeper effect (in which levels of belief in the rumor may dip soon after the rebuttal, but resurface after the passage of time)? Longitudinal designs will help explore the role of memory processes in the long-term effectiveness of rebuttals.

Much of the research on rebuttals has been conducted in laboratory settings; field studies are needed. Moreover, research on rumor management needs an interdisciplinary approach. Theoretical perspectives from cognitive psychology, social psychology, and rhetoric and communication need to combine with approaches in marketing, crisis management, and PR to arrive at context-relevant understanding of, and strategies for, rumor management.

Conclusion

Rumors continue to be a firm feature of social and organizational landscapes. We hope that we have put forth a clearer set of conceptualizations about rumor, its effects, motivations behind its transmission, its sense-making functions, its accuracy, the role of trust in rumor transmission, and how rumor may be managed. We have proposed an integrated model of rumor phenomena. We have outlined a comprehensive agenda for rumor research. We hope that this volume has served to highlight old and new questions surrounding rumor. We expect that it has served to put useful new frames—drawn from social and organizational literature—around the central aspects of rumor phenomena. We trust that this more integrated psychological and sociological approach to the study of rumor, the social and organizational frames offered, and the set of current research methods and questions put forth will be helpful to rumor researchers in the future.

References

10 die in Haiti as a false rumor is met by violent street protests. (1991, January 28). *The New York Times*, p. A3.

Abalakina-Paap, M., & Stephan, W. G. (1999). Beliefs in conspiracies. *Journal of Political Psychology, 20,* 637–647.

Abelson, R. P., & Lalljee, M. (1988). Knowledge structures and causal explanation. In D. J. Hilton (Ed.), *Contemporary science and natural explanation: Commonsense conceptions of causality* (pp. 175–203). New York: New York University Press.

Åckerström, M. (1988). The social construction of snitches. *Deviant Behavior, 9,* 155–167.

Adams, J. S. (1965). *Inequity in social exchange.* In L. Berkowitz (Ed.), *Advances in experimental social psychology* (Vol. 2, pp. 267–296). New York: Academic Press.

Agnes, M. (Ed.). (1996). *Webster's new world dictionary and thesaurus.* New York: Simon & Schuster.

Aiken, L. S., & West, S. G. (1991). *Multiple regression: Testing and interpreting interactions.* Newbury Park, CA: Sage.

Ajzen, I. (1977). Intuitive theories of events and the effects of base-rate information on prediction. *Journal of Personality and Social Psychology, 35,* 303–314.

Allport, F. H., & Lepkin, M. (1945). Wartime rumors of waste and special privilege: Why some people believe them. *Journal of Abnormal and Social Psychology, 40,* 3–36.

Allport, G. W., & Postman, L. J. (1947a). An analysis of rumor. *Public Opinion Quarterly, 10,* 501–517.

Allport, G. W., & Postman, L. J. (1947b). *The psychology of rumor.* New York: Holt, Rinehart & Winston.

Ambrosini, P. J. (1983). Clinical assessment of group and defensive aspects of rumor. *International Journal of Group Psychotherapy, 33,* 69–83.

Anderson, C. A. (1983). Abstract and concrete data in the perseverance of social theories: When weak data lead to unshakable beliefs. *Journal of Experimental Social Psychology, 19,* 93–108.

Anderson, C. A. (1985). Argument availability as a mediator of social theory perseverance. *Social Cognition, 3,* 235–249.

Anderson, C. A., Krull, D. S., & Weiner, B. (1996). Explanations: Processes and consequences. In E. T. Higgins & A. W. Kruglanski (Eds.), *Social psychology: Handbook of basic principles* (pp. 271–296). New York: Guilford Press.

Anderson, C. A., Lepper, M. R., & Ross, L. (1980). Perseverance of social theories: The role of explanation in the persistence of discredited information. *Journal of Personality and Social Psychology, 39,* 1037–1049.

Anderson, C. A., & Slusher, M. P. (1986). Relocating motivational effects: A synthesis of cognitive and motivational effects on attributions for success and failure. *Social Cognition, 4*, 270–292.

Andreassen, P. B. (1987). On the social psychology of the stock market: Aggregate attributional effects and the regressiveness of prediction. *Journal of Personality and Social Psychology, 53*, 490–496.

Antaki, C. (1988). Explanations, communication and social cognition. In C. Antaki (Ed.), *Analysing everyday explanation: A casebook of methods* (pp. 1–14). London: Sage.

Antaki, C., & Fielding, G. (1981). Research on ordinary explanations. In C. Antaki (Ed.), *The psychology of ordinary explanations of social behaviour: Vol. 23. European Monographs in Social Psychology* (pp. 27–55). London: Academic Press.

Anthony, S. (1973). Anxiety and rumour. *Journal of Social Psychology, 89*, 91–98.

Anthony, S. (1992). The influence of personal characteristics on rumor knowledge and transmission among the deaf. *American Annals of the Deaf, 137*, 44–47.

Arndt, J. (1967). *Word of mouth advertising: A review of the literature.* New York: Advertising Research Foundation.

Asch, S. E. (1955). Opinions and social pressure. *Scientific American, 193*, 31–35.

Ashford, S., & Black, J. (1996). Proactivity during organizational entry: The role of desire for control. *Journal of Applied Psychology, 81*, 199–214.

Austin, M. J., & Brumfield, L. (1991). P&G's run-in with the devil. *Business and Society Review, 78*(Summer), 16–19.

Back, K., Festinger, L., Hymovitch, B., Kelley, H., Schachter, S., & Thibaut, J. (1950). The methodology of studying rumor transmission. *Human Relations, 3*, 307–312.

Bacon, F. T. (1979). Credibility of repeated statements: Memory for trivia. *Journal of Experimental Psychology: Human Learning and Memory, 5*, 241–252.

Bandura, A. (2001). Social cognitive theory: An agentic perspective. *Annual Review of Psychology, 52*, 1–26.

Baron, R. M., & Kenny, D. A. (1986). The moderator–mediator variable distinction in social psychological research: Conceptual, strategic, and statistical considerations. *Journal of Personality and Social Psychology, 51*, 1173–1182.

Baron, R. S., David, J. P., Brunsman, B. M., & Inman, M. (1997). Why listeners hear less than they are told: Attentional load and the Teller-Listener Extremity effect. *Journal of Personality and Social Psychology, 72*, 826–838.

Bartlett, F. C. (1932). *Remembering.* Cambridge, England: Cambridge University Press.

Bauer, R. A., & Gleicher, D. B. (1953). Word-of-mouth communication in the Soviet Union. *Public Opinion Quarterly, 17*, 297–310.

Baumeister, R. F., Bratslavsky, E., Finkenauer, C., & Vohs, K. D. (2001). Bad is stronger than good. *Review of General Psychology, 5*, 323–370.

Baumeister, R. F., Campbell, J. D., Krueger, J. I., & Vohs, K. D. (2003). Does high self-esteem cause better performance, interpersonal success, happiness, or healthier lifestyles? *Psychological Science in the Public Interest, 4*(1), 1–44.

Baumeister, R. F., & Leary, M. R. (1995). The need to belong: Desire for interpersonal attachments as a fundamental human motivation. *Psychological Bulletin, 117*, 497–529.

Baumeister, R. F., Zhang, L., & Vohs, K. D. (2004). Gossip as cultural learning. *Review of General Psychology, 8*, 111–121.

Beal, D. J., Ruscher, J. B., & Schnake, S. B. (2001). No benefit of the doubt: Intergroup bias in understanding causal explanation. *British Journal of Social Psychology, 40*, 531–543.

Begg, I. M., Anas, A., & Farinacci, S. (1992). Dissociation of processes in belief: Source recollection, statement familiarity, and the illusion of truth. *Journal of Experimental Psychology: General, 121*, 446–458.

Belgion, M. (1939). The vogue of rumour. *Quarterly Review, 273*, 1–18.

Bennett, G. (1985). What's modern about the modern legend? *Fabula, 26*, 219–229.

Berger, C. R. (1987). Communicating under uncertainty. In M. E. Roloff & G. R. Miller (Eds.), *Interpersonal processes: New directions in communication research* (pp. 39–62). Newbury Park, CA: Sage.

Berger, C. R., & Bradac, J. J. (1982). *Language and social knowledge: Uncertainty in interpersonal relations*. London: Edward Arnold.

Bird, D. A. (1979). *Rumor as folklore: An interpretation and inventory*. Unpublished doctoral dissertation, Indiana University, Bloomington, IN.

Black beliefs on AIDS tallied. (1995, November 2). *Rochester Democrat and Chronicle*, p. B1.

Blake, R. H., McFaul, T. R., & Porter, W. H. (1974, November). *Authority and mass media as variables in rumor transmission*. Paper presented at the annual meeting of the Western Speech Communication Association, Newport Beach, CA.

Blake, R. R., & Mouton, J. S. (1983). The urge to merge: Tying the knot successfully. *Training and Development Journal, 37*, 41–46.

Blumenfeld, L. (1991, July 15). Procter & Gamble's devil of a problem: Anti-Satanism watchdogs turn up the heat. *Washington Post*, pp. B1, B6.

Bobo, L., & Kluegel, J. R. (1993). Opposition to race-targeting: Self-interest, stratification ideology, or racial attitudes. *American Sociological Review, 58*, 443–464.

Boehm, L. E. (1994). The validity effect—a search for mediating variables. *Personality and Social Psychology Bulletin, 20*, 285–293.

Bordia, P. (1996). Studying verbal interaction on the Internet: The case of rumor transmission research. *Behavior Research Methods, Instruments, & Computers, 28*, 149–151.

Bordia, P., & DiFonzo, N. (2002). When social psychology became less social: Prasad and the history of rumor research. *Asian Journal of Social Psychology, 5*, 49–61.

Bordia, P., & DiFonzo, N. (2004). Problem solving in social interactions on the Internet: Rumor as social cognition. *Social Psychology Quarterly, 67*, 33–49.

Bordia, P., & DiFonzo, N. (2005). Psychological motivations in rumor spread. In G. A.

Fine, C. Heath, & V. Campion-Vincent (Eds.), *Rumor mills: The social impact of rumor and legend* (pp. 87–101). New York: Aldine Press.

Bordia, P., DiFonzo, N., & Chang, A. (1999). Rumor as group problem-solving: Development patterns in informal computer-mediated groups. *Small Group Research, 30*(1), 8–28.

Bordia, P., DiFonzo, N., Haines, R., & Chaseling, L. (2005). Rumor denials as persuasive messages: Effects of personal relevance, source, and message characteristics. *Journal of Applied Social Psychology, 35*, 1301–1331.

Bordia, P., DiFonzo, N., Irmer, B. E., Gallois, C., & Bourne, M. (2005). *Consumer reactions to corporate rumor refutations*. Unpublished manuscript.

Bordia, P., DiFonzo, N., & Schulz, C. A. (2000). Source characteristics in denying rumors of organizational closure: Honesty is the best policy. *Journal of Applied Social Psychology, 11*, 2301–2309.

Bordia, P., DiFonzo, N., & Travers, V. (1998). Denying rumors of organizational change: A higher source is not always better. *Communications Research Reports, 15*, 189–198.

Bordia, P., Hobman, E., Jones, E., Gallois, C., & Callan, V. J. (2004). Uncertainty during organizational change: Types, consequences, and management strategies. *Journal of Business and Psychology, 18*, 507–532.

Bordia, P., Hunt, L., Paulsen, N., Tourish, D., & DiFonzo, N. (2004). Communication and uncertainty during organizational change: Is it all about control? *European Journal of Work and Organizational Psychology, 13*, 345–365.

Bordia, P., Jones, E., Gallois, C., Callan, V. J., & DiFonzo, N. (in press). Management are aliens! Rumors and stress during organizational change. *Group & Organization Management*.

Bordia, P., & Rosnow, R. L. (1998). Rumor rest stops on the information superhighway: A naturalistic study of transmission patterns in a computer-mediated rumor chain. *Human Communication Research, 25*, 163–179.

Brock, T. C. (1968). Implications of commodity theory for value change. In A. Greenwald, T. C. Brock, & T. M. Ostrom (Eds.), *Psychological foundations of attitudes* (pp. 243–276). New York: Academic Press.

Brunswik, E. (1952). The conceptual framework of psychology. *International encyclopedia of unified science.* Chicago: University of Chicago Press.

Brunvand, J. H. (1981). *The vanishing hitchhiker.* New York: Norton.

Brunvand, J. H. (1984). *The choking Doberman.* New York: Norton.

Buckner, H. T. (1965). A theory of rumor transmission. *Public Opinion Quarterly, 29,* 54–70.

Burlew, L. D., Pederson, J. E., & Bradley, B. (1994). The reaction of managers to the pre-acquisition stage of a corporate merger: A qualitative study. *Journal of Career Development, 21,* 11–22.

Burt, R., & Knez, M. (1996). Third-party gossip and trust. In R. M. Kramer & T. R. Tyler (Eds.), *Trust in organizations: Frontiers of theory and research* (pp. 68–89). Thousand Oaks, CA: Sage.

Calvo, M. G., & Castillo, M. D. (1997). Mood-congruent bias in interpretation of ambiguity: Strategic process and temporary activation. *The Quarterly Journal of Experimental Psychology, 50,* 163–182.

Cantera, K. (2002, January 3). Vigilant Utahns. *The Salt Lake Tribune,* p. A1.

Caplow, T. (1947). Rumors in war. *Social Forces, 25,* 298–302.

Cato, F. W. (1982). Procter & Gamble and the devil. *Public Relations Quarterly, 27,* 16–21.

Chapman, L. J., & Chapman, J. P. (1969). Illusory correlation as an obstacle to the use of valid psychodiagnostic signs. *Journal of Abnormal Psychology, 74,* 271–280.

Choe, S., Hanley, C. J., & Mendoza, M. (1999, October 17). GIs admit murdering civilians in S. Korea. *Rochester Democrat and Chronicle,* pp. 1A, 3A.

Chulov, M., Warne-Smith, D., & Colman, E. (2004, February 17). Rumour the spark that fired racial tinderbox. *The Australian,* pp. 1, 6.

Cialdini, R. B., & Trost, M. R. (1998). Social influence: Social norms, conformity, and compliance. In D. T. Gilbert, S. T. Fiske, & G. Lindzey (Eds.), *The handbook of social psychology* (4th ed., Vol. II, pp. 151–192). Boston: McGraw-Hill.

Clampitt, P. G., DeKoch, R. J., & Cashman, T. (2000). A strategy for communicating about uncertainty. *Academy of Management Executive, 14,* 41–57.

Cohen, G. L., Aronson, J., & Steele, C. M. (2000). When beliefs yield to evidence: Reducing biased evaluation by affirming the self. *Personality and Social Psychology Bulletin, 26,* 1151–1164.

Cohen, J. (1988). *Statistical power analysis for the behavioral sciences* (2nd ed.). Hillsdale, NJ: Erlbaum.

Cornwell, D., & Hobbs, S. (1992). Rumour and legend: Irregular interactions between social psychology and folklorists. *Canadian Psychology, 33,* 609–613.

Creed, W. E. D., & Miles, R. E. (1996). Trust in organizations: A conceptual framework linking organizational forms, managerial philosophies, and the opportunity costs of controls. In R. E. Kramer & T. R. Tyler (Eds.), *Trust in organizations: Frontiers of theory and research* (pp. 16–38). Thousand Oaks, CA: Sage.

Crick, N. R., Nelson, D. A., Morales, J. R., Cullerton-Sen, C., Casas, J. F., & Hickman, S. (2001). Relational victimization in childhood and adolescence: I hurt you through the grapevine. In J. Juvonen & S. Graham (Eds.), *School-based peer harassment: The plight of the vulnerable and victimized* (pp. 196–214). New York: Guilford Press.

Davis, K. (1972). *Human behavior at work.* San Francisco: McGraw-Hill.

Davis, K. (1975, June). Cut those rumors down to size. *Supervisory Management,* 2–6.

Davis, W. L., & O'Connor, J. R. (1977). Serial transmission of information: A study of the grapevine. *Journal of Applied Communication Research, 5,* 61–72.

Day, R. S. (1986). Overconfidence as a result of incomplete and wrong knowledge. In R. W. Scholz (Ed.), *Current issues in West*

German decision research (pp. 13–30). Frankfurt am Main, Germany: Lang.

DeClerque, J., Tsui, A. O., Abul-Ata, M. F., & Barcelona, D. (1986). Rumor, misinformation, and oral contraceptive use in Egypt. *Social Science and Medicine, 23,* 83–92.

Deener, B. (2001, September 20). Rumors rattle market. *The Dallas Morning News.*

De Fleur, M. L. (1962). Mass communication and the study of rumor. *Sociological Inquiry, 32,* 51–70.

DePaulo, B. M., & Kashy, D. A. (1998). Everyday lies in close and casual relationships. *Journal of Personality and Social Psychology 74,* 63–79.

Dewey, J. (1925). *Experience and nature.* Chicago: Open Court.

Dietz-Uhler, B. (1999). Defensive reactions to group-relevant information. *Group Processes and Intergroup Relations, 2,* 17–29.

DiFonzo, N. (1994). *Piggy-backed syllogisms for investor behavior: Probabilistic mental modeling in rumor-based stock market trading.* Unpublished doctoral thesis, Temple University, Philadelphia.

DiFonzo, N., & Bordia, P. (1997). Rumor and prediction: Making sense (but losing dollars) in the stock market. *Organizational Behavior and Human Decision Processes, 71,* 329–353.

DiFonzo, N., & Bordia, P. (1998). A tale of two corporations: Managing uncertainty during organizational change. *Human Resource Management, 37,* 295–303.

DiFonzo, N., & Bordia, P. (2000). How top PR professionals handle hearsay: Corporate rumors, their effects, and strategies to manage them. *Public Relations Review, 26,* 173–190.

DiFonzo, N., & Bordia, P. (2002a). Corporate rumor activity, belief, and accuracy. *Public Relations Review, 150,* 1–19.

DiFonzo, N., & Bordia, P. (2002b). Rumor and stable-cause attribution in prediction and behavior. *Organizational Behavior and Human Decision Processes, 88,* 329–353.

DiFonzo, N., & Bordia, P. (2006). Rumor in organizational contexts. In D. A. Hantula (Ed.), *Advances in psychology: A tribute to Ralph L. Rosnow* (pp. 249–274). Mahwah, NJ: Erlbaum.

DiFonzo, N., & Bordia, P. (in press). Rumors influence: Toward a dynamic social impact theory of rumor. In A. R. Pratkanis (Ed.), *The science of social influence.* Philadelphia: Psychology Press.

DiFonzo, N., Bordia, P., & Rosnow, R. L. (1994). Reining in rumors. *Organizational Dynamics, 23*(1), 47–62.

DiFonzo, N., Bordia, P., & Winterkorn, R. (2003, January). *Distrust is a key ingredient in negative rumor transmission.* Paper presented at the 4th Annual Meeting of the Society for Personality and Social Psychologists, Los Angeles, CA.

DiFonzo, N., Hantula, D. A., & Bordia, P. (1998). Microworlds for experimental research: Having your (control and collection) cake, and realism too. *Behavior Research Methods, Instruments, & Computers, 30,* 278–286.

Dirks, K. T., & Ferrin, D. L. (2001). The role of trust in organizational settings. *Organizational Science, 12,* 450–467.

Dirks, K. T., & Ferrin, D. L. (2002). Trust in leadership: Meta-analytic findings and implications for research and practice. *Journal of Applied Psychology, 87,* 611–628.

Donnelly, F. K. (1983, Spring). People's Almanac predictions: Retrospective check of accuracy. *Skeptical Inquirer,* 48–52.

Dunbar, R. I. M. (1996). *Grooming, gossip, and the evolution of language.* Cambridge, MA: Harvard University Press.

Dunbar, R. I. M. (2004). Gossip in evolutionary perspective. *Review of General Psychology, 8,* 100–110.

Dwyer, J. C., & Drew, C. (2005, September 29). Fear exceeded crime's reality in New Orleans. *The New York Times,* pp. A1, A22.

Eder, D., & Enke, J. L. (1991). The structure of gossip: Opportunities and constraints on collective expression among adolescents. *American Sociological Review, 56,* 494–508.

Edwards, O. (1989, April). Leak soup. *GQ Magazine,* p. 228.

Einhorn, H. J., & Hogarth, R. M. (1986). Judging probable cause. *Psychological Bulletin, 99,* 3–19.

Ellis, R. J., & Zanna, M. P. (1990). Arousal and causal attribution. *Canadian Journal of Behavioural Science, 22,* 1–12.

Emory, D. (n.d.) *Does Osama bin Laden own Snapple?* Retrieved December 13, 2005, from http://urbanlegends.about.com/library/blsnapple.htm

Esposito, J. L. (1986/1987). Subjective factors and rumor transmission: A field investigation of the influence of anxiety, importance, and belief on rumormongering (Doctoral dissertation, Temple University, 1986). *Dissertation Abstracts International, 48,* 596B.

Esposito, J. L., & Rosnow, R. L. (1983, April). Corporate rumors: How they start and how to stop them. *Management Review,* 44–49.

Fama, E. F., Fisher, L., Jensen, M. C., & Roll, R. (1969). The adjustment of stock prices to new information. *International Economic Review, 10,* 1–21.

Fearn-Banks, K. (2002). *Crisis communications: A casebook approach.* Mahwah, NJ: Erlbaum.

Fein, S., & Spencer, S. J. (1997). Prejudice as self-image maintenance: Affirming the self through derogating others. *Journal of Personality and Social Psychology, 73,* 31–44.

Festinger, L. (1957). *A theory of cognitive dissonance.* Evanston, IL: Row, Peterson.

Festinger, L., Cartwright, D., Barber, K., Fleischl, J., Gottsdanker, J., Keysen, A., et al. (1948). A study of rumor: Its origin and spread. *Human Relations, 1,* 464–485.

Fine, G. A. (1985). Rumors and gossiping. In T. Van Dijk (Ed.), *Handbook of discourse analysis* (Vol. 3, pp. 223–237). London: Academic Press.

Fine, G. A. (1992). *Manufacturing tales: Sex and money in contemporary legends.* Knoxville: University of Tennessee Press.

Fine, G. A. (2005, April 1–3). *Does rumor lie: Narrators and the framing of unsecured information.* Paper presented to the Sante Fe Institute's Conference on Deception: Methods, Motives, Contexts, and Consequences, Santa Fe, NM.

Fine, G. A., Heath, C., & Campion-Vincent, V. (Eds.) (2005). *Rumor mills: The social impact of rumor and legend.* Chicago: Aldine.

Fine, G. A., & Turner, P. A. (2001). *Whispers on the color line: Rumor and race in America.* Berkeley: University of California Press.

Firth, R. (1956). Rumor in a primitive society. *Journal of Abnormal and Social Psychology, 53,* 122–132.

Fisher, D. R. (1998). Rumoring theory and the Internet: A framework for analyzing the grass roots. *Social Science Computer Review, 16,* 158–168.

Fischle, M. (2000). Mass response to the Lewinsky scandal: Motivated reasoning or Bayesian updating? *Political Psychology, 21,* 135–159.

Fiske, S. T. (2003). Five core social motives, plus or minus five. In S. J. Spencer & S. Fein (Eds.), *Ontario Symposium on Personality and Social Psychology: Vol. 9. Motivated social perception* (pp. 233–246). Mahwah, NJ: Erlbaum.

Fiske, S. T. (2004). *Social beings: A core motives approach to social psychology.* Hoboken, NJ: Wiley.

Fiske, S. T., Lin, M., & Neuberg, S. L. (1999). The continuum model: Ten years later. In S. Chaiken & Y. Trope (Eds.), *Dual process theories in social psychology* (pp. 231–254). New York: Guilford Press.

Fiske, S. T., & Taylor, S. E. (1991). *Social cognition* (2nd ed.). New York: Random House.

Flanagan, J. C. (1954). The critical incident technique. *Psychological Bulletin, 51,* 327–358.

Foster, E. K. (2004). Research on gossip: Taxonomy, methods, and future directions. *Review of General Psychology, 8,* 78–99.

Foster, E. K., & Rosnow, R. L. (2006). Gossip and network relationships: The processes of constructing and managing difficult interaction. In D. C. Kirkpatrick, S. W. Duck, & M. K. Foley (Eds.), *Relating difficulty* (pp. 161–201). Mahwah, NJ: Erlbaum.

Freedman, A. M. (1991, May 10). Rumor turns fantasy into bad dream. *The Wall Street Journal,* pp. B1, B5.

Frith, B. (2001, August 29). AMP's silence on NAB merger rumours spoke volumes. *The Australian,* p. M1.

Fromkin, H. L. (1972). Feelings of interpersonal undistinctiveness: An unpleasant affective state. *Journal of Experimental Research in Personality, 6,* 178–185.

Gigerenzer, G., Hoffrage, U., & Kleinbölting, H. (1991). Probabilistic mental models: A Brunswikian theory of confidence. *Psychological Review, 98,* 506–528.

Gillin, B. (2005, September 28). Tales of mass murder, rape proving false. *Rochester Democrat and Chronicle,* p. 7A.

Gilovich, T., Vallone, R., & Tversky, A. (1985). The hot hand in basketball: On the misperception of random sequences. *Journal of Personality and Social Psychology, 17,* 295–314.

Gluckman, M. (1963). Gossip and scandal. *Current Anthropology, 4,* 307–316.

Goggins, S. M. (1979). *The wormburger scare: A case study of the McDonald's corporation's public relations campaign to stop a damaging rumor.* Unpublished master's thesis, Georgia State University, Athens.

Goleman, D. (1991, June 4). Anatomy of a rumor: It flies on fear. *The New York Times,* p. C5.

Goodwin, S. A., Operario, D., & Fiske S. T. (1998). Situational power and interpersonal dominance facilitate bias and inequality. *Journal of Social Issues, 54,* 677–698.

Goswamy, M., & Kumar, A. (1990). Stochastic model for spread of rumour supported by a leader resulting in collective violence and planning of control measures. *Mathematical Social Sciences, 19,* 23–36.

Green, D. F. (1984). *Rumor control strategies for corporations.* Unpublished master's thesis, University of Texas at Austin.

Grice, H. P. (1975). Logic and conversation. The William James Lectures. In P. Cole & J. L. Morgan (Eds.), *Syntax and semantics: Vol. 3. Speech acts* (pp. 41–58). New York: Academic Press.

Gross, A. E. (1990, October 22). Crisis management: How Popeyes and Reebok confronted product rumors. *Adweek's Marketing Week,* p. 27.

Gudykunst, W. B. (1995). Anxiety/uncertainty management (AUM) theory: Current status. In R. L. Wiseman (Ed.), *Intercultural communication theory* (pp. 8–57). Thousand Oaks, CA: Sage.

Guerin, B. (2003). Language use as a social strategy: A review and an analytic framework for the social sciences. *Review of General Psychology, 7,* 251–298.

Harcourt, J., Richerson, V., & Wattier, M. J. (1991). A national study of middle managers' assessment of organization communication quality. *Journal of Business Communication, 28,* 348–365.

Hardin, C. D., & Higgins, E. T. (1996). Shared reality: How social verification makes the subjective objective. In R. M. Sorrentino & E. T. Higgins (Vol. Eds.), *Handbook of motivation and cognition: Vol. 3. The interpersonal context* (pp. 28–84). New York: Guilford Press.

Hari, J. (2002, December 31). Well, they would say that, wouldn't they? *Australian Financial Review,* p. 42.

Harris, B., & Harvey, J. H. (1981). Attribution theory: From phenomenal causality to the intuitive social scientist and beyond. In C. Antaki (Ed.), *The psychology of ordinary explanations of social behaviour: Vol. 23. European Monographs in Social Psychology* (pp. 57–95). London: Academic Press.

Harris, S. G. (1994). Organizational culture and individual sensemaking: A schema-based perspective. *Organizational Science, 5,* 309–321.

Hasher, L., Goldstein, D., & Toppino T. (1977). Frequency and the conference of referential validity. *Journal of Verbal Learning and Verbal Behavior, 16,* 107–112.

Heath, C., Bell, C., & Sternberg, E. (2001). Emotional selection in memes: The case of urban legends. *Journal of Personality and Social Psychology, 81,* 1028–1041.

Heider, F. (1958). *The psychology of interpersonal relations.* New York: Wiley.

Hellweg, S. A. (1987). Organizational grapevines. In B. Dervin & M. J. Voigt, *Progress in communication sciences* (Vol. 8, pp. 213–230). Norwood, NJ: Ablex Publishing.

Hershey, R. (1956). Heed rumors for their meaning. *Personnel Journal, 34,* 299–301.

Hicks, R. D. (1990). Police pursuit of Satanic crime: Part 2: The Satanic conspiracy and urban legends. *Skeptical Inquirer, 14,* 378–389.

Higgins, E. T. (1981). The "communication game": Implications of social cognition. In E. T. Higgins, C. P. Herman, & M. P.

Zanna (Eds.), *Ontario Symposium on Personality and Social Psychology: Vol. 1. Social cognition* (pp. 343–392). Hillsdale, NJ: Erlbaum.

Higham, T. M. (1951). The experimental study of the transmission of rumour. *British Journal of Psychology, 42,* 42–55.

Hilton, D. J., & Slugoski, B. R. (1986). Knowledge-based causal attribution: The abnormal conditions focus model. *Psychological Review, 93,* 75–88.

Hirschhorn, L. (1983). *Cutting back: Retrenchment and redevelopment of human and community services.* San Francisco: Jossey-Bass.

Hogg, M., & Abrams, D. (1988). S*ocial identifications: A social psychology of intergroup relations and group processes.* London: Routledge.

Holtgraves, T., & Grayer, A. R. (1994). I am not a crook: Effects of denials on perceptions of a defendant's guilt, personality, and motives. *Journal of Applied Social Psychology, 24,* 2132–2150.

Hom, H., & Haidt, J. (2002, January). *Psst, Did you hear? Exploring the gossip phenomenon.* Poster presented at the Annual Meeting of the Society of Personality and Social Psychologists, Savannah, GA.

Horowitz, D. L. (2001). *The deadly ethnic riot.* Berkeley: University of California Press.

Houmanfar, R., & Johnson, R. (2003). Organizational implications of gossip and rumor. *Journal of Organizational Behavior Management, 23,* 117–138.

Hovland, C., & Weiss, W. (1951). The influence of source credibility on communication effectiveness. *Public Opinion Quarterly, 15,* 635–650.

Hunsaker, P. L., & Coombs, M. W. (1988). Mergers and acquisitions: Managing the emotional issues. *Personnel Journal, 67,* 56–78.

Iyer, E. S., & Debevec, K. (1991). Origin of rumor and tone of message in rumor quelling strategies. *Psychology and Marketing, 8,* 161–175.

Jaeger, M. E., Anthony, S., & Rosnow, R. L. (1980). Who hears what from whom and with what effect: A study of rumor. *Personality and Social Psychology Bulletin, 6,* 473–478.

JDBGMGR.EXE. (2002, September). Retrieved June 7, 2004, from http://www.snopes.com/computer/virus/jdbgmgr.htm

Jennings, D. L., Amabile, T. M., & Ross, L. (1982). Information covariation assessment: Data-based versus theory-based judgments. In D. Kahneman, P. Slovic, & A. Tversky (Eds.), *Judgment under uncertainty: Heuristics and biases* (pp. 211–230). New York: Cambridge University Press.

Jones, E. E., & Davis, K. E. (1965). From acts to dispositions: The attribution process in person perception. In L. Berkowitz (Ed.), *Advances in experimental social psychology* (Vol. 2, pp. 220–226), New York: Academic Press.

Jung, C. G. (1916). Ein beitrag zur psycholgie des gerüchtes [A contribution in the psychology of rumor]. In C. E. Long (Trans.), *Collected papers on analytical psychology* (pp. 176–190). New York: Wiley. (Original work published 1910)

Jung, C. G. (1959). A visionary rumour. *Journal of Analytical Psychology, 4,* 5–19.

Jungermann, H., & Thüring, M. (1993). Causal knowledge and the expression of uncertainty. In G. Strube & K. F. Wender (Eds.), *The cognitive psychology of knowledge* (pp. 53–73). Amsterdam: Elsevier Science.

Kahneman, D., & Tversky, A. (1973). On the psychology of prediction. *Psychological Review, 80,* 237–351.

Kahneman, D., & Tversky, A. (1979). Prospect theory: An analysis of decision under risk. *Econometrica, 47,* 263–291.

Kahneman, D., & Tversky, A. (1982). Subjective probability: A judgment of representativeness. In D. Kahneman, P. Slovic, & A. Tversky (Eds.), *Judgment under uncertainty: Heuristics and biases* (pp. 32–47). New York: Cambridge University Press.

Kakar, S. (2005). Rumors and religious riots. In G. A. Fine, V. Campion-Vincent, & C. Heath (Eds.), *Rumor mills: The social impact of rumor and legend* (pp. 53–59). New York: Aldine.

Kamins, M. A., Folkes, V. S., & Perner, L. (1997). Consumer responses to rumors: Good news, bad news. *Journal of Consumer Psychology, 6,* 165–187.

Kapferer, J.-N. (1989). A mass poisoning rumor in Europe. *Public Opinion Quarterly, 53,* 467–481.

Kapferer, J.-N. (1990). Rumor in the stock exchange. *Communications, 52,* 61–84.

Kapferer, J.-N. (1990). *Rumors: Uses, interpretations, and images* (B. Fink, Trans.). New Brunswick, NJ: Transaction Publishers. (Original work published 1987)

Kelley, H. H. (1973). The processes of causal attribution. *American Psychologist, 28,* 107–128.

Kelley, S. R. (2004). *Rumors in Iraq: A guide to winning hearts and minds.* Unpublished master's thesis, Naval Postgraduate School, Monterey, CA. Retrieved November 16, 2004, from http://theses.nps.navy.mil/04Sep_Kelley.pdf

Kenrick, D. T., Maner, J. K., Butner, J., Li, N. P., Becker, D. V., & Schaller, M. (2002). Dynamical evolutionary psychology: Mapping the domains of the new interactionist paradigm. *Personality and Social Psychology Review, 6,* 347–356.

Kerner, O., Lindsay, J. V., Harris, F. R., Abel, I. W., Brooke, E. W., Thornton, C. B., et al. (1968). *Report of the National Advisory Commission on Civil Disorders* (Report No. 1968 O - 291-729). Washington, DC: U.S. Government Printing Office.

Kimmel, A. J. (2004a). *Rumors and rumor control: A manager's guide to understanding and combating rumors.* Mahwah, NJ: Erlbaum.

Kimmel, A. J. (2004b). Rumors and the financial marketplace. *Journal of Behavioral Finance, 5,* 134–141.

Kimmel, A. J., & Keefer, R. (1991). Psychological correlates of the transmission and acceptance of rumors about AIDS. *Journal of Applied Social Psychology, 21,* 1608–1628.

Kirkpatrick, C. (1932). A tentative study in experimental social psychology. *American Journal of Sociology, 38,* 194–206.

Knapp, R. H. (1944). A psychology of rumor. *Public Opinion Quarterly, 8,* 22–27.

Knapp, S. D. (Ed.). (1993). *The contemporary thesaurus of social science terms and synonyms: A guide for natural language computer searching.* Phoenix, AZ: Oryx.

Knobloch, L. K., & Carpenter-Theune, K. E. (2004). Topic avoidance in developing romantic relationships: Associations with intimacy and relational uncertainty. *Communication Research, 31,* 173–205.

Knopf, T. A. (1975). *Rumor, race and riots.* New Brunswick, NJ: Transaction Publishers.

Koenig, F. W. (1985). *Rumor in the marketplace: The social psychology of commercial hearsay.* Dover, MA: Auburn House.

Koller, M. (1992). Rumor rebuttal in the marketplace. *Journal of Economic Psychology, 13,* 167–186.

Koller, M. (1993). Rebutting accusations: When does it work, when does it fail. *European Journal of Social Psychology, 23,* 373–389.

Komarnicki, M., & Walker, C. J. (1980, March). *Reliable and valid hearsay: Convergent and divergent rumor transmission.* Paper presented at the Eastern Psychological Association meeting, Hartford, CT.

Kramer, R. M. (1999). Trust and distrust in organizations: Emerging perspectives, enduring questions. *Annual Review of Psychology, 50,* 569–598.

Krull, D. S., & Anderson, C. A. (1997). The process of explanation. *Current Directions in Psychological Science, 6,* 1–5.

Kuhn, T. S. (1996). *The structure of scientific revolutions* (3rd ed.). Chicago: University of Chicago Press.

Kunda, Z. (1987). Motivated inference: Self-serving generation and evaluation of causal theories. *Journal of Personality and Social Psychology, 53,* 636–647.

Kunda, Z. (1990). The case for motivated reasoning. *Psychological Bulletin, 108,* 480–498.

Kunda, Z. (1999). *Social cognition: Making sense of people.* Cambridge, MA: MIT Press.

Kurland, N. B., & Pelled, L. H. (2000). Passing the word: Toward a model of gossip and power in the workplace. *Academy of Management Review, 25,* 428–438.

Latané, B., & Bourgeois, M. J. (1996). Experimental evidence for dynamic social impact: The formations of subcultures in electronic groups. *Journal of Communication, 46,* 35–47.

Lazar, R. J. (1973). Stock market price movements as collective behavior. *International Journal of Contemporary Sociology, 10,* 133–147.

Leary, M. R. (1995). *Self-presentation: Impression management and interpersonal behavior.* Boulder, CO: Westview Press.

Leavitt, H. J., & Mueller, R. A. (1951). Some effects of feedback on communication. *Human Relations, 4,* 401–410.

Lerbinger, O. (1997). *The crisis manager: Facing risk and responsibility.* Mahwah, NJ: Erlbaum.

Lev, M. (1991, February 6). Carter stock drops again on rumors. *The New York Times,* p. D4.

Levin, J., & Arluke, A. (1987). *Gossip: The inside scoop.* New York: Plenum Press.

Litman, J. A., & Pezzo, M. V. (2005). Individual differences in attitudes towards gossip. *Personality and Individual Differences, 38,* 963–980.

Litwin, M. L. (1979, January). Key communicators—They lock out rumors. *National Association of Secondary School Principals Bulletin,* 17–22.

London, I. D., & London, M. B. (1975). Rumor as a footnote to Chinese national character. *Psychological Reports, 37,* 343–349.

Lord, C. G., Lepper, M. R., & Ross, L. (1979). Biased assimilation and attitude polarization: The effects of prior theory on subsequently considered information. *Journal of Personality and Social Psychology, 46,* 1254–1266.

Lorenzi-Cioldi, F., & Clémence, A. (2001). Group processes and the construction of social representations. In M. A. Hogg & S. Tindale (Eds.), *Group processes* (pp. 311–333). Malden, MA: Blackwell.

Lott, B. E., & Lott, A. J. (1985). Learning theory in contemporary social psychology. In G. Lindzey & E. Aronson (Eds.), *The handbook of social psychology* (3rd ed., Vol. 1, pp. 109–135). New York: Random House.

Lowenberg, R. D. (1943). Rumors of mass poisoning in times of crisis. *Journal of Criminal Pathology, 5,* 131–142.

Lynch, R. D. (1989). Psychological impact of AIDS on individual, family, community, nation, and world in a historical perspective. *Family Community Health, 12*(2), 52–59.

Lynn, M. (1991). Scarcity effects on desirability: A quantitative review of the commodity theory literature. *Psychology and Marketing, 8,* 43–57.

Lyons, A., & Kashima, Y. (2001). The reproduction of culture: Communication processes tend to maintain cultural stereotypes. *Social Cognition, 19,* 372–394.

MacLeod, C., & Cohen, I. L. (1993). Anxiety and the interpretation of ambiguity: A text comprehension study. *Journal of Abnormal Psychology, 102,* 238–247.

Maines, D. R. (1999). Information pools and racialized narrative structures. *The Sociological Quarterly, 40,* 317–326.

Malkiel, B. G. (1985). *A random walk down Wall Street* (4th ed.). New York: Norton.

Marks, A. (2001, October 23). From survival tales to attack predictions, rumors fly. *The Christian Science Monitor,* p. 2.

Marting, B. (1969). *A study of grapevine communication patterns in a manufacturing organization.* Unpublished doctoral dissertation, Arizona State University, Tempe.

Marty, E. M. (1982). Satanism: No soap. *Across the Board, 19*(11), 8–14.

Matthews, L., & Sanders, W. (1984). Effects of causal and noncausal sequences of information on subjective prediction. *Psychological Reports, 54,* 211–215.

Mausner, J., & Gezon, H. (1967). Report on a phantom epidemic of gonorrhea. *American Journal of Epidemiology, 85,* 320–331.

McAdam, J. R. (1962). *The effect of verbal interaction on the serial reproduction of rumor.* Unpublished doctoral dissertation, Indiana University, Bloomington, IN.

McEvily, B., Perrone, V., & Zaheer, A. (2003). Introduction to the special issue on trust in an organizational context. *Organization Science, 14,* 1–4.

McGee, G. W., & Ford, R. C. (1987). Two (or more?) dimensions of organizational commitment: Reexamination of the affective and continuance commitment scales. *Journal of Applied Psychology, 72,* 638–642.

McMillan, S. (1991). Squelching the rumor mill. *Personnel Journal, 70*(10), 95–99.

Merton, R. K. (1968, January 5). The Matthew effect in science. *Science, 159,* 56–63.

Michelson, G., & Mouly, S. (2000). Rumour and gossip in organizations: A conceptual study. *Management Decision, 38,* 339–346.

Michelson, G., & Mouly, V. S. (2004). Do loose lips sink ships? The meaning, antecedents and consequences of rumour and gossip in organizations. *Corporate Communications: An International Journal, 9,* 189–201.

Mihanovic, M., Jukic, V., & Milas, M. (1994). Rumours in psychological warfare. *Socijalna Psihijatrija, 22,* 75–82.

Mikkelson, B. (1999, November 19). *The unkindest cut.* Retrieved November 2, 2004, from http://www.snopes.com/horrors/robbery/slasher.asp

Mikkelson, B. (2001, November 24). *Citibank rumor.* Retrieved December 2, 2005, from http://www.snopes.com/rumors/citibank.htm

Mikkelson, B. (2002, April 28). *You've got to be kidneying.* Retrieved June 7, 2004, from http://www.snopes.com/horrors/robbery/kidney.htm

Mikkelson, B. (2003, January 12). *Trademark of the devil.* Retrieved November 22, 2004, from http://www.snopes.com/business/alliance/procter.asp

Mikkelson, B. (2004a, July 8). *Deja 'roo.* Retrieved November 9, 2004, from http://www.snopes.com/critters/malice/kangaroo.htm

Mikkelson, B. (2004b, September 23). *Lights out!* Retrieved November 2, 2004, from http://www.snopes.com/horrors/madmen/lightout.asp

Mikkelson, B. (2005, September 27). *Killer dolphins.* Retrieved November 22, 2005, from http://www.snopes.com/Katrina/rumor/dolphins.asp

Mikkelson, B., & Mikkelson, D. P. (2004, August 23). *Verses, foiled again.* Retrieved November 25, 2005, from http://www.snopes.com/politics/bush/bibleverse.asp

Miller, D. L. (1985). *Introduction to collective behavior.* Belmont, CA: Wadsworth.

Miller, M. W. (1991, May 1). Computers: 'Prodigy' headquarters offered peeks into users' private files. *The Wall Street Journal,* p. B1.

Mirvis, P. H. (1985). Negotiations after the sale: The roots and ramifications of conflict in an acquisition. *Journal of Occupational Behaviour, 6,* 65–84.

Modic, S. J. (1989, May 15). Grapevine rated most believable. *Industry Week, 238*(10), 11.

Monday, Monday. (2002, October 1). Retrieved December 16, 2005, from http://www.snopes.com/rumors/fema.htm

Monge, P. R., & Contractor, N. S. (2000). Emergence of communication networks. In F. M. Jablin & L. L. Putnam (Eds.), *The new handbook of organizational communication: Advances in theory, research, and methods* (pp. 440–502). Thousand Oaks, CA: Sage.

Morin, E. (1971). *Rumour in Orléans.* New York: Pantheon Books.

Mullen, B. (1989). *Advanced BASIC meta-analysis.* Hillsdale, NJ: Erlbaum.

Mullen, P. B. (1972). Modern legend and rumor theory. *Journal of the Folklore Institute, 9,* 95–109.

Newman, M. E. J. (2003). The structure and function of complex networks. *SIAM Review, 45,* 167–256.

Newstrom, J. W., Monczka, R. E., & Reif, W. E. (1974). Perceptions of the grapevine: Its value and influence. *Journal of Business Communication, 11,* 12–20.

Nisbett, R., & Ross, L. (1980). *Human inference: Strategies and shortcomings of social judgment.* Englewood Cliffs, NJ: Prentice-Hall.

Nkpa, N. K. U. (1977). Rumors of mass poisoning in Biafra. *Public Opinion Quarterly, 41,* 332–346.

Noon, M., & Delbridge, R. (1993). News from behind my hand: Gossip in organizations. *Organization Studies, 14,* 23–36.

Ojha, A. B. (1973). Rumour research: An overview. *Journal of the Indian Academy of Applied Psychology, 10,* 56–64.

Pendleton, S. C. (1998). Rumor research revisited and expanded. *Language & Communication, 18,* 69–86.

Peters, H. P., Albrecht, G., Hennen, L., & Stegelmann, H. U. (1990). "Chernobyl" and the nuclear power issue in West

German public opinion. *Journal of Environmental Psychology, 10,* 121–134.

Peterson, W. A., & Gist, N. P. (1951). Rumor and public opinion. *American Journal of Sociology, 57,* 159–167.

Pettigrew, T. F. (1979). The ultimate attribution error: Extending Allport's cognitive analysis of prejudice. *Personality and Social Psychology Bulletin, 5,* 461–476.

Petty, R. E., & Cacioppo, J. T. (1981). *Attitudes and persuasion: Classic and contemporary approaches.* Dubuque, IA: Brown.

Petty, R. E., & Wegener, D.T. (1998). Attitude change: Multiple roles for persuasion variables. In D. T. Gilbert, S. T. Fiske, & G. Lindzey (Eds.), *The handbook of social psychology* (4th ed., Vol. I, pp. 323–390). Boston: McGraw-Hill.

Pezzo, M. V., & Beckstead, J. (2006). A multi-level analysis of rumor transmission: Effects of anxiety and belief in two field experiments. *Basic and Applied Social Psychology, 28,* 91–100.

Pinsdorf, M. K. (1987). *Communicating when your company is under siege: Surviving public crisis.* Lexington, MA: Lexington Books.

Ponting, J. R. (1973). Rumor control centers: Their emergence and operations. *The American Behavioral Scientist, 16,* 391–401.

Popper, K. R. (1962). *Conjectures and refutations: The growth of scientific knowledge.* New York: Basic Books.

Porter, E. G. (1984). Birth control discontinuance as a diffusion process. *Studies in Family Planning, 15,* 20–29.

Pound, J., & Zeckhauser, R. (1990). Clearly heard on the street: The effect of takeover rumors on stock prices. *Journal of Business, 63,* 291–308.

Prasad, J. (1935). The psychology of rumour: A study relating to the great Indian earthquake of 1934. *British Journal of Psychology, 26,* 1–15.

Prasad, J. (1950). A comparative study of rumours and reports in earthquakes. *British Journal of Psychology, 41,* 129–144.

Pratkanis, A. R., & Aronson, E. (1991). *Age of propaganda: The everyday use and abuse of persuasion.* New York: Freeman.

Pratkanis, A. R., & Aronson, E. (2001). *Age of propaganda: The everyday use and abuse of persuasion* (Rev. ed.). New York: Freeman.

Pratkanis, A. R., & Greenwald, A. G. (1989). A socio-cognitive model of attitude structure and function. In L. Berkowitz (Ed.), *Advances in experimental social psychology* (Vol. 22, pp. 245–285). New York: Academic Press.

Priester, J. R., & Petty, R. E. (1995). Source attributions and persuasion: Perceived honesty as a determinant of message scrutiny. *Personality and Social Psychology Bulletin, 21,* 637–654.

Quist, R. M., & Resendez, M. G. (2002). Social dominance threat: Examining social dominance theory's explanation of prejudice as legitimizing myths. *Basic and Applied Social Psychology, 24,* 287–293.

Rajecki, D. W. (1990). *Attitudes* (2nd ed.). Sunderland, MA: Sinauer Associates.

Rawlins, W. (1983). Openness as problematic in ongoing friendships: Two conversational dilemmas. *Communication Monographs, 50,* 1–13.

Robinson, S. L. (1996). Trust and breach of the psychological contract. *Administrative Science Quarterly, 41,* 574–599.

Rose, A. M. (1951). Rumor in the stock market. *Public Opinion Quarterly, 15,* 461–486.

Rosenberg, L. A. (1967). On talking to a newspaper reporter: A study of selective perception, distortion through rumor, professional gullibility, or how to ride the zeitgeist for all it is worth. *American Psychologist, 22,* 239–240.

Rosenthal, M. (1971). Where rumor raged. *Trans-Action, 8*(4), 34–43.

Rosenthal, R. (1979). The "file drawer problem" and tolerance for null results. *Psychological Bulletin, 86,* 638–641.

Rosenthal, R. (1991). *Meta-analytic procedures for social research* (Rev. ed.). Newbury Park, CA: Sage.

Rosenthal, R., & Rosnow, R. L. (1991). *Essentials of behavioral research: Methods and data analysis* (2nd ed.). New York: McGraw-Hill.

Rosnow, R. L. (1974). On rumor. *Journal of Communication, 24*(3), 26–38.

Rosnow, R. L. (1980). Psychology of rumor reconsidered. *Psychological Bulletin, 87,* 578–591.

Rosnow, R. L. (1988). Rumor as communication: A contextualist approach. *Journal of Communication, 38,* 12–28.

Rosnow, R. L. (1991). Inside rumor: A personal journey. *American Psychologist, 46,* 484–496.

Rosnow, R. L. (2001). Rumor and gossip in interpersonal interaction and beyond: A social exchange perspective. In R. M. Kowalski (Ed.), *Behaving badly: Aversive behaviors in interpersonal relationships* (pp. 203–232). Washington, DC: American Psychological Association.

Rosnow, R. L., Esposito, J. L., & Gibney, L. (1988). Factors influencing rumor spreading: Replication and extension. *Language & Communication, 8,* 29–42.

Rosnow, R. L., & Fine, G. A. (1976). *Rumor and gossip: The social psychology of hearsay.* New York: Elsevier.

Rosnow, R. L., & Foster, E. K. (2005, April). Rumor and gossip. *Psychological Science Agenda, 19*(4). Retrieved April 21, 2005, from http://www.apa.org/science/psa/apr05gossip.html

Rosnow, R. L., & Georgoudi, M. (1985). "Killed by idle gossip": The psychology of small talk. In B. Rubin (Ed.), *When information counts: Grading the media* (pp. 59–74). Lexington, MA: Lexington Books.

Rosnow, R. L., & Kimmel, A. J. (2000). Rumor. In A. E. Kazdin (Ed.), *Encyclopedia of psychology* (Vol. 7, pp. 122–123). New York: Oxford University Press & American Psychological Association.

Rosnow, R. L., Yost, J. H., & Esposito, J. L. (1986). Belief in rumor and likelihood of rumor transmission. *Language & Communication, 6,* 189–194.

Ross, L., Lepper, M. R., & Hubbard, M. (1975). Perseverance in self-perception and social perception: Biased attributional processes in the debriefing paradigm. *Journal of Personality and Social Psychology, 32,* 880–892.

Ross, L., Lepper, M. R., Strack, F., & Steinmetz, J. (1977). Social explanation and social expectation: Effects of real and hypothetical explanations on subjective likelihood. *Journal of Personality and Social Psychology, 35,* 817–829.

Rothbaum, F., Weisz, J. R., & Snyder S. S. (1982). Changing the world and changing the self: A two-process model of perceived control. *Journal of Personality and Social Psychology, 42,* 5–37.

Rousseau, D. M., Sitkin, S. B., Burt, R. S., & Camerer, C. (1998). Not different after all: A cross-discipline view of trust. *Academy of Management Review, 23,* 393–404.

Rousseau, D. M., & Tijoriwala, S. A. (1999). What's a good reason to change? Motivated reasoning and social accounts in promoting organizational change. *Journal of Applied Psychology, 84,* 514–528.

Roux-Dufort, C., & Pauchant, T. C. (1993). Rumors and crisis: A case study in the banking industry. *Industrial and Environmental Crisis Quarterly, 7,* 231–251.

Rudolph, E. (1971). *A study of informal communication patterns within a multi-shift public utility organizational unit.* Unpublished doctoral dissertation, University of Denver, Denver, Colorado.

Rudolph, E. (1973). Informal human communication systems in a large organization. *Journal of Applied Communication Research, 1,* 7–23.

Ruscher, J. B. (2001). *Prejudiced communication: A social psychological perspective.* New York: Guilford Press.

Sabini, J., & Silver, M. (1982). *Moralities of everyday life.* New York: Oxford University Press.

Salancik, G. R., & Pfeffer, J. (1977). A social information processing approach to job attitudes and task design. *Administrative Science Quarterly, 23,* 224–253.

Scanlon, T. J. (1977). Post-disaster rumor chains: A case study. *Mass Emergencies, 2,* 121–126.

Schachter, S., & Burdick, H. (1955). A field experiment on rumor transmission and distortion. *Journal of Abnormal and Social Psychology, 50,* 363–371.

Scheper-Hughes, N. (1990). Theft of life. *Society, 27*(6), 57–62.

Schweiger, D. M., & DeNisi, A. S. (1991). The effects of communication with employees following a merger: A longitudinal field experiment. *Academy of Management Journal, 34,* 110–135.

Sedikides, C., & Anderson, C. A. (1992). Causal explanations of defection: A knowledge structure approach. *Personality and Social Psychology Bulletin, 18,* 420–429.

Sedikides, C., & Skowronski, J. J. (1991). The law of cognitive structure activation. *Psychological Inquiry, 2,* 169–184.

Sedivec, D. J. (1987). *Network analysis of the accuracy process within the grapevine.* Unpublished master's thesis, North Dakota State University, Fargo.

Seligman, M. E. P., Abramson, L. Y., Semmel, A., & von Baeyer, C. (1979). Depressive attributional style. *Journal of Abnormal Psychology, 88,* 242–247.

Shadish, W. R., & Haddock, C. K. (1994). Combining estimates of effect size. In H. Cooper & L. V. Hedges (Eds.), *The handbook of research synthesis* (pp. 261–282). New York: Russell Sage Foundation.

Shanker, T. (2004, March 23). U.S. team in Baghdad fights a persistent enemy: Rumors. *The New York Times,* p. A1.

Sherif, M. (1936). *The psychology of social norms.* Oxford, England: HarperCollins.

Shibutani, T. (1966). *Improvised news: A sociological study of rumor.* Indianapolis, IN: Bobbs-Merrill.

Sinha, D. (1952). Behaviour in a catastrophic situation: A psychological study of reports and rumours. *British Journal of Psychology, 43,* 200–209.

Sinha, D. (1955). Rumours as a factor in public opinion during elections. *The Eastern Anthropologist, 8,* 63–73.

Skarlicki, D. P., & Folger, R. (1997). Retaliation in the workplace: The roles of distributive, procedural, and interactional justice. *Journal of Applied Psychology, 82,* 434–443.

Slackman, M. (2003, June 14). A tale of two cities. *The Gazette* (Montreal, Quebec, Canada), p. F1.

Smeltzer, L. R. (1991). An analysis of strategies for announcing organization-wide change. *Group and Organization Studies, 16,* 5–24.

Smeltzer, L. R., & Zener, M. F. (1992). Development of a model for announcing major layoffs. *Group and Organization Studies, 17,* 446–472.

Smith, E. R. (1994). Social cognition contributions to attributional theory and research. In P. G. Devine, D. L. Hamilton, & T. M. Ostrom (Eds.), *Social cognition: Impact on social psychology* (pp. 77–108). San Diego, CA: Academic Press.

Smith, G. H. (1947). Beliefs in statements labeled fact and rumor. *Journal of Abnormal and Social Psychology, 42,* 80–90.

Smith, L. C., Lucas, K. C., & Latkin, C. (1999). Rumor and gossip: Social discourse on HIV and AIDS. *Anthropology & Medicine, 6,* 121–131.

Steele, C. M. (1988). The psychology of self-affirmation: Sustaining the integrity of the self. In L. Berkowitz (Ed.), *Advances in experimental social psychology* (Vol. 21, pp. 261–302). San Diego, CA: Academic Press.

Stevens, L. E., & Fiske, S. T. (1995). Motivation and cognition in social life: A social survival perspective. *Social Cognition, 13,* 189–214.

Struthers, C. W., Menec, V. H., Schonwetter, D. J., & Perry, R. P. (1996). The effects of perceived attributions, action control, and creativity on college students' motivation and performance: A field study. *Learning and Individual Differences, 8,* 121–139.

Sugiyama, M. S. (1996). On the origins of narrative: Storyteller bias as a fitness-enhancing strategy. *Human Nature, 7,* 403–425.

Suls, J. M., & Goodkin, F. (1994). Medical gossip and rumor: Their role in the lay referral system. In R. F. Goodman & A. Ben-Ze'ev (Eds.), *Good gossip* (pp. 169–179). Lawrence: University Press of Kansas.

Tabachnick, B. G., & Fidell, L. S. (1996/2001). *Using multivariate statistics* (4th ed.). Boston: Allyn & Bacon.

Teenager arrested after cyber hoax causes chaos. (2003, April 3). Retrieved May 22, 2003, from http://www.thestandard.com.hk/thestandard/txtarticle_v.cfm?articleid=38028

Terry, D. J., Tonge, L., & Callan, V. J. (1995). Employee adjustment to stress: The role of coping resources, situational factors and coping responses. *Anxiety, Stress, and Coping, 8,* 1–24.

Tesser, A., & Rosen, S. (1975). The reluctance to transmit bad news. In L. Berkowitz (Ed.), *Advances in experimental social psychology* (Vol. 18, pp. 193–232). New York: Academic Press.

Tommy rumor: The truth behind the rumor. (1999, January 11). Retrieved April 15, 2005, from http://www.tommy.com/help/rumor/rumorOprah.jsp

Trope, Y., & Liberman, A. (1996). Social hypothesis testing: Cognitive and motivational mechanisms. In E. T. Higgins & A. W. Kruglanski (Eds.), *Social psychology: Handbook of basic principles* (pp. 239–270). New York: Guilford Press.

Trope, Y., & Thompson, E. P. (1997). Looking for truth in all the wrong places? Asymmetric search of individuating information about stereotyped group members. *Journal of Personality and Social Psychology, 73,* 229–241.

Turner, P. A. (1993). *I heard it through the grapevine: Rumor in African-American culture.* Berkeley: University of California Press.

Turner, R. H. (1964). Collective behavior. In R. E. L. Faris (Ed.), *Handbook of modern sociology* (pp. 382–425). Chicago: Rand McNally.

Turner, R. H. (1994). Rumor as intensified information seeking: Earthquake rumors in China and the United States. In R. R. Dynes & K. J. Tierney (Eds.), *Disasters, collective behavior, and social organization* (pp. 244–256). Newark: University of Delaware Press.

Turner, R. H., & Killian, L. M. (1972). *Collective behavior* (2nd ed.). Englewood Cliffs, NJ: Prentice-Hall.

Tybout, A. M., Calder, B. J., & Sternthal, B. (1981). Using information processing theory to design marketing strategies. *Journal of Marketing Research, 18,* 73–79.

Unger, H. (1979, June). Psst—heard about Pop Rocks? Business rumors and how to counteract them. *Canadian Business,* p. 39.

U.S. Department of State Bureau of International Information Programs. (2005, January 14). *The 4000 Jews rumor.* Retrieved December 18, 2005, from http://usinfo.state.gov/media/Archive/2005/Jan/14-260933.html

Van der Linden, P., & Chan, T. (2003). *What is an urban legend?* Retrieved August 2003 from http://www.urbanlegends.com/afu.faq/index.htm

Van Dijk, T. A. (1987). *Communicating racism: Ethnic prejudice in thought and talk.* Newbury Park, CA: Sage.

Van Groezen, B., Leers, T., & Meijdam, L. (2002). The vulnerability of social security when fertility is endogenous. *Journal of Institutional and Theoretical Economics, 158,* 715–730.

Verma, S. K. (2003, February 21). I would rather die than eat beef, says PM. *The Statesman* (India). Retrieved March 3, 2003, from LexisNexis database.

Victor, J. S. (1989). A rumor-panic about a dangerous Satanic cult in western New York. *New York Folklore, 15,* 23–49.

Vigoda, R. (1993, November 5). Heard about the headlights? The big lie comes sweeping into town. *Philadelphia Inquirer,* pp. B1, B8.

Walker, C. J. (1996, March). *Perceived control in wish and dread rumors.* Poster presented at the Eastern Psychological Association Meeting, Washington, DC.

Walker, C. J. (2003, January). *If you can't say something good, say something bad.* Paper presented at the 4th annual meeting of the Society for Personality and Social Psychologists, Los Angeles, CA.

Walker, C. J., & Beckerle, C. A. (1987). The effect of anxiety on rumor transmission. *Journal of Social Behavior and Personality, 2,* 353–360.

Walker, C. J., & Blaine, B. (1991). The virulence of dread rumors: A field experiment. *Language & Communication, 11,* 291–297.

Walker, C. J., & Struzyk, D. (1998, June). *Evidence for a social conduct moderating function of common gossip.* Paper presented to the International Society for the Study of Close Relationships, Saratoga Springs, NY.

Walton, E. (1961). How efficient is the grapevine? *Personnel, 38,* 45–49.

Weenig, M. W. H., Groenenboom, A. C. W. J., & Wilke, H. A. M. (2001). Bad news transmission as a function of the definitiveness of consequences and the relationship between communicator and recipient. *Journal of Personality and Social Psychology, 80,* 449–461.

Wegner, D. M., Coulton, G. F., & Wenzlaff, R. (1985). The transparency of denial: Briefing in the debriefing paradigm. *Journal of Personality and Social Psychology, 49,* 338–346.

Wegner, D. M., Wenzlaff, R., Kerker, R. M., & Beattie, A. E. (1981). Incrimination through innuendo: Can media questions become public answers? *Journal of Personality and Social Psychology, 40,* 822–832.

Weinberg, S. B., & Eich, R. K. (1978). Fighting fire with fire: Establishment of a rumor control center. *Communication Quarterly, 26,* 26–31.

Weinberg, S. B., Regan, E. A., Weiman, L., Thon, L. J., Kuehn, B., Mond, C. J., et al. (1980). Anatomy of a rumor: A field study of rumor dissemination in a university setting. *Journal of Applied Communication Research, 8,* 156–160.

Weiner, B. (1985). An attributional theory of achievement motivation and emotion. *Psychological Review, 92,* 548–573.

Weiss, W. H. (1982). *The supervisor's problem solver.* New York: American Management Association.

Werner, W. P. (1976). *The distortion of rumor as related to prejudice and stereotypes.* Unpublished thesis, Montclair State College, Montclair, NJ.

Wert, S. R., & Salovey, P. (2004). A social comparison account of gossip. *Review of General Psychology, 8,* 122–137.

Wheelan, S. A., Verdi, A. F., & McKeage, R. (1994). *The Group Development Observation System: Origins and applications.* Philadelphia: PEP Press.

White, R. W. (1959). Motivation reconsidered: The concept of competence. *Psychological Review, 66,* 297–333.

Wilke, J. R. (1986). *Rumor as a social phenomenon: An analysis of three crisis rumors of the 1970's.* Unpublished master's thesis, Auburn University, Auburn, AL.

Wood, W. (1999). Motives and modes of processing in the social influence of groups. In S. Chaiken & Y. Trope (Eds.), *Dual process theories in social psychology* (pp. 547–570). New York: Guilford Press.

Wood, W. (2000). Attitude change: Persuasion and social influence. *Annual Review of Psychology, 51,* 539–570.

Worth, R. F. (2005, September 1). *Stampede: 950 die as Iraqi crowd panics.* Retrieved September 1, 2005, from http://www.sltrib.com

Yandell, B. (1979). Those who protest too much are seen as guilty. *Personality and Social Psychology Bulletin, 5,* 44–47.

Zaremba, A. (1988). Working with the organizational grapevine. *Personnel Journal, 67,* 38–42.

Zaremba, A. (1989, September/October). Management in a new key: Communication networks. *Industrial Management, 31,* 6–11.

Zingales, F. (1998, February). What's a company's reputation worth? *Global Finance,* p. 17.

Author Index

Subject Index

About the Authors

Nicholas DiFonzo earned his PhD in social and organizational psychology from Temple University in 1994, where he was awarded the Marianthi Georgoudi Dissertation Award for philosophical and theoretical contributions to the field of psychology. He is currently professor of psychology at the Rochester Institute of Technology. He is a member of numerous professional associations including the American Psychological Association, the American Psychological Society, and the Society for Personality and Social Psychologists. Dr. DiFonzo currently serves as consulting editor for *The Journal of Social Psychology*.

He has published approximately 30 articles, book chapters, and technical reports pertaining to the topic of rumor. He has studied how rumors propagate through networks in social space and across time, the mechanisms by which rumors become accurate or distorted, motivations involved in rumor transmission, processes involved in believing a rumor, how rumor is differentiated from other forms of communication, how rumor processes are affected by organizational trust, and how rumors influence social and economic behavior. He has also pursued practical applications of rumor theory including how harmful rumors may be most effectively refuted. Dr. DiFonzo has also given approximately 30 presentations and invited addresses at academic conferences on these topics, as well as several seminars to business audiences on the topic of managing rumors.

Dr. DiFonzo recently received a grant from the National Science Foundation to investigate how rumors propagate through social networks over time. He has also received grants from the Institute for Public Relations to study corporate rumors, their effects, and how top corporate public relations officers handle them. He has investigated rumor attributional processes and boomerang effects in rumor refutation in projects funded by the Australian Research Council. Dr. DiFonzo organized and maintains an Internet discussion group, Rumor-Gossip Research@listserver.rit.edu, for scholars interested in the topics of rumor and gossip. Dr. DiFonzo is currently serving as expert witness for the Procter & Gamble Corporation on the topic of the famous (and false) Satanism rumor and product rumors.

Prashant Bordia is an associate professor in the School of Management at the University of South Australia. He obtained his PhD in social and organizational psychology from Temple University in 1996, where he was awarded the Vanderveer Fellowship in 1995. He is a member of the U.S. Academy of Management and the Australian Psychological Society and an international affiliate of the American Psychological Association. He is a consulting editor for *The Journal of Social Psychology* and on the editorial boards of *Group & Organization Management,* the *Journal of Business and Psychology,* and the *Journal of Business Communication.*

Dr. Bordia has studied rumor as collective sense making on the Internet, effectiveness of rumor rebuttal strategies, rumors during organizational change and, more recently, the role of motivations in rumor spread. He was awarded the University of Queensland Foundation Early Career Research Excellence Award in 2003. Dr. Bordia has published over 40 articles in refereed journals and book chapters and has presented numerous papers in international conferences. He has received best paper awards at the Academy of Management and the Australian I/O Psychology conferences. He has received competitive research grant funding from the Australian Research Council and the U.S. National Science Foundation to study rumors and has conducted research and consulting projects with several public and private sector organizations. Dr. Bordia is currently serving as expert witness for the Procter & Gamble Corporation on the topic of the famous (and false) Satanism rumor and product rumors.